汉语语言文字启蒙

A Key to Chinese Speech and Writing

II

Joël Bellassen
University Paris 7

With the Collaboration of
Zhang Pengpeng
Beijing Language and Culture University

Translator
Christian Artuso

华语教学出版社　北京
SINOLINGUA　BEIJING

First edition 1997

Original title published in French
Perfectionnement à la Langue et à I'Écriture chinoises
@La Compagnie/Bellassen 1991

The character 字 on the front cover is the original handwriting of Yan Zhenqing,
a great calligraper of the Tang Dynasty

ISBN 7-80052-508-2

Copyright © Sinolingua Beijing 1997
Published by Sinolingua
24 Baiwanzhuang Road, Beijing 100037, China

Printed by Beijing Foreign Languages Printing House
Distributed by China International Book Trading Corporation
35 Chegongzhuang Xilu, P. O. Box 399
Beijing 100044, China

Printed in the People's Republic of China

Preface to the English Edition

The two volumes that make up this method of learning Chinese were published in France at the end of 1989 (I) and 1991 (II) respectively. They are intended for students with no previous knowledge of the language.

We would like to express our gratitude to those colleagues in Germany, America, England, China and Scandinavia who, acquainted with the French manuals, first put forth the idea of an English edition. Our thanks go to them for the continued interest they have shown in the present volumes, in which there is, no doubt, room for improvement. This interest, we feel, has been kindled by an entirely different conception of learning Chinese. Departing from the usual form of teaching in vogue for the last forty years, this new approach is nevertheless intrinsically traditional, in that it shows a great respect for the originality of the Chinese language.

In every aspect of life, only when we chose to look reality in the face, can we avoid encounters with conflict and disorder. In terms of learning Chinese, the written language is not merely a graphic duplicate of the oral sounds. Bearing this consideration in mind, Chinese students as well as their professors must adopt two separate approaches of the language which consist of distinguishing two systems of logic of thought. Those two systems are not identical and they may even conflict with each other. Meanwhile, one has to keep in mind that the Chinese characters as fundamental unit of written language should always be entitles to a specific place and that is what I strove to do in this book. We would like to thank Mrs. Anne Alexis and Ms Jocelyne Finazzi for their attentive editing.

J. B.

TABLE OF LESSONS

TABLE OF CONTENTS

ABBREVIATIONS

adj	adjective
adv	adverb
conj	conjunction
const	construction
el	element
exp	expression
fig	figuratively speaking
Fn	family name
int	interrogative
loc	locative
Mw	measure word
n	noun
neg	negation
phon	phonetic
Pn	proper noun
prep	preposition
pro	pronoun
Qvb	qualifying verb
s. o.	someone
sth.	somthing
suf	suffix
Tw	time word
vb	verb
v-o	verb-object

INTRODUCTION

The present volume is designed to continue along the same lines established in Volume I. From the very beginning our ambition was to present a way of learning Chinese that respects the characteristic genius of this language and its writing system. This task was both easy and arduous. "Easy" because it was simply a matter of allowing the nature of Chinese to emerge i. e. to try to realise the role (lexical, syntactical and cultural) played by sinograms in the Chinese universe in general. The task was at the same time "arduous" because the reading of most textbooks, especially Chinese textbooks, reveals in fact that, to use the words of Heraclites "Nature loves to conceal itself from our view". Such textbooks were in fact influenced by Western schools of thought at the beginning of this century which saw Chinese writing as a "primitive and out of date" tool that only served to "sow confusion in the mind". These textbooks, thus believing it wise to follow the approach of textbooks written in Western languages, closely adopted a course of supressing signs in favour of words (often going so far as not to distinguish the two notions) and refusing to consider the frequency, origin and cursive writing styles of sinograms * . One must admit that such a step cannot be without drastic consequences upon, for example, the multiple meanings of signs which is so vital for the understanding of written work. We were therefore required to ask ourselves what could serve as a didactic for languages that don't use a phonetic system, and then, in conceiving this second volume to adapt our subject matter to the level that was intended.

Completing this volume allows a student to attain a level corresponding to that of having completed second year university.

This volume introduces through 25 lessons 500 supplementary characters, still chosen for their high frequency rate, which are included in more than 4, 000 words. The 900 sinograms of the two volumes thus enable a recognition of 90% of characters found in modern readings.

Built upon the base acquired in Volume I, the texts of this volume were conceived within a much less rigid framework. They are either narratives or dialogues on a theme and thus lend themselves naturally to oral exploitation. The contents of these texts are equally divided among literature or stories (including the appearence of original texts such as Tang poems, Lao She and Lu Xun), customs (Chinese given names, Yin and Yang, . . .) and from modern life (letters to newspapers, "Are you an auditive or a visual person?" . . .).

The task of learning the words made up from those new sinograms presented in each lesson can be approached in many different ways ranging from merely reading the words and trying to guess their meaning to completely mastering them.

The "Snowball" sections which in Voume I appeared after every three lessons have been adapted to suit this new level and are now integrated into every lesson. They now take the form of an extremely effective pedagogic process i. e. explaining Chinese words by "recycling" vocabulary already acquired.

Just as learning Chinese is an adventure, so too is formulating a textbook. The thirst to learn and observations of our own students as well as the welcome given to our first volume by those who have used it , have all been of great encouragement to us. We hope they will be rewarded here.

Joël Bellassen and Zhang Pengpeng
Paris, July 1991

---

* These beginners' textbooks published in China "forgot" to teach the stroke order of the characters that would burden the memory with sinograms of limited use.

TABLE OF 900 CHARACTERS

	A	B	C	D	E	F	G	H	I	J	K	L	M	N	O	P	Q	R	S	T	U	V	W	X	Y	Z	A'	B'	C'	D'
1	啊	爱	安	暗	按	八	把	爸	吧	白	百	拜	班	般	板	半	办	帮	包	保	抱	报	爆	杯	北	被	背	备	本	鼻
2	比	笔	避	必	边	便	遍	辨	变	标	表	别	病	并	补	不	部	布	步	才	材	采	彩	菜	参	草	层	曾	茶	察
3	查	差	产	长	常	场	厂	唱	车	彻	称	成	城	承	程	吃	冲	虫	出	初	除	楚	处	川	穿	传	船	窗	床	创
4	春	词	此	次	从	村	存	错	答	达	打	大	带	待	代	单	但	淡	蛋	当	党	导	到	道	的	得	灯	等	低	底
5	地	第	弟	点	典	电	店	掉	调	丁	定	冬	东	懂	动	都	读	独	度	短	断	段	对	队	多	朵	躲	饿	儿	而
6	耳	二	发	乏	法	反	饭	范	方	房	防	访	放	非	飞	费	分	坟	份	风	封	夫	服	福	府	父	副	复	富	妇
7	该	改	概	敢	感	干	刚	钢	高	搞	告	哥	歌	革	隔	格	个	给	跟	根	更	工	公	功	共	狗	够	构	姑	古
8	骨	故	顾	固	瓜	刮	挂	怪	关	观	官	馆	管	惯	光	广	规	鬼	贵	国	果	过	还	孩	海	害	含	汉	好	号
9	喝	河	和	何	合	黑	很	恨	红	后	候	呼	忽	乎	湖	胡	虎	户	互	护	花	华	划	画	化	话	怀	坏	欢	环
10	换	黄	回	会	婚	活	火	或	货	获	机	鸡	积	基	极	及	集	级	急	几	己	寄	继	际	记	济	纪	技	计	季
11	家	加	假	架	价	间	简	见	建	健	件	江	将	讲	交	饺	脚	角	叫	教	较	接	街	阶	结	节	解	姐	介	界
12	今	金	斤	仅	紧	近	进	尽	京	经	精	睛	景	静	境	究	九	酒	久	就	旧	救	居	局	举	句	具	据	剧	拒
13	觉	绝	决	军	开	看	康	考	靠	科	可	课	刻	客	肯	空	孔	口	苦	哭	快	筷	块	况	困	拉	来	浪	劳	老
14	乐	了	累	类	冷	离	李	里	理	礼	立	丽	利	历	力	例	连	联	脸	练	凉	两	辆	亮	量	谅	疗	料	烈	林
15	零	○	领	另	龙	留	流	六	楼	路	旅	绿	虑	论	落	妈	马	吗	买	卖	满	慢	忙	毛	么	没	美	每	门	们
16	猛	梦	迷	米	密	面	民	名	明	命	某	母	木	目	拿	哪	那	男	南	难	脑	闹	呢	内	能	你	年	念	娘	鸟
17	您	牛	农	弄	怒	女	暖	怕	排	派	判	旁	跑	培	朋	皮	篇	片	票	品	平	评	漂	破	普	七	期	骑	其	奇
18	齐	起	气	汽	器	千	前	钱	强	墙	桥	巧	切	且	亲	轻	青	清	情	请	庆	穷	秋	求	球	区	取	去	趣	全
19	缺	却	确	然	让	扰	热	人	认	任	日	容	肉	如	入	三	色	杀	山	善	商	伤	上	少	绍	蛇	设	社	谁	身
20	深	什	神	甚	生	声	升	省	师	诗	十	时	识	实	食	始	使	史	是	事	市	室	示	似	视	适	式	士	试	世
21	势	收	手	守	首	受	书	舒	熟	数	术	树	双	水	睡	顺	说	思	司	私	死	四	送	拆	算	虽	随	岁	碎	所
22	索	他	她	它	台	太	态	谈	特	疼	提	题	体	替	天	田	条	铁	听	庭	停	通	同	统	头	突	图	土	团	推
23	托	外	完	玩	晚	碗	万	王	往	忘	望	为	围	委	位	卫	味	温	文	闻	问	我	屋	无	五	午	武	舞	物	务
24	西	息	希	析	习	喜	洗	细	系	下	吓	夏	先	鲜	显	现	线	限	香	乡	相	想	响	象	向	像	项	消	小	校
25	笑	效	些	鞋	写	谢	新	心	信	星	行	形	醒	姓	兴	幸	性	休	修	需	许	续	选	学	雪	血	寻	牙	呀	言
26	研	颜	眼	演	验	阳	羊	养	样	要	药	爷	也	夜	叶	业	一	医	衣	依	疑	以	已	意	义	艺	忆	易	议	因
27	音	阴	印	应	英	影	硬	映	用	优	由	油	有	友	又	右	鱼	于	语	雨	与	遇	育	欲	元	园	原	员	圆	远
28	院	愿	约	月	越	云	运	杂	在	再	咱	早	造	则	怎	增	展	站	张	丈	章	招	找	照	者	这	着	真	诊	正
29	整	政	证	知	之	支	织	直	职	值	只	指	纸	止	至	制	治	致	志	中	钟	终	种	重	众	周	洲	州	竹	主
30	住	祝	注	著	助	专	转	庄	装	壮	准	资	子	仔	字	自	总	走	租	族	足	组	嘴	最	昨	左	作	做	坐	座

TABLE OF RADICALS

	A	B	C	D	E	F	G	H	I	J	K	L	M	N
1	丶	一	丨	丿	乙	亠	冫	冖	讠	二	十	厂	匚	卜
2	刂	冂	八	人	亻	勹	夕	几	儿	厶	又	廴	卩	阝
3	阝	凵	刀	力	巳	氵	忄	宀	门	辶	寸	扌		工
4	土	士	艹	大	廾	尤	弋	小	口	囗	巾	山	彳	彡
5	夕	夂	犭	忄	彐	尸	巴	己	弓	子	屮	女	幺	纟
6	马	巛	灬	斗	文	方	火	心	户	礻	王	韦	木	犬
7	歹	车	戈	比	瓦	小	止	支	日	曰	水	贝	见	父
8	牛	手	毛	气	攵	片	斤	爪	月	欠	风	殳	爿	毋
9	穴	立	疒	衤	示	石	龙	业	目	田	罒	皿	钅	矢
10	禾	白	瓜	鸟	用	矛	卩	足	皮	母	衣	羊	米	耒
11	老	耳	臣	西	页	卢	虫	缶	舌	竹	臼	自	血	舟
12	羽	聿	艮	糸	辛	言	麦	走	赤	豆	酉	辰	豕	卤
13	里	足	豸	谷	采	身	角	青	其	雨	齿	龟	食	金
14	佳	鱼	音	革	骨	鬼	髟	麻	鹿	黑	鼠	鼻		

The radicals from the dictionary 新华字典 Xīnhuá Zìdiǎn (Commercial Press, Beijing, 1979) are used as references here.

1A graphic element; **1B** (idem)GE; **1C** GE; **1D** GE; **1E** GE; **1F** GE; **1G** ice; **1H** cover; **1I** word; **1J** two; **1K** ten; **1L** shelter; **1M** basket; **1N** divination;

2A knife; **2B** GE; **2C** separation; **2D** person; **2E** person; **2F** to envelope; **2G** GE (knife or kneeling person); **2H** tea table; **2I** person (two legs); **2J** private; **2K** right hand; **2L** elongated step; **2M** stamp/seal; **2N** mound ;

3A city; **3B** GE; **3C** knife; **3D** force; **3E** GE(seal or kneeling person); **3F** water; **3G** vertical heart; **3H** roof; **3I** wide; **3J** door; **3K** walking; **3L** thumb; **3M** hand; **3N** work;

4A searth; **4B** scholar; **4C** grass; **4D** big; **4E** joint hands; **4F** lame; fault; **4G** arrow on a string; **4H** little; **4I** mouth; **4J** wall; **4K** towel; **4L** mountain; **4M** step with left foot; **4N** ornament;

5A sunset; **5B** reverse foot; **5C** clawed animal; **5D** food; **5E** head of pork or a hand seen from side on; **5F** corpse; **5G** GE; **5H** oneself; **5I** bow(archery); **5J** child; **5K** seedling/sprout; **5L** woman; **5M** thread; **5N** silk;

6A horse; **6B** watercourse; **6C** fire; **6D** decalitre; **6E** written sign; **6F** square; **6G** fire; **6H** heart; **6I** door flap; **6J** ritual; **6K** king or jade; **6L** tanned hide; **6M** tree; **6N** dog, clawed animal;

7A death; **7B** chariot (vehicle); **7C** halberd; **7D** comparison; **7E** tile; **7F** heart; **7G** stop/foot; **7H** to hit; **7I** sun; **7J** to say; **7K** water; **7L** shell; **7M** see; **7N** father;

8A buffalo; **8B** hand; **8C** hair; **8D** breath; **8E** hand holding stick; **8F** slice; **8G** axe; **8H** claws; **8I** meat or moon; **8J** open-mouthed person; **8K** wind; **8L** pole, mace; **8M** plank; **8N** prohibit;

9A cave; **9B** standing up; **9C** illness; **9D** clothing; **9E** sacred revelation(ritual); **9F** stone; **9G** dragon; **9H** activity; **9I** eye; **9J** field; **9K** net; **9L** vessel; **9M** metal; **9N** arrow;

10A cereal(rice); **10B** white; **10C** melon; **10D** bird; **10E** use; **10F** spear; **10G** hardness; **10H** to match; Mw; **10I** skin; **10J** mother; **10K** clothing; **10L** sheep; **10M** rice; **10N** plouth;

11A old age; **11B** ear; **11C** servant; **11D** nest (west); **11E** head(page); **11F** tiger **11G** reptile; **11H** vessel; **11I** tongue; **11J** bamboo; **11K** mortar; **11L** nose(oneself); **11M** blood; **11N** boat;

12A feathers; **12B** brush; **12C** hardness; **12D** silk; **12E** bitterness; **12F** word; **12G** wheat; **12H** hurried walk; **12I** red; **12J** stemmed bow, bean; **12K** alcohol; **12L** cyclical sign; **12M** pig; **12N** salting;

13A hamlet; **13B** foot; **13C** feline; **13D** valley; **13E** to distinguish; **13F** body; **13G** born; **13H** blue-green **13I** winnowing basket; **13J** rain; **13K** tooth; **13L** turtle; **13M** food; **13N** metal;

14A short-tailed bird; **14B** fish; **14C** sound **14D** leather; **14E** bone; **14F** ghost; **14G** long hair; **14H** hemp; **14I** deer; **14J** black; **14K** rat; **14L** nose.

1

第一课　画龙点睛

传说古代有一位画家在墙上画了四条龙，每条龙画得都很好，像真的一样，可是都没有画眼睛。人们看了都觉得特别奇怪，问他为什么不画眼睛。画家很自信地说："要是我画上眼睛，龙马上就会飞起来。"人们都不相信，要求他把龙眼睛画上去。他说："我只画一条。"画家提起笔来在一条龙上画了眼睛。画家刚一画完，立刻下起大雨来。这时，那条有眼睛的龙突然动了起来。过了一会儿，这条龙离开了墙，飞到天上去了。那几条没有眼睛的龙还留在墙上。

这个成语常常指写文章或说话的时候用一两句重要的话，把意思说得更清楚。如：这句话起到了'画龙点睛'的作用。

VOCABULARY

传说	n, vb	chuánshuō	it is said that; legend has it
古代	n	gǔdài	ancient times
墙	n	qiáng	wall
条	Mw	tiáo	[Mw for long slender objects]; clause
眼睛	n	yǎnjīng	eyes
特别	adv	tèbié	especially, particularly
奇怪	Qvb	qíguài	strange; to be amazed
自信	Qvb	zìxìn	self-confident
相信	vb	xiāngxìn	to believe in , to be sure of
要求	vb, n	yāoqiú	to want, to request; request
突然	adv	tūrán	suddenly
留	vb	liú	to stay
经常	adv	jīngcháng	often
指	vb	zhǐ	to show, to point out
文章	n	wénzhāng	article, text
句	Mw, n	jù	sentence
清楚	Qvb, vb	qīngchu	clear; understand

Use

| 传说 | ◆ 传说他去国外了。 |
| | ◆ 这是一个传说，不是真的。 |

| 条 | ◆ 一条龙，一条鱼，一条路，一条意见 |

特别	◆ 他的名字很特别。
	◆ 我特别喜欢吃中国饭。
	◆ 他汉语说得特别好。

奇怪	◆ 他是一个奇怪的人。
	◆ 没有人来，一点儿也不奇怪。
	◆ 他的问题提得很奇怪。
	◆ 真奇怪，都五月了，天气还这么冷！
	◆ 我们都奇怪他今天怎么没有来。

| 自信 | ◆ 这个人很自信。 |
| | ◆ 他自信能找到那个地方。 |

| 要求 | ◆ 这是我的要求。 |
| | ◆ 我要求你们马上回家！ |

提	◆ 他提着很多东西。
	◆ 我提了三个问题。
	◆ 一提起去美国的事，他就不高兴。

突然	◆ 他来得很突然。
	◆ 他突然不高兴了。
	◆ 突然，他打了我一下。

留	◆ 他留在学校工作了。
	◆ 我朋友想留我在他家吃晚饭。
	◆ 他把书都留在我这儿了，没有带走。

| 经常 | ◆ 这是经常的工作。 |
| | ◆ 他经常去看电影。 |

| 或 | ◆ 明天你来或不来都行。 |

清楚	◆ 他的汉字写得很清楚。
	◆ 这个问题，你清楚不清楚？
	◆ 他把这个问题讲清楚了。

起	◆ 你要从头学起。[从…起:from. . .]
	◆ 这猫太娇气了,我养不起。
	◆ 太贵了!我买不起。Used as potential, 起 indicates that one has the means to do something.

作用	◆ 这是化学作用。
	◆ 在学校里你们要起好作用。
	◆ 他说的话是有作用的。

v + 上	◆ 我爱上她了。
	◆ 他把我的名字写上了。
	◆ 请把门关上!Resultative, 上 can indicate the idea of joining, adequate.

v + 上去	◆ 你把东西拿上去!
	◆ 东西太多,我拿不上去。
	◆ 他们走上去了。
	The directionals 去 and 来 can be combind with basic movements(上,下,出,进,回,过,起) to form complex verbs (the combination 起去 is impossible). When the direct object is a place the only possible construction is vb + movement + 去/来.

v + 起来	◆ 那个人站起来了。
	◆ 他拿起一本书来对我说。
	◆ 雨下起来了。
	◆ 学习汉语的人多起来了。
	◆ 说起来,我们还是同学呢。
	◆ 天气冷起来了。The combination 起来 can have a literal meaning (lift up)and a figurative meaning (to go about doing something).

楚	chǔ	clear, neat; Kingdom of Chu 楚国
传 傳	chuán zhuàn	to transmit, to propagate 传道,传教,传热,传真,电传真,口传 biography 自传
代	dài	era, dynasty; to replace 代办,代言人,代用,当代,汉代,近代,明代,年代,千秋万代,时代,现代,现代化,元代, * 仉 an instrument for counting, to put in order
怪	guài	strange 怪不得,怪物,古怪,见怪,难怪,千奇百怪,作怪
或	huò	or; someone; perhaps * 或 borders, the earth and a halberd: territory (see 域)
经 經	jīng	acupunctural meridian, scripture, canon; to cross 经常化,经过,经书,经心,经意,念经,书经,月经 * 經 silk radical and a loom
睛	jīng	eye 定睛

句	jù	sentence; [Mw for sentences, remarks]

句法，句子，病句，名句

留	liú	to stay, to keep

留给，留念，留下，留学，留学生，久留，

*卯＋田： phonetic element and a "field", symbol of a location

奇	qí	extraordinary, strange

传奇，好奇，好奇心

* 　a rider on a horse (see 骑)

墙 牆	qiáng	wall

墙报，城墙

* 土＋嗇： "earth" + "petty, stingy" (two ripe ears of wheat in a field)

清	qīng	clear , distinct; completely

清白，清代，清明，清算，清真，分清，冷清，认清，一清早

求	qiú	to beg, to demand

求和，求亲，求情，求人不如求己，求学，讲求，请求

* 　a fur coat (see 裘)

特	tè	special, exceptional

特别，特长，特殊，特等，特地，特点，特色，特意，奇特

*牛＋寺： "ox" and "temple"

条	條	tiáo	[Mw for long and thin objects]; article, clause

条文，条子，教条，面条

突	tū	sudden; to dash forward

突出

* a "dog" coming out of a cave

相	xiāng	mutual, reciprocal

相比，相传，相当，相等，相对，相关，相
亲相爱，相识，相同，老相识

	xiàng	physical features

相机，相片，相声，看相，长相，真相

* an "eye" observing a "tree"

眼	yǎn	eye

眼看，眼明手快，眼皮，眼前，眼下，眼中
钉，白眼，开眼，亲眼

章	zhāng	chapter, rule, badge, seal

章法，公章，章回小说，会章，图章，第一章

*音＋十："ten" "sounds" forming a musical composition

指	zhǐ	finger; to point

指出，指点，指定，指东画西，指教，指
明，指名，指南，指事，指头，指正，手
指，无名指，小指，中指

单句

1. 楚国是中国古代的一个国家。
2. 怪物指奇怪的人或动物。
3. 语法上不对的句子叫病句。
4. 名句就是很有名的句子。
5. 到外国去上学叫留学。
6. 在外国留学的学生叫留学生。
7. 分清就是区分清楚。
8. 长相就是一个人长的样子。
9. 相同就是一样。
10. 两个人认识叫相识。
11. 眼看是马上的意思。
12. "指"有指头的意思,无名指,小指,中指都是手指头的名字。
13. 今天是我的生日,我母亲特地为我做了面条。
14. 他指定我作他的代言人。
15. 我想把这个相机留给我哥哥用。
16. 这是一所现代化医院。
17. 这是我最近写的一本书,请您多多指教!
18. 有不对的地方,请王先生指正。
19. 他是中国明代的传奇人物。
20. 你怎么那么教条呀!
21. 这本书第一章讲的是我们这个时代的一些千奇百怪的现象。
22. 这是一本法国当代最有名的作家写的自传。
23. 父亲常常对我说:要做一个清白的人,最重要的是要能分清是非。

24. 他们办公室有一台传真机，可以打传真。
25. 水可以传热。
26. 那位老人过去在中国传教。
27. 我想一定是有人在作怪。
28. 和你不相关的事就少问。
29. 我祝你们相亲相爱，白头到老。
30. 这上面的不少条文我看不懂。
31. 今天晚上他不来，你也别见怪。他就是这么一个奇怪的人。
32. 他眼前一黑什么也看不见了。
33. 他给了我一张画儿，上面写着"北京留念"四个字。
34. 中国三十年代有很多人到国外去求学。
35. 他把我看成是他的眼中钉。
36. 传说这个湖里有个怪物，长得很大，样子像条龙。
37. 校长指名让我到他办公室去工作。

会 话

1　—这个句子对不对？
　　—不对，是一个病句。

2　—你想到哪个国家去留学？
　　—到中国，这是我特意买的《中国留学指南》。
　　—怪不得你现在那么认真学中文呢！

3　—你会刻图章吗？
　　—会刻。你看这是我给一个学校刻的公章。

4　—那个人是学什么的？
　　—是学中国明代文学的，但对清代、元代和现代文学也知
　　　道一些。
　　—他有什么特长？
　　—他书法相当好。

9

5 —明天我们去看看北京的城墙，怎么样？

—你这人，好奇心怎么那么重！对什么都好奇！城墙有什么
看头？

—听说北京的城墙很有特色。

6 —小张，你们班的墙报办得不错，特点很突出。

—哪儿的话，和你们班相比还差得远呢！

7 —我最喜欢看中国三十年代作家写的小说，你呢？

—我喜欢看当代作家写的小说。

8 —这个人是有点儿古怪，难怪他爱人老说他。

—我不这么看。我倒觉得，他干事，眼明手快的。

9 —你打算什么时候走？

—眼看要下雨了，我不想在这儿久留，想吃了饭就走。

10 —老王在家吗？

—不在，一清早就到地里去了。他给你留了个条，说有什
么特殊的事让你到地里去找他。

11 —你听过相声吧？

—没听过，这次去中国我想去听听。

12 —今天我可开眼了！

—你看到什么了？

—我亲眼看到《清明上河图》了。这张画儿画得真是特别好！

13 —我这次回国，要经过几个国家，我不想带很多东西。这些书
太重，眼下我又用不上，想把它给你留下。

—好，就留在我这儿吧！

2

第二课　中国文字

王：你认为汉语和其它语言的最大区别是什么？

马：我认为是文字。因为只有汉字是表意文字，其它文字都是表音文字。

王：那日文呢？

马：日文中使用了两千多个汉字，同时日文还使用假名，假名只表音不表意，所以不能说日文也是表意文字。

王：一个汉字就是一个词吗？

马：不一定。有的词是一个汉字，有的词是由几个汉字组成的。

王：常用汉字有多少？

马：有三千多。由这三千多汉字可以构成几万个词。用字构词，这是汉语的一个特点。

王：有人说汉字是一种落后的文字，你同意这种看法吗？

马：我不同意。我认为汉字有很多优点，汉字的优点会越来越被人们认识到。现在有一些科学家说，西方人学习汉字可能对大脑有好处。

王：是吗？那学汉语就太有意义了！

马：我对汉字感兴趣还有一个原因。

王：什么原因？

马：我觉得汉字是一种艺术。你看，这是昨天我朋友送我的一份礼物。

王：几个毛笔字。

马：对！这是中国的书法，多好看！

Presentation

汉字	type	pinyin	English
其它	pro	qítā	other
表意	v-o	biǎoyì	expressing meaning, semantic
表音	v-o	biǎoyīn	expressing sound, phonetic
使用	vb	shǐyòng	to use
假名	n	jiǎmíng	kana (Japanese syllabic signs)
词	n	cí	word
由	prep	yóu	by, from
组成	vb	zǔchéng	to make up, to compose
构成	vb	gòuchéng	to form, to constitute
构	vb	gòu	to compose
特点	n	tèdiǎn	particularity, speciality
落后	Qvb	luòhòu	to be backward
优点	n	yōudiǎn	quality, strong point
越来越…	const	yuèláiyuè	more and more...
被	prep	bèi	by
科学家	n	kēxuéjiā	scientist
大脑	n	dànǎo	brain
好处	n	hǎochù	good point, advantage
意义	n	yìyì	meaning, sense, value
感	vb	gǎn	to feel, to experience
兴趣	n	xìngqu	interest, motivation
原因	n	yuányīn	cause
艺术	n	yìshu	art
送	vb	sòng	to give, to send
礼物	n	lǐwù	present, gift

其它	◆ 你先看这本书，再看其它的书。 其它 indicates "other things" over and above a thing already mentioned.
只有	◆ 只有这个地方我没去过。 ◆ 只有坐十路汽车才可以到那儿。 ◆ 只有他一个人会开车。
那	◆ 那是我朋友。 ◆ 那本书很好。 ◆ 如果明天天气不好，那就不去了。 ◆ 他不同意，那你呢？
由	◆ 我们班由两个国家的学生组成。 ◆ 明天的会由早上八点开到十一点。 ◆ This preposition introduces what/where something is done or who/what it is done by.
vb + 成	◆ 我把'太'字写成'大'了。 ◆ 他不来，这个会就开不成了。 ◆ 下雨就去不成了。 This resultative expresses the process of transformation.
多	◆ 十多个人，两个多月，三年多 ◆ 你要多说汉语。 ◆ 我今天多喝了一杯酒。 ◆ 去中国，坐飞机比坐火车快多了。 ◆ 今天多热啊！

| 越来越… | ◆ 天气越来越热。 |
| | ◆ 他汉语说得越来越好。 |

| 越…越… | ◆ 这本书我越看越爱看。 |
| | ◆ 天气越热，买汽水的人越多。 |

| vb + 到 | ◆ 我们学到第二课了。 |
| | ◆ 他找到他的钱包了。 |

This resultative expresses the act of reaching or achieving.

对	◆ 他说的都对。
	◆ 他说对了,你说错了。
	◆ 我们家的门对着汽车站。
	◆ 他对老师说了些什么？
	◆ 我对中国文化很感兴趣。
	◆ 有人说喝茶对身体有好处。

被	◆ 那本书被我朋友拿走了。
	◆ 他被谁打了？
	◆ 我刚出门又被叫了回来。

被 introduces the agent (which can be understood). The verb often carries a sign of completion or a result. The context of the sentence often implies opposition or adversity.

送	◆ 他送给我两本书。
	◆ 我把这些东西送到他家去。
	◆ 我送你去飞机场。

被	bèi	quilt; [indicates passive action] by	

被动，被子

* 衣＋皮： "clothing" and "skin", to cover with a piece of clothing

---

表	biǎo	outside, to show；table, form, watch

表白，表哥，表里如一，表面，表明，表现，代表，代表大会，发表，课表，手表，钟表，字母表

* 裘 fur clothing, the hairs on the outside

处 處	chǔ	to be in a certain position

处分，处女，处女作，处事

	chù	place, office

处处，处所，处长，办事处，长处，难处，用处，住处

* 処 a person and a reversed foot (movement)

词 詞	cí	word

词句，词头，词语，代词，动词，歌词，连词，名词，生词，题词，祝词

* 詞 words and "to be in charge of" (a person and a mouth)

感	gǎn	to feel; feelings

感到，感动，感化，感觉，感人，感想，感谢，感知，好感，快感，语感

构 構	gòu	to construct, to arrange

构思，构图，机构

假	jiǎ	false	
		假发，假话，假如，假山，假使	
	jià	holidays	
		假期，病假，放假，请假，休假	

科	kē	section, field (of studies), branch (of a department etc.)
		科教片，科学，科学院，儿科，教科书，外科，文科，眼科
		*禾＋斗："cereal" + "a measure for grain"

礼 禮	lǐ	ceremony, convention
		礼花,礼教
		* 示豊 "rites" and a sacrificial vase with two strings of jade on top

落	luò	to fall
		落成，落花生，落日，没落

其	qí	that, such; his (her, its, their)
		其次，其间，其中，文如其人
		* a sieve

趣	qù	interest; pleasing
		风趣，有趣

使	shǐ	to employ, to use
		使不得,使得,使馆,大使,大使馆,好使,天使
		*亻＋吏："person" + "bureaucrat"

术 術	shù	technique, art
		术语，美术，手术，算术，学术，艺术家

送		sòng	to send, to give, to accompany

送别，送给，送行，欢送
* （图） to accompany, a torch in hand

义	義	yì	justice, meaning

义气，爱国主义，本义，定义，个人主义，广义，机会主义，讲义，教条主义，名义，人道主义，起义，同义词，要义，正义，主义

艺	藝	yì	art, talent

艺名，艺人，艺术家，工艺，手艺，文艺，园艺
* （图） a person taking care of plants, the art of gardening

优	優	yōu	excellent, outstanding

优等，优美，优生学，优先

由		yóu	cause, reason, due to , by

由不得，由来，不由自主，自由
* （图） what is born in a field, germination

原		yuán	origin, prairie

原本，原来，原始，原文，原先，原子，原子能
* （图） a spring

越		yuè	to get over, to exceed; more

越过，越南，越 ... 越 ...，优越，优越感

组	組	zǔ	to form, to organize; group

组长，词组，小组

单句

1. 词头、词组、词语、名词、动词等都是语法术语。
2. "表里如一"是一个成语，指的是一个人心里想的和口头说的、做的都一样。
3. 上课的时间表叫课表。
4. 长处就是优点的意思。
5. 住处就是住的地方。
6. 使人很感动叫感人。
7. 因为生病请的假叫病假。
8. 学校上课时用的书叫教科书。
9. 落花生也叫花生，是吃的东西。
10. 落日就是太阳落下去。
11. "其"是代词，其间就是这中间。
12. 好使就是好用的意思。
13. 一个词本来的意义叫本义。
14. 越南是一个国家，在中国的南边。
15. 词组是由词构成的。
16. 我朋友很讲义气，我刚到法国时他送给我一条被子和一块手表，当时我真不知怎么感谢他。
17. 你能不能给爱国主义下个定义？
18. 雨果是一位法国人道主义作家。
19. 我感到他从外国留学回来后有种优越感。
20. 看科教片可以从中学到不少科学知识。
21. 他表哥是学文科的。从去年他在《文艺报》上发表的文章看，他爱说假话，爱从表面看问题，我对他没有什么好感。

23. 那位艺人的动作很优美，表现得也很自然。
24. 离我们组长的住处不远有一个钟表店。
25. 上海原子能发电站明天落成。
26. 他写过几本教科书，其中一本是用法文写的，但是他在学术上没有很大成就。
27. 看落日和看日出给人的感觉不一样。
28. 这个人有很多长处，说话也很风趣，我们小组的人都喜欢他。
29. 我想代表老师们讲两句话。
30. 他不由自主地说："我很想去天安门看礼花。"
31. 这个打字机不太好使。
32. 你这么说话使我们很被动。
33. 以后你有什么难处来找我。

会话

1　—老师，这个词是什么词？是动词还是名词？
　　—是动词。
　　—这两个词呢？
　　—一个是代词，一个是连词。

2　—"生词"是什么意思？
　　—没学过的词叫"生词"。这课有二十几个生词。

3　—"原来" 和"原先"是不是同义词？
　　—是同义词。

4　—这个医院有眼科吗?我要看眼科。
　　—有，往前走不远是外科和儿科，再往前走就是眼科。

5　—李先生，你的病要做手术。

—差不多。

6　—你们什么时候开始放假？
　　—从七月份开始放假。
　　—假期你想到哪儿去？
　　—假如能买到飞机票的话，我想去中国和越南。

7　—你去过中国大使馆吗？
　　—没去过。听说中国大使馆很大，还有假山，是吗？
　　—是的。你见过中国大使吗？
　　—见过一次。是在欢送中国艺术家回国的晚会上。

8　—这是什么机构？
　　—这是中国科学院在法国的办事处。
　　—你认识办事处处长吗？
　　—认识。他原先是北京大学的老师。这是当年他写的讲义。

9　—你看过这本小说吗？
　　—看过。这是一位中国女作家的处女作。小说构思奇特，
　　　写得很生动很感人，让人越看越爱看。

10　—到国外以后你感到很自由吗？
　　　—很难说，和我原来的想法不一样。

11　—你看了他的题词有什么感想？
　　　—表面上看，这个人有点教条主义。

12　—为什么给他处分？他不是优等生吗？
　　　—休假完以后他没有马上回国。

13　—你觉得我这几个菜做得怎么样？
　　　—还可以，你的手艺不错。

3

第三课　中国人的习惯

王：你来中国已经几个月了，你觉得哪些事情使你感到有点儿奇怪？

马：一次我去看一个老朋友，我们已经五年多没见面了。我送给他一张画。为了买这张画，我差不多花了一天时间，不知跑了多少家商店，可是当我送给他时，他怎么连看都不看！

王：这是中国人的习惯。中国人接受礼物后，往往不马上打开看，只是向送礼的人表示感谢。他们觉得当着人的面打开看，不太好。

马：原来是这样！还有我对中国朋友在见到我时问的一些问题有时不理解。他们常问我一些很具体的事。比如你吃饭了吗？你去哪儿呀？

王：这是在向你打招呼。中国人之间见面时很少说"你好！"、"你身体好吗？"。在吃饭前后，你的朋友遇到你，问你吃饭了没有，就是在向你打招呼。

马：那在路上遇到我呢？

王：可能会说"去哪儿了？"、"进城呀？"什么的。

马：那中国人打招呼的用语就太多了！

王：是呀！多极了！

马：据说中国人孩子对父母不说"谢谢！"，是吗？

王：是的！对爱人也不说。你们西方人太爱说"谢谢！"了。

马：这太有意思了！我真想写一本书，叫《论中国人的习惯》。

VOCABULARY

习惯	n, vb	xíguàn	habit;, to be used to
已经	adv	yǐjīng	already
事情	n	shìqing	affair, business, event
感到	vb	gǎndào	to feel
见面	vb	jiànmiàn	to meet
为了	prep	wèile	for
连…都…	exp	lián…dōu…	even...
跑	vb	pǎo	to run
接受	vb	jiēshòu	to receive
往往	adv	wǎngwǎng	often
打开	vb	dǎkāi	to open
表示	vb	biǎoshì	to express
感谢	vb	gǎnxiè	to thank
当着	vb	dāngzhe	facing
原来	adv	yuánlái	former; originally
理解	vb, n	lǐjiě	to understand, to interpret
具体	Qvb	jùtǐ	concrete, precise
比如	conj	bǐrú	for example
打招呼	v – o	dǎzhāohu	to greet
…之间	loc	zhījiān	between
…极了	suf	jíle	extremely
遇到	vb	yùdào	to meet, to run into, to come across
用语	n	yòngyǔ	expression
据说	vb	jùshuō	it is said that
论	n, v	lùn	view; to discuss

Use

已经

◆ 老师已经走了。

◆ 他的孩子已经大了。

◆ 我已经喝了三杯酒了。

◆ 现在已经三点了。

使

◆ 他说的话使我很高兴。

◆ 去他家可以使你认识更多新朋友。

The complement of this verb is a proposition that produces an effect on somebody or something.

有点儿

◆ 他今天有点儿不高兴。

◆ 今天天气有点儿冷。

◆ 我有点儿想去又有点儿不想去。

◆ Distinguish 有一点儿大 (it's a little big) from 有没有大一点儿的 (Aren't there any bigger ones?).

次

◆ 有一次,我去上海,在那儿住了三天。

◆ 我去过一次上海。

◆ 下一次会是在星期五开。

差不多

◆ 他和他父亲长得差不多。

◆ 这儿的人我差不多都认识。

◆ 这两个手提包差不多一样重。

◆ 我们一年差不多学五百个汉字。

◆ 他到法国差不多三年了。

家

◆ 一家商店,一家医院

◆ 文学家,音乐家,歌唱家,作家,道家,法家

当

◆ 当我回来的时候,他已经走了。

◆ 你有什么意见,可以当着我的面说。

怎么

◆ 你们怎么去中国?

◆ 他今天怎么那么高兴?

◆ 怎么,你不认识我了?

◆ 这个字我怎么写也写不好。

◆ 上次怎么做的,这次还怎么做。

◆ 汉语我刚学,还不怎么会说。

连…都…	◆ 连我都知道了，他当然知道。
	◆ 这么奇怪的动物，过去我连见都没见过。
	◆ 连他叫什么名字我都不知道。
	◆ 他家我连一次都没去过。

往往	◆ 他往往星期天到我家来。
	在北京，骑自行车往往比坐汽车方便。
	Unlike 常常, 往往 is only used for the repetition of habitual and objective actions or actions that have been maintained up to the present. The conditions of the action must be mentioned.

向	◆ 你要向他学习。
	◆ 去火车站,你要向东走。
	◆ 飞机飞向东边了。

原来	◆ 他还住在原来的地方。
	◆ 我原来不住在这个地方。
	◆ 原来是你,我还以为是老王呢。

会	◆ 他很会做饭。
	◆ 明天他会来的。
	◆ 你怎么会知道的?
	会 indicates capacity and future probability.

| …什么的 | ◆ 他买了很多东西,有鱼、肉、白菜什么的。 |
| | ◆ 他不喜欢看书、看报什么的,就爱看电影。 |

Qvb + 极了	◆ 这本书好极了。
	◆ 北京的夏天热极了。
	◆ 他跑得快极了。

惯 惯	guàn	to get used to, to become accustomed to; habitual	

惯用语

呼	hū	to exhale air, to call out aloud

呼叫，欢呼

* 吁 a mouth and breath being exhaled

极 極	jí	extreme; extremely

极点，极其，极为，北极，南极，太极

* 木 + 及： "tree" + "to reach"

接	jiē	to join, to receive, to make welcome, to connect

接班，接班人，接见，接近，接连，接生，
接收，接头，接着，间接

解	jiě	to undo(buttons etc.), to understand

解饿，解放，解开，解手，解说，解体，和解，百思
不解，见解，讲解，了解，《说文解字》

* 解 a knife cutting up the horns of a bull

据 據	jù	according to

据点，收据，字据

* 扌 + 居: hand radical + "residence"

具	jù	tool, utensil, to possess, to provide

具有，茶具，道具，工具，家具，面具，文
具，用具

* 具 two hands holding a vase

理		lǐ	to order things, to arrange, to take notice of

理发，理发馆，理会，理科，理事，理所当然，理想，理想主义，理由，办理，处理，代理，道理，地理，讲理，经理，情理，生理，说理，条理，无理，物理，心理，心理学，有理，原理，真理，自理

连 連	lián	in succession, even...

连带，连接，连忙，连年，连日，连同，黄连，接二连三，接连，相连

* 絭 a person walking, attached to and pulling a chariot

论 論	lùn	to mention, to discuss, to determine

论点，论据，论理，论说，论文，不论，定论，二元论，理论，无论，相对论，言论，一元论

	lún	short for 《论语》

跑	pǎo	to run

跑表，跑道，跑电，跑马场，跑鞋，长跑，起跑

情	qíng	feeling, situation

情报，情感，情歌，情理，情人，事情，情书，爱情，表情，感情，感情用事，国情，难为情，热情，手下留情，同情，心情

示	shì	to manifest, to notify

示意图，请示

* Ⅱ a monolith (menhir), symbol of spiritual appearances

受	shòu	to receive, to bear	

受不了，受话机，受气，感受，难受

* 爱 a hand putting a container in another hand

| 习 習 | xí | custom; to get used to |

习非成是，习见，习气，习题，习以为常，习字，学习，自习

| 向 | xiàng | toward |

方向，面向，一向

* 向 a house with an open window facing north

| 已 | yǐ | already |

已知

| 遇 | yù | to encounter, to meet by chance |

遇见，遇难，礼遇，奇遇，相遇

| 招 | zhāo | to recruit, to beckon |

招生，招收，招手

* 招 to greet a person with both mouth and hand

| 之 | zhī | [determination marker]; to go to |

之后，之前，百分之一，自知之明

* 之 a foot, symbol of walking

单句

1. 喝茶的用具叫茶具。
2. 表示爱情的歌叫情歌。
3. 黄连是一种中药。
4. 之前就是以前。
5. 解手就是解大小便。
6. 汉语中有些惯用语很难讲解。
7. 这些人中有百分之五的人心理上不正常。
8. 老吃这样的东西我真有点儿受不了了。
9. 这个人没有自知之明。
10. 他昨天接收到了来自美国的情报。
11. 连日来他先后接见了法国、美国和中国大使。
12. 这个城市是一九四五年解放的。
13. 接近他的人都知道他对人很热情。
14. 五年之后我想人们对这个问题能作出定论。
15. 他对中国很有感情，也非常同情中国人民。
16. 我想在自习课上把这几道习题做完。
17. 你接你父母的班是理所当然的。
18. 在法国有言论自由。
19. 今天我有点儿难受，可能是吃多了。
20. 人们大声欢呼："法国万岁!"
21. 《相对论》是物理学上的一种理论。
22. 我不了解受话机的原理。
23. 请你手下留情。
24. 那个带面具的人向你招手呢。

会话

1　—什么叫"文具"？
　　—办公和学习用具叫文具。

2　—听说你现在正在学习心理学，是吗？
　　—是的，我想在今年写完我的论文。

3　—你知道哪儿有理发馆吗？我想理个发。
　　—前面不远就有一个。

4　—昨天我在你们商店买了一些家具和一块跑表，你们能不能
　　　给我开个收据？
　　—请等一下，我去请示一下经理。

5　—你了解南极和北极吗？
　　—我是学地理的，看过不少有关的书，了解一点儿。

6　—为什么让他去处理这些事你不放心？
　　—因为他一向爱感情用事。

7　—让你在这样的地方解手，我有点儿难为情。
　　—没什么，我已经习以为常了。

8　—你同意他的论点和论据吗？
　　—不同意，因为他对中国的国情不了解。

9　—看你的表情，你今天心情不好。
　　—是的，今天早上我爱人接连给我打了几个电话说我孩子病
　　　了。

10   —你们大学什么时候招生？

       —从下星期一开始。今年要招收五百名理科学生。

11   —昨天在跑马场你遇见谁了？

       —我中学时的物理老师。

12   —你的理想是什么？

       —我的理想是有一天让天下的人都过上好日子。

13   —北京图书馆在哪个方向？

       —在北京西边，离动物园不远。

14   —天天跑长跑对人的生理和心理都有好处。

       —你说的有道理。

4

第四课　怕不怕鬼？

王：你怕不怕鬼？

马：我不怕，我不相信有鬼。

王：那么，你家门上挂着一块红木板，这是怎么一回事？

马：一个算命的告诉我，鬼怕红色，门口挂块红木板，鬼就不敢来。

王：这都是迷信说法，根本没那么回事！我是个彻底的无神论者。

马：那你家为什么有那么多乐器、闹钟之类的东西？

王：听说鬼怕声音，一有声音，鬼就吓跑了。

马：这有什么根据呢？这不也是迷信吗？

王：我也说不清楚，总觉得有这些东西心里才放心。有些事情说不出道理，只是一种感觉。

马：总之，我不信鬼，可是不知怎的，经常注意人背后有没有影子！

王：我也不信鬼，可是一见到漂亮的女人，就怀疑她会不会是鬼！

V Ocabulary

Presentation

汉字	class	pinyin	English
怕	vb	pà	to be afraid of
鬼	n	guǐ	ghost, devil
挂	vb	guà	to hang
块	Mw	kuài	[Mw meaning piece of]; piece
木板	n	mùbǎn	wooden plank
怎么一回事	exp	zěnmeyìhuíshì	What's up? What's all this/that about?
算命	vb	suànmìng	to tell someone's fortune
告诉	vb	gàosu	to tell, to warn
红色	n	hóngsè	red
敢	vb	gǎn	to dare
迷信	n	míxìn	superstition
根本	n, adj	gēnběn	base; fundamental, radically
彻底	adj	chèdǐ	thorough
无神论者	n	wúshénlùnzhě	athiest
乐器	n	yuèqì	musical instrument
闹钟	n	nàozhōng	alarm-clock
…之类	const	zhīlèi	of that sort, of the genre
吓	v	xià	to frighten, to scare
根据	n	gēnjù	on the basis of, according to
放心	vb	fàngxīn	to be reassured, to be relieved, at ease
道理	n	dàolǐ	reason, principle, truth
感觉	n	gǎnjué	feeling
总之	conj	zǒngzhī	in brief, in short
注意	vb	zhùyì	to pay attention to, to look out for, look out!
背	n	bèi	back

影子	n	yǐngzi	shadow
漂亮	Qvb	piàoliang	beautiful
怀疑	vb	huáiyí	to doubt, to suspect

Use

怕	◆ 我怕老虎。
	◆ 南方人很怕冷。
	◆ 他怕喝凉水。
	◆ 他怕我不来，今天给我打了两次电话。

Sentences expressing "existence":

◆ 学校里有很多学生。
◆ 门上挂着一块木板。
◆ 本子上写着三个字。

| 根本 | ◆ 他根本不认识我。 |
| | ◆ 这是一个国家落后的根本原因。 |

回	◆ 这回事我不知道。
	◆ 你们两个人说的不是一回事。
	◆ 上回我是在南京遇见他的。
	◆ 有一回，他请我和我爱人去吃饭。

| vb + n + 的 | ◆ 算命的，教书的，卖东西的，卖票的 |
| | 他是教书的。 |

那么 + Qvb	◆ 今天的天气为什么那么热？
	◆ 你像他那么学习一定可以学好。
	◆ 他家我就去过那么两次。

根据	◆ 你有没有科学根据？
	◆ 你根据什么说他是医生？

……之类	◆ 这儿不能放吃的之类的东西。
	◆ 我买了一些书、画报之类的东西。

注意	◆ 路上要注意安全。
	◆ 张老师很注意学生们的发音。

一…就…	◆ 他一到家就打电话。
	◆ 你一讲我就懂了。
	◆ 他在中国一住就住了十年。
	This construction indicates a close connection, a linking of two actions [一 and 就 are adverbs, their subjects being placed before them].

总之	◆ 这种现象美国有，法国有，日本有，总之，很多国家都有。
	◆ 你高兴也好，不高兴也好，总之，我不能同意你的意见。

才	◆ 他才从学校回来。
	◆ 你怎么才来就要走？
	◆ 晚上十点他才能回来。
	◆ 这个孩子才六岁，已经认识不少字了。
	◆ 只有去这家书店，才能买到这本书。
	◆ 他今天不来才好呢！

板	bǎn	plank, stiff	

板板六十四，板子，黑板，快板儿，老板

背	bèi	back; to turn one's back, to recite from memory

背地里，背面，背心

	bēi	to carry on one's back

背包，背着

* 𦥑 two people, back to back + flesh radical

彻 徹	chè	thorough, penetrating

彻夜

底	dǐ	bottom, base, end

底片，底下，底子，到底，年底，有底，月底

敢	gǎn	to dare

敢作敢为，不敢当

告	gào	to tell, to accuse, to announce

告别，报告，被告，被告人，公告，广告

* 告 a cow in a place for sacrifice

根	gēn	root, origin

根据地

挂 掛	guà	to hang, to worry

挂面，挂念，挂图

鬼	guǐ	ghost, devil

鬼子，酒鬼，小鬼，心里有鬼

* 鬼 a being with a big head (a mask)

怀 懷	huái	bosom; to hold against one's chest, to keep in mind

怀表，怀念，关怀

类 類	lèi	type, species	类比，类别，词类，分类，门类，人类，同类，有教无类，种类
亮	liàng	bright, clear	亮光，明亮，漂亮话，心明眼亮，月亮
迷	mí	to be fascinated by, to be confused, to be lost	迷路，迷人，迷住，影迷
命	mìng	to order; order, fate, life, mandate of heaven	命根子，命名，命题，活命，生命，使命，天命，要命

* 命 a person listening to words emitted from a mouth

木	mù	tree, wood	木工，木头，红木
闹 鬧	nào	noisy; to create a disturbance, to be troubled by, to go in for	闹病，闹事，闹市，闹意见，热闹
怕	pà	to be afraid	怕人，怕生，怕事，可怕，生怕
漂	piào	see 漂亮	
	piǎo	漂白 (piǎobái)	
器	qì	utensil	器具，器物，机器，家用电器，热水器，乐器

* 器 objects guarded by a dog

色	sè	colour	色情，白色，出色，黑色，黄色，金色，特色，五色
	shǎi		色酒，色子，掉色

神		shén	spirit

神话，神经，神经病，神经学，神色，眼神

* 祁 the rite radical and a field struck by lightning (supernatural action)

诉	訴	sù	to tell, to accuse

诉说，公诉，起诉书，上诉

算		suàn	to count, to be regarded as

算法，算了，算是，清算

* 算 two hands manipulating an abacus and the bamboo radical

无	無	wú	without

无比，无不，无从，无法，无法无天，无非，无关，
无论，无论怎样，无能，无为，无中生有，有无

吓	嚇	xià	to frighten

吓人，惊吓

疑		yí	to doubt

疑问，无疑

* 疑 a person with an open mouth, hesitating at an inter-section

者		zhě	[suffix: the person who. . .]

爱国主义者，笔者，工作者，后者，或者，前者，
使者，先行者，学者，再者，作者

注		zhù	to direct (one's thoughts), notes

注解，注明，注视，注音，注重，关注

总	總	zǒng	to assemble; general, always, anyway

总共，总会，总机，总理，总算

* 總 a tuft of hair tied up (joined)

单 句

1. 月底是指一个月的最后几天。
2. 挂在墙上的图叫挂图。
3. 用机器做的面条叫挂面。
4. 喝酒能喝得很多的人叫酒鬼。
5. 词类就是对词的分类。词分动词、名词、代词等。
6. 非常喜欢看电影的人叫电影迷。
7. 走错了路，不知道怎么走了，叫迷路。
8. 闹病就是生病的意思。他闹病了，也可以说他生病了。
9. 城市里经常很热闹的地方叫闹市。
10. 色情电影、色情画报也叫黄色电影、黄色画报。
11. 说一个人有神经病就是说这个人神经有些不正常。
12. 写书或写文章的人是书和文章的作者。
13. 类别和种类是同义词。
14. 快板儿不是用木头做的。
15. 这个人老爱背着人干事，一定心里有鬼。
16. 乐器的种类很多。
17. 我的父母十分挂念我，生怕我在国外得病。
18. 那个女人的眼神很迷人。
19. 月亮上没有生命。
20. 大家都很关注在北京发生的事情。
21. 文章最后要注明作者是一位外国人。
22. 这几条注解写得不太清楚。

会话

1 —你什么时候能写完这份报告?
　—年底以前。

2 —你们老板喜欢什么样的人?
　—喜欢工作出色、敢作敢为的人，不喜欢爱说漂亮话的人。

3 —能不能把我的背心和这块怀表放到你的背包里?
　—对不起，我背包里有一个热水器，没有地方了。

4 —听说你们国家以前的总理是位学者，是吗?
　—是的，人民都很怀念他。

5 —学生闹事可怕不可怕?
　—没什么可怕的，无能的人才怕学生闹事。

6 —中国到底有多少文艺工作者?
　—总共有几十万名。

7 —中国家用电器贵吗?
　—很贵。

8 —黑板上的句子你们都看懂了吗?还有疑问没有?
　—没有了。

9 —你做什么工作?
　—我是木工。

10 —你跟你的房东告别了吗？
    —还没有呢。我想今天晚上去告别。

11 —人类和动物的最重要的区别是什么？
    —人类有语言，动物没有。

12 —这是一份什么广告？
    —电影广告。

13 —解这道题有几种算法？
    —有三种。

14 —今天还去他家吗？
    —算了，太晚了。明天再去吧。

15 —这些机器是从哪国进口的？
    —美国。

5

第五课　中国人的名字(一)

王：我想向您请教几个有关中国人起名字的问题。听说你是个中国通！

马：不敢当，不敢当！什么问题？

王：据说中国人的名字都具有一定的含义，是吗？

马：是的！姓一般是继承父亲的，名字却是由家人或者请朋友起的。

王：中国人的名字都表示哪些含义?换句话说孩子的父母怎样给孩子起名呢？

马：我发现中国人的名字所表示的含义有这样几类：一类是表达了父母对子女的期望；一类是表示子女出生的地点；一类是和子女出生的时间或时代有关系。

王：中国人一般对子女都抱有什么期望呢？

马：期望可太多了！你看这几个名字：李成才、张富贵、王国强。成才就是成为有才能的人；富贵就是将来成为高贵而富有的人；国强就是国家富强，父母希望国家富强。

王：看来有的名字不仅表达了父母对子女的期望，还表达了对国家的期望。

马：是的！人们往往把对国家的希望寄托在孩子身上。

王：我从报上随便选一个中国人的名字，你都能讲出它的含义吗？

马：要看情况。有的可以，有的要问他本人才知道。

VOCABULARY

请教	vb	qǐngjiào	to ask for advice, to consult
有关	vb	yǒuguān	to have something to do with, to relate to
起	vb	qǐ	to give (a name)
中国通	suf	zhōngguótōng	specialist on Chinese affairs
不敢当	exp	bùgǎndāng	you flatter me!
具有	vb	jùyǒu	to possess, to have
含义	n	hányì	meaning
一般	Qvb, adv	yìbān	in general, ordinary
继承	vb	jìchéng	to inherit
却	adv	què	but
或者	conj	huòzhě	or
换句话说	exp	huànjùhuàshuō	in other words
所 + vb	pro	suǒ	that which...
类	Mw	lèi	type, species
表达	vb	biǎodá	to express
期望	n	qīwàng	wish
时代	n	shídài	era
关系	n	guānxi	relationship, connection
抱	vb	bào	to hold, to harbour (a feeling etc.)
成才	Pn	Chéngcái	Chengcai [given name]
富贵	Pn	Fùguì	Fugui [given name]
国强	Pn	Guóqiáng	Guoqiang [given name]
成为	vb	chéngwéi	to become
将来	n	jiānglái	future
高贵	Qvb	gāoguì	to be noble
富有	Qvb	fùyǒu	rich; to have plenty

42

富强	Qvb	fùqiáng	to be rich and powerful
希望	vb	xīwàng	to hope for
不仅	conj	bùjǐn	not only
寄托	vb	jìtuō	to confide, to put one's hope in
随便	adv, Qvb	suíbiàn	casually; random
选	vb	xuǎn	to choose
情况	n	qíngkuàng	situation
看情况	exp	kànqíngkuàng	that depends

Use

有关	◆ 这是一些有关中国文化的书。 ◆ 他学中文和他父亲有关。
据说	◆ 据说他去过中国。 ◆ 这个人据说很有学问。
一定	◆ 我说他是日本人，是有一定根据的。 ◆ 明天我一定要把这本书看完。
一般	◆ 他和我一般高。 ◆ 他飞一般地向前跑去。 ◆ 一般的人这么晚不出去。 ◆ 下午我一般在图书馆看书。 ◆ 这本小说写得很一般。
却	◆ 他虽然是法国人，中文却说得很好。 ◆ 他是中国人，却不会说中文。

换句话说	◆ 常用汉字有多少?换句话说,要学多少汉字才可以看懂中文书?
	◆ 从这儿到学校坐汽车要多长时间?换句话说,从这儿到学校有多远?

所	◆ 我所认识的人都喜欢吃中国饭。
	◆ 我所知道的就是这些。
	Used here to enclose a relative clause with 的.

可	◆ 在中国骑自行车可方便呢!
	◆ 你可回来了,我都等了三个小时了。
	This adverb is used to reinforce certain intonations.

而	◆ 他写的字大而清楚。
	◆ 学生们都走了,而老师们还在工作。

看来	◆ 看来,他会同意我们的意见。
	◆ 看来,他来过这个地方。

不仅…还…	◆ 这次去中国我不仅看了很多地方,还认识了不少朋友。
	◆ 他不仅会中文, 还会日文、法文。

S INOGRAMS

般	bān	type

一般地，一般化，一般来说，一般人

* 𦐖 a hand holding a boat hook to move a boat(see 搬)

抱	bào	to hold in the arms, to harbour (a feeling)

抱不平，怀抱

* 㧱 a child in its mother's womb, with the addition of a hand radical

---

承	chéng	to admit, to accept

承办，承包，承当，承认，承受，承望，继承人

* 㞑 a person kneeling down, two hands receiving or offering something

---

达 達	dá	to reach

达成，达到，传达，到达，发达，马达，四通八达

富	fù	rich, abundant

富贵，富人

含	hán	to hold in the mouth, to contain

含有，包含

换	huàn	to change

换班，换车，换工，换钱

寄	jì	to mail, to entrust, to depend upon

寄放，寄钱，寄生，寄信

继 繼	jì	to continue, to follow	

继承人，继而，继父，继母，继往开来，后继无人

* 㡭 a graphic inversion of 㡭 "to break", and silk

将 將　jiāng　to be just about to , to want to

将错就错，将近，将就，将要

jiàng　a general

干将，主将

仅 僅　jǐn　only

仅仅

况　kuàng　circumstances, moreover

近况

强　qiáng　strong

强大，强国，强化，强人，强行，强硬，刚强，好强

qiǎng　to strive for

强求，强使

却　què　to retreat; but, however

忘却

随 隨　suí　to follow, to comply with

随从，随地，随和，随口，随身，随时，随手，随意

通　tōng　through; to lead to, to connect, to understand well

通报，通病，通常，通车，通道，通电，通风，通告，通过，通信，通行，通用，通知，不通，打通

托	tuō	to hold in the palm of the hand, to entrust to	

托词，托儿所，托人情，托生，托子，假托，请托，日托，受托，信托

望	wàng	to gaze into the distance, to hope, to expect	

大喜过望，看望，名望，无望

希	xī	rare; to hope	

希奇，希少，希有

系 係 繫	xì	system, series, department (of a university etc.); to tie	

父系，母系，体系，语系，中文系

* ⺼ a lock of hair

选 選	xuǎn	to choose	

选民，选票，选手，选种，人选，文选

单句

1. 富人就是有钱的人。
2. 马达是一种机器。
3. 继父、继母不是亲生父母。
4. 近况就是最近的情况。
5. 强国就是强大的国家。
6. 忘却是书面语词，口语就是忘了的意思。
7. 日托就是指白天送孩子去托儿所，晚上接孩子回家。
8. 无望就是没有希望。
9. "后继无人"是一个成语，指以后没有继承人了。
10. 希有动物是指这种动物很希少。
11. 一般来说，选民都喜欢选有名望的人。
12. 请随手关门。
13. 法语和汉语不是同一个语系。
14. 通过看这个电影，我对日本更了解了。
15. 飞机到达上海的时间是下午三点。
16. 这张月票，地铁和汽车通用。
17. 这些东西，我这次拿不了了，先寄放在你这儿。
18. 一般人都认为中国是一个不发达国家。
19. 这所房子通风不好。
20. 酒里含有不少化学成分。
21. 他得了将近一百万张选票。
22. 这本《文选》有点儿一般化。

1 —请问，到北京大学在哪儿换车？
   —下一站换车。

2 —这儿能换钱吗？
   —换什么钱？
   —换美元。
   —你换多少？
   —换五百美元。

3 —你在哪个系学习？
   —中文系。

4 —你朋友好强吗？
   —她非常好强，人们都叫她女强人。

5 —我什么时候给你打电话最好？
   —一般来说，我晚上不出去，你随时可以给我打电话。

6 —你承认这句话你说错了吗？
   —不承认。

7 —明天你想干什么？
   —我想去看望我的一个老朋友。

8 —这个城市的人口不少吧？
   —是的，快达到五百万了。

9 —这句话包含几个意思？
   —包含两个意思。

10 —昨天下午传达室有人吗？我怎么打了几次电话都没 打通？
   —星期六传达室通常没有人。

11 —你接到学校的通知了吗？
   —接到了。

12 —你觉得这本教科书的语法体系怎么样？
   —看来有点儿问题！

Extract from the short story
Kong Himself (Kong Yiji)
by Lu Xun
(see Lesson 12, page 112)
[translation J. B. → C. A.]

"He had a long, greyish and very bushy beard. He was dressed in a long tunic; however, it was so dirty and worn that it seemed as though it had not been washed in over ten years. Whenever he spoke to anyone, he would always splurt out words like "thither", "thine" and "thence" which were hardly understandable. Since his surname was Kong, he was given the nickname "Kong Himself" which came from an unintelligible sentence extracted from a piece of calligraphy that read: "The great man Confucius (Kong), alone, himself. "

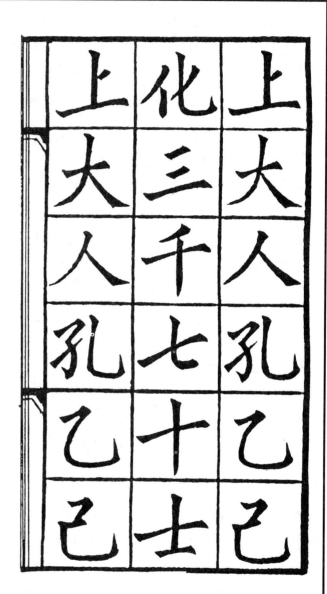

The 24 Periods of the Year

The traditional Chinese calendar is both lunar and solar. It divides the year into 12 lunar months and at the same time into 24 fifteen-day periods (jiéqì 节气). Even though the Gregorian calendar was officially adopted in China in 1912 these 24 periods are still seen as references when matters related to climate and farm work are considered.

(The dates mentioned below can vary by one day)

立春	lìchūn	Beginning of Spring	4th February
雨水	yǔshuǐ	Rainwater	20th February
惊蛰	jīngzhé	the Waking of Insects	5th March
春分	chūnfēn	Spring Equinox	20th March
清明	qīngmíng	Pure Brightness	5th April
谷雨	gǔyǔ	Grain Rain	20th April
立夏	lìxià	Beginning of Summer	6th May
小满	xiǎomǎn	Grain Full	21st May
芒种	mángzhòng	Grain in Ear	5th June
夏至	xiàzhì	Summer Solstice	21st June
小暑	xiǎoshǔ	Slight Heat	7th July
大暑	dàshǔ	Great Heat	23rd July
立秋	lìqiū	Beginning of Autumn	8th August
处暑	chǔshǔ	End of the Dog Days	23rd August
白露	báilù	White Dew	7th September
秋分	qiūfēn	Autumn Equinox	23rd September
寒露	hánlù	Cold Dew	8th October
霜降	shuāngjiàng	Frost's Decent	23rd October
立冬	lìdōng	Beginning of Winter	7th November
小雪	xiǎoxuě	Slight Snow	22nd November
大雪	dàxuě	Great Snow	7th December
冬至	dōngzhì	Winter Solstice	22nd December
小寒	xiǎohán	Slight Cold	6th January
大寒	dàhán	Great Cold	21st January

6

第六课　中国人的名字(二)

王：给男孩儿起名和给女孩儿起名有什么不同？

马：刚才讲的三个名字一般是给男孩儿起的，给女孩儿起名中国人常爱用一些美丽的字眼如：何文静、夏丽花、周小香。

王：也就是说他们希望女孩儿将来长得漂亮。

马：是呀！人之常情吗！

王：我有一个中国朋友叫田京生，这么说他可能是在中国首都生的。

马：很有可能。

王：你能不能给我介绍几个和时间、时代有关系的名字？

马：李春光这个名字就表示这个孩子是春天生的。王雪这个名字表示这个孩子出生时可能正在下雪。林建国这个名字一看就知道这个孩子是一九四九年生的。

王：那么文化革命中出生的孩子一定爱用红卫、立新之类的词了。

马：可不是吗！

王：看来中国人的名字很有时代特色。

马：仔细研究的话还会发现中国城里人和乡下人，北京人和上海人，知识分子和一般市民在起名上都有些差别。

王：是吗？这太有意思了，真能写篇论文了！

V OCABULARY

Presentation

汉字		词性	拼音	English
美丽		Qvb	měilì	beautiful
字眼		n	zìyǎn	wording, diction
何		Pn	Hé	He [surname]
文静		Pn	Wénjìng	Wenjing [given name]
夏		Pn	Xià	Xia [surname]
丽花		Pn	Lìhuā	Lihua [given name]
周		Pn	Zhōu	Zhou [surname]
小香		Pn	Xiǎoxiāng	Xiaoxiang [given name]
人之常情		exp	rénzhīchángqíng	way of the world, what everybody wants, normal
京生		Pn	Jīngshēng	Jingsheng [given name]
首都		n	shǒudū	capital
介绍		vb	jièshào	to introduce
春光		Pn	Chūnguāng	Chunguang [given name]
林		Pn	Lín	Lin [surname]
建国		Pn	Jiànguó	Jianguo [given name]
下雪		vb	xiàxuě	to snow
革命		n	gémìng	revolution
红卫		Pn	Hóngwèi	Hongwei [given name]
立新		Pn	Lìxīn	Lixin [given name]
可不是吗!		exp	Kěbúshìma!	Of course!
特色		n	tèsè	characteristic, distinguishing feature
仔细		Qvb	zǐxì	in detail, carefully
研究		vb, n	yánjiū	research; to research
乡下		n	xiāngxià	countryside

市民	n	shìmín	residents of a city, townspeople
差别	n	chābié	difference
篇	Mw	piān	[Mw for written works]
论文	n	lùnwén	thesis, dissertation

Use

给	◆ 我给他一本书。 ◆ 那本书你给我看不给我看？ ◆ 他给我打了一个电话。 ◆ 王大夫给我看病。 ◆ 我把这些东西留给他。
刚才	◆ 刚才你干什么去了？ ◆ 刚才说话的那个人是谁？ ◆ 吃了药，我觉得比刚才好多了。 ◆ 他把刚才的事儿忘了。
也就是说	◆ 星期六学校里一个人也没有，也就是说，星期六不上课。 ◆ 一块钱可以买十张票，也就是说，票不贵。
这么说	◆ 这么说他可能认识我父亲。 ◆ 这么说最好是秋天去北京。
人之常情	◆ 父母希望子女生活得好是人之常情。 ◆ 买东西希望买又好又不贵的是人之常情。
有可能	◆ 我有可能明年去美国。 ◆ 他很有可能吃了饭来我们家。

| 介绍 | ◆ 我给您介绍一下，他是我的朋友。 |
| | ◆ 他已经向老师们作了介绍。 |

| 可不是吗! | ◆ 听说昨天晚上你是走着回家的。——可不是吗! |
| | ◆ 现在的东西比过去贵多了。——可不是吗! |

| 在 . . . 上 | ◆ 在这个问题上我同意他的意见。 |
| | ◆ 他在学习上没有问题。 |

| 篇 | ◆ 一篇文章,一篇论文 |

革	gé	to change, to expel; leather

革命家，革新

*   leather being prepared, the fur removed

光	guāng	light, brilliant

光明，光明正大，光学，不光，发光，风光，
日光，时光，阳光，月光

*   a kneeling person and a flame where the head should
be (holding a torch under torture?)

何	hé	who? what? how?

何不，何处，何等，何地，何况，何如，何
时，何以，如何，无论如何

建	jiàn	to build, to found

建国，建立

介	jiè	to separate, to interpose

介词，介意，介绍

*   a person held between the two flaps of a breast-plate
(from which: "to be situated between")

静	jìng	silently, peaceful

静坐，安静，动静，冷静，平静

究	jiū	to examine thoroughly

讲究

丽	麗	lì	beautiful

风和日丽，美丽

* 丽丽 a pair

林	lín	forest, woods

林区

* 林林 two trees

篇	piān	a piece of writing, [Mw for writings]

长篇小说，连篇，中篇小说

* 篇 a horizontal tablet with inscriptions

绍	紹	shào	to carry on, to continue

绍兴，绍兴酒，介绍信

首	shǒu	head; to begin; first

首次，首脑，首先，首相，首要，首长，元
首

* 首 the eye and hair

卫	衛	wèi	to defend, to guard

卫生，卫生间，卫生所，卫星

* 韦 two feet on either side of a place

细	細	xì	fine, thin, meticulous

细长，细小，细心

* 細 a skull and a silk radical

| 夏 | xià | summer |
| | | 夏时，夏天，夏雨雨人 |

| 乡 乡 | xiāng | countryside, village |
| | | 乡亲，乡下，城乡，家乡，老乡，同乡，下乡 |

香	xiāng	aromatic, tasty
		香菜，香水，吃香，丁香
		* 香 a pleasureable perfume（甘）emitted from a grain

雪	xuě	snow
		雪花，雪人
		* 雪 rain held in the hand

| 研 | yán | to grind, to study |
| | | 研究生，研究员，教研室，科研 |

| 周 | zhōu | circuit, week, [Fn] |
| | | 周报，周代，周到，周年，周期，周岁 |

| 仔 | zǐ | (of domestic animals or fowls) young |

单句

1. 日光和阳光是同义词，都指的是太阳光。
2. 时光就是时间的意思。
3. "何"是文言词，是"什么"的意思。
4. 何时就是什么时候，何地就是什么地方。
5. 如何是怎么样的意思。
6. 建国就是建立一个国家。
7. 从、在、跟、把等都是介词。
8. 美丽是好看的意思。
9. 绍兴是一个地名，是中国南方的一个城市。
10. 绍兴酒也叫黄酒。
11. 首次就是第一次的。
12. 首要就是最重要的。
13. 把自己家乡的人叫做老乡或同乡。
14. 用雪做的人叫雪人。
15. 科研就是科学研究。
16. 一周出一次的报叫周报。
17. 作为一个革命家要光明正大。
18. 随地大小便很不卫生。
19. 一九八九年是法国大革命二百周年。
20. 中国的城乡差别还很大。
21. 在广场上静坐的人越来越多。
22. 他是一个很讲究吃的人。
23. 法国国家元首今天会见了日本首相。
24. 每个大学都有卫生所。

会话

1 —你是学什么的？
   —学光学的。

2 —你喜欢看长篇小说还是中篇小说？
   —我都喜欢看。

3 —你有介绍信吗？
   —有，这是我们学校开的介绍信。

4 —你在哪个教研室工作？
   —我在汉语教研室工作。

5 —他做什么工作？
   —他是中国科学院的研究员。

6 —你是哪个系的研究生？
   —我是中文系的。

7 —你今年多大了？
   —我今年三十五周岁了。

8 —你喜欢用香水吗？
   —很喜欢用。

9 —这是什么菜？
   —是香菜，我很喜欢吃香菜。

10　　—你下过乡吗？
　　　　—下过。文化大革命中，中学生都要上山下乡。

11　　—听说北京的夏天很热，是吗？
　　　　—是的。

12　　—他工作细心不细心？
　　　　—很细心，做事情也很周到。

13　　—今天大学里怎么这么安静？一点儿动静也没有。
　　　　—现在大学放假了。

14　　—你喜欢看什么电影？
　　　　—我喜欢看风光片，了解各国的风光。

7

第七课　有用和无用之间

　　庄子是中国古代的思想家。庄子的思想对中国传统文化和思想影响很大。至今人们还在不断研究他的思想。下面这个故事反映了庄子所抱的处世态度和做人标准。

　　有一天，庄子和他的学生到树林里去，看见有的树被砍了，有的没有被砍。他的学生问他：

　　"为什么有的树没有被砍呢？"

　　庄子回答说：

　　"因为这些树不成材，没有用。"

　　他们从树林里出来，来到一位朋友家。这位朋友养了两只鸟，一只会叫，一只不会叫。为了招待庄子和他的学生，这位朋友就让人把那只不会叫的鸟杀了去做菜。这时，庄子的学生又问庄子：

　　"为什么要杀不会叫的那只呢？"

　　庄子说：

　　"因为它不会叫，没有用。"

　　学生听了不解地问：

　　"有用的树被砍掉，而无用的鸟却被杀。那么，一个人是有才有用好呢？还是无才无用好？"

　　庄子说：

　　"两者都不好，最好是处于有才和无才、有用和无用之间。"

The hermit turns away from direct action and prefers to blend in with natural movements. (see Lesson 7)

Presentation

汉字		词类	拼音	英文
子	庄	Pn	Zhuāngzǐ	Zhuangzi
统	传	n	chuántǒng	tradition
响	影	n, vb	yǐngxiǎng	influence; to influence
今	至	exp	zhìjīn	up to the present
断	不	adv	búduàn	nonstop, incessantly
事	故	n	gùshi	story
映	反	vb	fǎnyìng	to reflect, to depict, to report
世	处	vb	chǔshì	to conduct oneself in social life
度	态	n	tàidu	attitude
准	标	n	biāozhǔn	standard, criterion
林	树	n	shùlín	forest
	树	n	shù	tree
砍		vb	kǎn	to chop down, to cut
答	回	vb	huídá	to reply
材	成	v-o	chéngcái	to become a useful person
	养	vb	yǎng	to raise, to bring up
	鸟	n	niǎo	bird
待	招	n, vb	zhāodài	welcome; to entertain (guest)
	杀	vb	shā	to kill
解	不	vb	bùjiě	not to understand
掉	砍	vb	kǎndiào	to chop down
	无	neg	wú	without
于	处	vb	chǔyú	to be in a certain position

影响	◆ 这篇文章很有影响。
	◆ 他在法国的影响很大。
	◆ 你们在这儿不要影响他休息。

不断	◆ 他从去年开始就不断给我来信。
	◆ 这几天不断有人去中国。

下面	◆ 车的下面什么也没有。
	◆ 下面我问你们一个问题。
	◆ 你念下面的。

... 之间	◆ 我们学校老师和学生之间的关系不错。
	◆ 这个城市在北京和上海之间。
	◆ 下午三点到四点之间我在办公室。

有一天	◆ 有一天我在路上遇见了我的中学老师。

只	◆ 一只鸟，一只鸡，一只羊，一只大象，一只鞋，两只手

为了	◆ 为了写这篇论文,他去了两次日本。
	◆ 你父母不让你晚上出去是为了你好。

让	◆ 他比你小,你要让着他点儿。
	◆ 车来了,大家让一让。
	◆ 谁让你把这些东西都吃了?
	◆ 让我仔细想一想。

S INOGRAMS

标 標	biāo	mark, sign; to put a mark or label on	标点，标明，标题，标语，标准时间，路标，商标
材	cái	material	教材，木材，器材，身材，题材，药材
答	dá	to reply	答题，解答，问答
待	dài	to wait, to treat somebody	待人接物，待遇，等待，对待，接待，期待，招待会，招待所
掉	diào	to fall, to loose	掉过儿，掉色(shǎi)，掉头，掉下，去掉，忘掉
度	dù	to pass; degree, measure	度过，度假，度日如年，长度，风度，高度，过度，难度，能见度
断 斷	duàn	to break, to decide, to split	断定，断气，断然，断送，断言，打断，果断，间断，论断，中断 * 斷 to cut thread with an axe
而	ér	therefore, but, then	而后，而今，而已，从而，然而，因而，总而言之 * 而 a beard hanging from the chin

反		fǎn	opposite, reverse; to oppose

反常，反动，反对，反而，反感，反话，反面，反问，反义词，反正，反作用，平反，相反，相反相成

* 反 a hand in front of an object

故		gù	event, cause, old

故意，病故，事故，无故

砍		kǎn	to cut (with an axe), to chop

砍大山

杀	殺	shā	to kill

自杀

世		shì	generation, era, world

世代，世道，世面，世上，不可一世，出世，问世

* 世 three knots, each one symbolising ten years

树	樹	shù	tree; to plant

树立，树木，果树

* 樹 a tree, the earth, a container (symbol of stability) and a hand

态	態	tài	attitude

表态，动态

统	統	tǒng	in succession; to direct; global

统一，系统，正统，总统

响 響	xiǎng	to make a sound; sound	

响亮，反响，回响

| 养 養 | yǎng | to provide for, to foster |

养成，养活，养老院，养路，教养

* 羊食 food and a sheep

| 映 | yìng | to reflect |

放映，上映

| 于 | yú | at, in, by, from, to |

等于，对于，敢于，关于，由于

| 至 | zhì | until |

至多，至少，至于

* 至 an arrow stuck in (having reached) the ground

| 准 準 | zhǔn | to allow, to permit; standard, norm |

准时，水准

单句

1. 解答就是讲解和回答。
2. 问答就是有问有答。
3. 答题就是回答问题。
4. 忘掉就是忘了的意思。
5. 度假的假是假期的意思，度假就是过假期。
6. 总而言之就是总之的意思。
7. 反常就是不正常。
8. 反对革命就是反动。
9. 无故就是没有原因。
10. 果树是一种树木。
11. 表态就是表示态度。
12. 总统是国家元首。
13. 响亮就是声音很大。
14. 养老院是不工作的老人们住的地方。
15. 反作用就是相反的作用。
16. 法国进口外国的木材和药材。
17. 我敢断言这个电影一定会在美国反响很大。
18. 三年来我从来没有中断过汉语学习。
19. 孔子的思想以前是中国的正统思想。
20. 语言是一个系统。
21. 明年他要到法国去留学，因而他现在天天在学法文。
22. 那个养路工人快断气了。
23. 他处理问题很果断。
24. 待人要在有疑处不疑，做学问要在不疑处找疑。

会话

1　—你觉得这篇文章写得怎么样？
　　—题材选得不错，标题用得也很好，就是有几个标点用得不对。

2　—这条标语是谁写的？
　　—是那个身材高大的大学生。

3　—你们用的是哪个学校的教材？
　　—是北京大学的教材。

4　—你觉得他父亲这个人怎么样？
　　—他父亲很会待人接物，是位有风度有教养的人。

5　—中国知识分子的待遇高不高？
　　—不高。

6　—今天你怎么没准时到？
　　—路上出了点儿小事故。

7　—你在你家接待你的朋友吗？
　　—不，我家太小。我想让他住学校招待所。

8　—明天上映的影片是关于什么方面的？
　　—是关于中国文化方面的。

9　—对待中国统一的问题，你的态度是什么？
　　—我希望中国早日统一。国家的统一对人民有好处。

10 　—在日本，一年有多少人自杀？
　　　—至少有几百人吧。

11 　—你父亲是什么时候平反的？
　　　—是一九七九年。

12 　—你现在对这个人怎么这么反感？
　　　—由于这几年他养成了一些不好的习惯。

13 　—你是不是故意说反话？
　　　—不是，这是我的真心话。

14 　—你为什么常常打断他的话？他会不高兴的。
　　　—没关系，反正他已经不喜欢我了。

第八课　比老虎还利害

　　孔子是中国古代的大教育家和思想家。《论语》是他的弟子记录他言行的著作。孔子的思想过去被看成是中国的正统思想。尽管孔子已经死了二千多年了，可是孔子的思想还影响着中国人的行为。

　　有一天，孔子和他的弟子到齐国去，从一座大山旁边经过，看到一位妇女在路旁哭，而且哭得很伤心。于是，孔子就让他的弟子上前去问这位妇女，看看发生了什么事。

　　孔子的弟子问那位妇女：

　　"您为什么哭得这么伤心啊？一定是遇到了什么不幸吧？"

　　那位妇女答道：

　　"是呀！我们这个地方有老虎，前几天老虎吃了我公公。昨天我丈夫和我儿子又被老虎吃了。我怎么能不伤心呢？"

　　孔子的弟子感到很奇怪，又问：

　　"你们明知道这儿有老虎，但为什么不离开这个地方，到别的地方去住呢？"

　　妇女答道：

　　"虽然这里有老虎，但是没有专制统治。"

　　孔子的弟子把这位妇女说的话告诉了孔子，孔子对他的弟子们说：

　　"你们听到了吗？专制统治比老虎还利害呀！"

VOCABULARY

Presentation

教育家	n	jiàoyùjiā	pedagogue, educator
《论语》	Pn	lúnyǔ	*Analects of Confucius*
记录	vb	jìlù	to record
言行	n	yánxíng	words and deeds
著作	n	zhùzuò	work, book, writing
正统	Qvb	zhèngtǒng	orthodox
尽管	conj	jǐnguǎn	even though, in spite of
死	vb	sǐ	to die
行为	n	xíngwéi	behaviour, acts
利害	Qvb	lìhai	terrible, formidable
弟子	n	dìzǐ	disciple
齐国	Pn	Qíguó	the Qi Kingdom
座	Mw	zuò	[Mw for seats, mountains, pagodas...]
经过	vb	jīngguò	to pass through, to go across
妇女	n	fùnǚ	woman
哭	vb	kū	to cry
而且	conj	érqiě	but also
伤心	Qvb	shāngxīn	sad
于是	conj	yúshì	hence, so
发生	vb	fāshēng	to happen
不幸	n	búshìng	misfortune
答道	vb	dádào	to reply
公公	n	gōnggong	father-in-law (husband's father)
丈夫	n	zhàngfu	husband
但是	conj	dànshì	but
专制	n	zhuānzhì	despotism, autocracy
统治	n	tǒngzhì	rule, domination

75

尽管	◆ 你有什么问题尽管对我说。
	◆ 尽管这本书很贵，可是我还是要买。
	◆ 这个地方我没去过，尽管我在北京住了很长时间。

经过	◆ 我把昨天事情的经过告诉了他们。
	◆ 从北京坐火车到上海要经过山东。
	◆ 经过研究，大家同意让我先去问问他。
	◆ 这是经过老师同意的。

而且	◆ 今天来的人都是我的朋友，而且有的还是我的小学同学。
	◆ 他不但会法文，而且还会中文和日文。
	◆ 他做的饭好吃，而且花钱不多。

| 于是 | ◆ 这个问题我还是不懂，于是我又问了老师一遍。 |
| | ◆ 那本书卖完了，于是我就买了这本。 |

| 明 | ◆ 你明知道下午有事，为什么还出去呢？ |
| | ◆ 明明是你忘了，怎么说是我没说呢？ |

| 虽然…但是… | ◆ 虽然他说这是真的，但是我不相信。 |
| | ◆ 这个孩子虽然不大，但是懂的事情却不少。 |

但	dàn	but
		不但

弟	dì	younger brother
		弟弟，表弟，高干子弟

* 𡕡 a cord coiled at different levels, symbol of the rank of brotherhood

---

妇 婦	fù	married woman
		妇科，夫妇，主妇

* 𡚸 a woman holding a broom

管	guǎn	to bother, to mind, to manage, to be in charge of; pipe, tube

管理，管事，管用，管子，别管，不管，看管，气管，水管，主管

害	hài	to harm, to hurt

害处，害鸟，害人，受害，无害，要害，有害

尽 盡	jǐn	to the greatest extent, to give priority to
		尽快，尽先，尽早，尽着
	jìn	to exhaust, to the limit

尽其所长，尽其所有，尽头，尽心，尽兴，尽意，用尽

* 𦥔 a hand stirring a fire in a container

哭	kū	to cry
		哭声，大哭

* 𡘜 a barking dog

利	lì	sharp, interest, favourable	

利落，利息，利用，利于，便利，不利，名利，有利

* 𥝢 a knife and grain

齐 齊	qí	uniform, together, complete

齐唱，齐名，齐心，百花齐放

* 𠧎 three ears of grain growing in a straight and orderly fashion

---

且	qiě	and , for the moment

且说，不但...而且...

伤 傷	shāng	wound; to wound

伤风，伤感，伤害，伤口，伤人，伤天害理，受伤

死	sǐ	to die

死板，死得其所，死活，死路，死去，死人，死心，饿死，生死

* 𣦵 a person kneeling before a skeleton

幸	xìng	fortunate, lucky, happy

幸得，幸而，幸好

育	yù	to give birth to , to raise, to bring up

发育，教育，生育，体育

* 育 a child, head downwards and a flesh radical

丈	zhàng	a unit of length = 3. 33 metres, husband

* 丈 a hand holding a stick, symbol of measure

制	zhì	to make, to manufacture, to control

制定，制动器，制度，制革，制片人，制作，法制，公有制，机制，所有制，特制，体制

* 㓞 a knife cutting a vegetable

治	zhì	to administer, to treat, to cure, to control

治安，治病，自治区

著	zhù	outstanding; to show, to write a book; book

著名，著书立说，著者，名著，原著

专 專	zhuān	specially, concentrated; to monopolize

专长，专场，专车，专机，专家，专科，专门，专题，专心，专利

座	zuò	seat, seating, [Mw for objects with a stable base]

座次，座位，座钟，座子，讲座，让座，在座

单句

1. 医院里看妇女病的科室叫妇科。
2. 丈夫和他的夫人叫夫妇。
3. 有害的鸟叫害鸟。
4. 受害就是受到伤害。
5. 无害就是没有害处。
6. 哭声就是哭的声音。
7. 大哭就是大声哭。
8. 便利和方便是同义词。
9. 有利就是有好处，不利就是没有好处。
10. 齐唱就是同时一起唱。
11. 齐名就是有同样的名望。
12. 伤风是一种常见病。
13. 使人受到伤害叫伤人。
14. 生育就是生孩子。
15. 著名和有名是同义词。
16. 很有名的著作叫名著。
17. 一个人的特长也叫专长。
18. 电影院里或飞机上人们坐的位子叫座位。
19. 把座位让给别人坐叫让座。
20. 中国有五个自治区。
21. 公有制是一种所有制。
22. 管理一个大学比管理一个图书馆难得多。
23. 水管是一种管子。
24. 我孩子小时候常常有病，发育不太好。
25. 没有法制就没有民主。
26. 我们班的同学都很齐心。
27. 今天在座的有各方面的专家。

会话

1 —我给你介绍一下，他是我弟弟，大学体育老师。
   —你好，认识你很高兴。

2 —你觉得这个城市的治安怎么样？
   —我不太了解，他主管治安工作，你最好去问他。

3 —你喜欢高干子弟吗？
   —不喜欢。一般来说，高干子弟的名利思想都很重。

4 —你同意让你孩子喝酒吗？
   —我不但不同意，而且反对他喝酒。我觉得喝酒对身体有
    害。

5 —听说有好多人受伤了？
   —是的，至少有几百名。我想利用星期天专门去看望他们一
    次。

6 —明天学校有一个专题讲座，你去听吗？
   —什么讲座？
   —介绍法国的教育制度。

7 —什么叫著书立说？
   —就是把自己的学说写成书。

8 —饭怎么还没做好？我都快饿死了！
   —马上就好了，再等五分钟我们就吃饭。

9　—这个人工作怎么样？

　　—不怎么样，干事情一点儿也不专心，而且还很死
　　　板。

10　—你父亲的病怎么样了？如果还不好，最好去找专家
　　　看看。

　　—找专家看过了，吃了不少药也不管用。

11　—这是谁的飞机？

　　—这是总统的专机。

第九课　古诗三首

〔王安石〕

京口瓜洲一水间
钟山只隔数重山
春风又绿江南岸
明月何时照我还

〔李白〕

床前明月光
疑是地上霜
举头望明月
低头思故乡

〔王之涣〕

白日依山尽
黄河入海流
欲穷千里目
更上一层楼

Li Bai(Li Po)(701-762), lived at the beginning of the Tang Dynasty and along with his contemporary Du Fu(712-770) is traditionally considered as one of China's greatest poetic geniuses. He had a Taoist mentality and rebelled against the established order. After he left Sichuan (as an adult), the province where he grew up, he lived a marginal life. Legend has it that this great lover of alcohol drowned when, drunk, he tried to catch the moon's reflection on the water of the Yangtze River.

Wang Zhihuan (668-742), a native of Shanxi, lived at the beginning of the Tang Dynasty. Member of a circle of poets which included Wang Changling, he excelled in short poems, characterized by their musicality.

Wang Anshi (1021-1086), a native of Jiangxi, and a great statesman of the Song Dynasty who initiated economic and social reforms that eliminated a number of privileges of the rich and powerful.

岸	àn	river bank, shore, coast

岸边，对岸，海岸，河岸

* The original pictogram 厂 has been enhanced by the mountain radical and a phonetic element 干

层 層	céng	storey, floor, layer

层次，层次分明，上层，下层

床	chuáng	bed

起床

低	dī	to lower; low

低声，高低

隔	gé	to separate; partition

隔断，隔开，隔离

瓜	guā	melon

瓜分，瓜田李下，爪子儿，地瓜，冬瓜，黄瓜，木瓜，南瓜，西瓜，香瓜

* 瓜 a melon on the vine

举 舉	jǔ	to lift

举办，举杯，举手，举行，一举两得

* several hands offering an object

流	liú	to flow

流传，流动，流放，流利，流通，流行，流行病，电流，风流，河流，落花流水，水流，下流，主流

绿	綠	lǜ	green

绿色

目	mù	eye, item, catalogue

目标，目不识丁，目的，目的地，目前，面目，条目，心目

* 👁 an eye

穷	窮	qióng	poor; thoroughly; to limit

穷尽，穷人，无穷

* 穴 + 力 : a cave (hole) and force, "shackled"

入	rù	to enter

入口，入门，入手，入学，出入，进入，收入

* 入 an arrow like object

诗	詩	shī	poem

诗词，诗歌，诗人

石	shí	stone

石板，石刻，石头

* 石 a cliff and a rock

数	數	shù	number

数目，数学，数字

shǔ to count

数数

霜	shuāng	frost
		下霜

依	yī	to lean on, to depend upon, to comply with; according to
		依据，依然

欲	yù	to want; desire
		欲望

照	zhào	to shine, to illuminate, to take a photograph; according to
		照办，照常，照旧，照片，照相，照相机，关照，依照

洲	zhōu	continent, islet in a river
		非洲，美洲，南极洲
		* 氵 land surrounded by water and the water radical

1. 瓜子儿就是瓜的种子。
2. 举杯就是举起杯子，举手就是举起手。
3. 低的反义词是高。
4. 穷人就是没有钱的人，它的反义词是富人。
5. 照常就是和平常一样。
6. 照相机就是照相用的机器。
7. 进学校学习叫入学。
8. 出入就是出来进去。
9. 石板是用石头作的。
10. 我的家住在河对岸。
11. 长江和黄河是中国两条最大的河流。
12. 现在中国正在流行这首歌。
13. 他很喜欢石刻艺术。
14. 这条路高低不平，你开车不要开得太快。
15. 这篇文章层次分明。
16. 你在他心目中是一个了不起的人物。
17. 低声就是说话的声音很低。
18. 我第一次来中国，请您多多关照！
19. 他的欲望是将来能买一所房子。

1   —你每天早上几点起床？
     —我一般是七点半起床。

2 —你住十八楼几层？
　—我住十八楼一层。

3 —你喜欢吃什么瓜？
　—我喜欢吃冬瓜和黄瓜。夏天的时候我最喜欢吃西瓜和香瓜。

4 —招待会什么时候举行？
　—明天晚上七点半。

5 —这个晚会是谁举办的？
　—是大学工会举办的。

6 —他的法语说得怎么样？
　—他不但发音很好，而且说得也很流利。

7 —你学习汉语的目的是什么？
　—将来我想去中国工作。

8 —你去过非洲吗？
　—去过。你看，这是我在非洲照的照片。

9 —目前法国想学数学的大学生多不多？
　—不太多，而且一年比一年少。

10 —这个病人要马上隔离。
　—为什么？
　—因为他得的是流行病。

11 —北京的流动人口有多少？
　—数目很大，至少有二百万。

12   —你一个月的收入有多少？

　　　　—五百三十元。

13   —你为什么对他反感?

　　　　—他说话很下流，一点儿也没有教养。

14   —听说这位诗人很风流?

　　　　—不知道，我只知道他的诗写得很好。

15   —你说这个数字不对，依据是什么?

　　　　—这个数字和这本书上的不一样。

第十课　走马观花

人们传说，从前有个叫贵亮的年轻人，他的脚有毛病，走路很困难。可是，他却想找一个长得好看的爱人，于是就让他的朋友何汉替他介绍一个姑娘。正好，有个名叫叶青的姑娘，鼻子有些毛病，也要何汉给她找个满意的情人。何汉想：让她和贵亮结婚，不是很好吗？

有一天，何汉让贵亮骑着马从叶青家门前走过，又叫叶青手里拿着一朵花，站在家门口，装作闻花的样子。

叶青看到贵亮骑在马上，样子好看极了，心里非常喜欢。贵亮也爱上了这个很好看的闻花姑娘。

结婚那天，两人又见了面，说起"走马观花"的情景，双方这时才明白为什么一个骑马，一个闻花。

现在人们常用这个成语来形容，一个人参观一个地方，很快地看了一遍，但没有仔细观察。

V OCABULARY

走马观花	exp	zǒumǎguānhuā	to skim the surface
从前	n	cóngqián	formerly, in the past
贵亮	Pn	Guìliàng	Guiliang [given name]
脚	n	jiǎo	foot
毛病	n	máobìng	fault, imperfection
困难	n, Qvb	kùnnan	difficulty; to be in difficulty
何汉	Pn	Hé Hàn	He Han [a name]
替	prep	tì	on someone's behalf, instead of
叶青	Pn	Yè Qīng	Ye Qing [a name]
姑娘	n	gūniang	girl
鼻子	n	bízi	nose
满意	Qvb	mǎnyì	to be satisfied
情人	n	qíngrén	lover
结婚	vb	jiéhūn	to marry
朵	Mw	duǒ	[Mw for flowers]
装作	vb	zhuāngzuò	to pretend
闻	vb	wén	to smell, to hear
样子	n	yàngzi	appearance, manner, aspect
情景	n	qíngjǐng	situation
双方	n	shuāngfāng	both sides, both parties
明白	vb	míngbai	to understand
形容	vb	xíngróng	to describe
参观	n, vb	cānguān	visit; to visit
遍	Mw	biàn	[verbal Mw] time (i. e. one time, two times, etc.)
观察	vb	guānchá	to observe, to examine

93

走马观花	◆ 今天我没有时间，只是走马观花看了一遍。
困难	◆ 他现在生活很困难。 ◆ 你有什么困难可以来找我。
替	◆ 你休息一下，我替你干一会儿。 ◆ 大家都替你高兴。
正好	◆ 今天我正好有时间。 ◆ 正好，我买了两张票，你一张我一张。 ◆ 你来得正好，我正想给你打电话呢。
满意	◆ 他对这个房子很满意。 ◆ 这是他最满意的一本书。
遍	◆ 这本书我看了一遍。 ◆ 这本书我一遍也没看过。 like 一次,the verbal measure word 一遍 means "once" however it incorporates the idea of "from beginning to end".

鼻	bí	nose
		鼻孔，鼻音

遍	biàn	everywhere, [verbal Mw]

参 参	cān	to participate, to join, to consult
		参看，参照，人参(rénshēn)

察	chá	to examine
		察觉，察看
		* 𥜒 a roof and a hand putting meat on a sacrificial altar

朵	duǒ	[Mw for flowers]
		花朵

姑	gū	paternal aunt; girl
		姑父，姑姑，姑妈，姑母，姑且，姑息

观 觀	guān	to observe, to inspect
		观察家，观点，观光，观看，观念，察言观色，乐观，旁观者清，人生观，主观

婚	hūn	marriage
		婚期，婚事，婚书，定婚，离婚，求婚，晚婚，再婚，早婚

脚	jiǎo	foot
		脚本，脚跟

结 **結**	jié	to knot, to attach, to end	结成，结构，结果，结合，结论，结算，结业，总结
景	jǐng	scenery, view, circumstance	景色，景山，景象，背景，大杀风景，风景，光景，前景，夜景
困	kùn	to be hard pressed, difficult, sleepy	穷困
满	mǎn	full	满城风雨，满怀，满满当当，满面春风，满期，满人，满月，满洲，满座，不满，美满，完满，自满
娘	niáng	mother, a young woman	老大娘，新娘
青	qīng	blue-green, black	青菜，青春，青海，青年，青衣，万古长青 * 靑 生＋丹："to grow" + "cinnabar", symbol of colour
容	róng	to hold, to contain, to tolerate, to allow; appearance	容器，从容，面容
双 **雙**	shuāng	pair	双边，双重，双打，双关语，双名，双亲，双喜 * 雙 a hand holding two birds

替		tì	to replace, in the place of 替代,替换,代替,交替,接替
闻 聞		wén	to hear, to smell 闻风而动,闻名,百闻不如一见,传闻,新闻
形		xíng	form, aspect 形成,形而上学,形容词,形声字,形态,形体, 形象,形形色色,形影不离,词形,得意忘形,方 形,情形,无形,象形字
叶 葉		yè	leaf, [Fn] 叶公好龙,叶子,茶叶,落叶,树叶
装 裝		zhuāng	clothing, costume; to pretend, to install 装出,安装,服装,化装,西装,中山装

单句

1. 从鼻子里发出的音叫鼻音。
2. 人参是一种名贵的中药。
3. 姑姑也叫姑妈。
4. 婚事就是男女结婚的事。
5. 结婚的日期叫婚期。
6. 一个男子请求一个女子和他结婚叫求婚。
7. 在中国男二十五岁以后女二十三岁以后结婚叫晚婚。
8. 晚上的景色叫夜景。
9. 景山是北京的一个公园，在北海公园旁边。
10. 穷困指一个人很穷，而且在生活上困难很多。
11. 中国的东北以前叫满洲。
12. 一个孩子出生后过完第一个月叫满月。
13. 满座是指座位都坐满了人。
14. 小孩和青年人对六十岁以上的妇女可以叫老大娘。
15. 新结婚的女人叫新娘。
16. 青海是一个地区的名字，在中国西北地区。
17. 一句话同时包含两个意思叫双关语。
18. 双亲就是指父亲和母亲两个亲人。
19. 双喜指同时有两个喜事。
20. 闻名和有名、著名是同义词。
21. "百闻不如一见"是一条成语，意思是听一百次不如亲眼见一次。
22. 从树上落下的叶子叫落叶。
23. 对待人生的态度叫人生观。

24. 他的人生观对不对，现在下结论还太早。

25. 假期我想把学习总结一下。

26. 他们结婚后生活得很美满。

27. 这个问题请参看本书第三章。

会话

1 ——"不满"这个词怎么用？
　——"不满"这个词是形容词，可以说，我对他很不满。

2 ——你们定婚了吗？
　——已经定婚了，我们打算明年五月份结婚。

3 ——你觉得他这个人怎么样？
　——他很乐观，而且从不自满。

4 ——你同意不同意他的观点？
　——我不同意，他的看法有些主观。

5 ——今天你看报了吗？有什么重要新闻？
　——看了，美国总统明天将到达法国。

6 ——你去过黄山吗？
　——去过，我觉得黄山的风景真是美极了。

7 ——"妈"是不是象形字？
　——不是，是形声字。"女"是形旁，"马"是声旁。

8   —你怎么老买青菜呀?

　　　—我不喜欢吃肉。《观察家》报上有一篇文章说，多吃青菜
　　　　对身体有好处。

9   —听说法国离婚的人数很多，是吗?

　　　—是的，越来越多。

10   —你去哪儿了?

　　　—我去服装店了，买了一身西装和一身中山装。

11   —你走了，谁接替你的工作?

　　　—可能是新来的那个青年人。

12   —你们家安装电话了吗?

　　　—还没有。

13   —你看过这个电影的脚本吗?

　　　—看过，脚本写得不错。

CIVILISATION

The Elements

As is shown in Lesson 20 on traditional Chinese medicine, Chinese thought has a global view on a world full of things that correspond and interact. . .

NUMBERS	1	2	3	4	5
ELEMENTS	water	fire	wood	metal	earth
ORIENTATION	north	south	east	west	centre
HUMAN ACTIVITIES	gesture gravity	word order	sight wisdom	hearing understanding	willingness holiness
HEAVENLY SIGNS	rain	Yang	heat	cold	wind
COLOURS	black	red	green	white	yellow
TASTES	salt	bitter	acidic	acrid	sweet
SMELLS	rotten	burnt	rancid	raw meat	perfume
PLANT FOODSTUFFS	yellow millet	beans	wheat	oil seeds	white millet
DOMESTIC ANIMALS	pig	chicken	sheep	dog	cow
ANIMAL CLASS	hard skin	feathers	scales	hair	bare skin
PARTS OF THE HOUSE	alley or well	heath	inside door	main gate	impluvium (pool for collecting rain water)
MUSIC NOTES	Yu	Zhi	Jiao	Shang	Gong
ORGANS	kidneys	lungs	spleen	liver	heart

11

第十一课 杯弓蛇影

古时候，有个人叫乐广。他很喜欢帮助人，也很会用道理说服人。乐广有个好朋友，和他住在同一条街上。两个人常常在一起喝酒、谈天。可是后来，那个朋友有一个多月没到乐广家来了。乐广就派人去了解情况。派去的人回来说，那个朋友病了。原来上一次他在乐广家喝酒，看见酒杯里有一条小蛇。可是酒已经喝下去了，有什么办法呢！他当时心里很不舒服，回到家里就病了。

乐广听了，觉得很奇怪，酒杯里怎么会有小蛇呢？他走到上一次喝酒的地方，仔仔细细地看了一遍，忽然看见墙上挂着一张弓，他立刻明白了。于是，他又派人去请那个朋友来喝酒，而且还说他能治好他的病。

那个朋友开始很不愿意来，最后他还是来了。乐广已经准备好了酒菜，让他朋友还坐在老地方。那个朋友本来就很不放心，他往酒杯里一看，啊！那条小蛇还在酒杯里呢！他吓得出了一身冷汗。乐广指着墙上的弓笑着说："酒杯里没有什么蛇，这是墙上弓的影子。"

他把墙上的弓拿下来，酒杯里的小蛇立刻不见了。他朋友这才明白是怎么一回事，病也就好了。

这个成语用来形容有人怀疑这个、怀疑那个，实际上并没有那么一回事。

西方人看了这个成语故事之后，可能会觉得这和现代精神分析学所使用的方法类似。精神分析医生在给某一个病人治病时，往往要这个人回忆他过去所经历的事情。

VOCABULARY

杯弓蛇影	exp	bēigōngshéyǐng	unreasonable fear
乐广	Pn	Yuè Guǎng	Yue Guang [given name]
帮助	vb, n	bāngzhù	to help; help
说服	vb	shuōfú	to convince
街	n	jiē	street
谈天	vb	tántiān	to chat
派	vb, n	pài	to send; faction
蛇	n	shé	snake
舒服	Qvb	shūfu	to be comfortable, to feel at ease
忽然	adv	hūrán	suddenly
弓	n	gōng	bow (archery)
立刻	adv	lìkè	immediately
治	vb	zhì	to treat, to cure
愿意	vb	yuànyì	to wish , to be willing
汗	n	hàn	sweat
笑	vb	xiào	to laugh
影子	n	yǐngzi	shadow
实际	n	shíjì	reality, in practice
精神分析学	n	jīngshénfēnxīxué	psychoanalysis
精神	n	jīngshén	spirit
分析	n, vb	fēnxī	analysis; to analyse
类似	adj	lèisì	similar, analogous
某	pro	mǒu	certain···, some
回忆	vb	huíyì	to recollect, to call to mind
经历	n	jīnglì	experience
准备	vb	zhǔnbèi	to prepare

103

帮助	◆ 他常常帮助别人。 ◆ 谢谢你的帮助。
后来	◆ 他去年三月来过一次，后来就再没有来过。 ◆ 他起先在小学当老师，后来到商店工作去了。
vb + 下去	◆ 你从楼上走下去。 ◆ 这本小说没有意思，我不想看下去了。 This directional construction can have the figurative sense of "to continue to..."
vb + 下来	◆ 他们走下飞机来。 ◆ 你把楼上的东西拿下来。 ◆ 你把你的名字写下来。 ◆ 天慢慢地黑了下来。
仔仔细细	◆ 仔细—仔仔细细　认真—认认真真　高兴—高高兴兴　舒服—舒舒服服 ◆ 他高高兴兴地去学校。
忽然	◆ 他说着说着，忽然不说了。 ◆ 不知为什么，他忽然大笑起来。
立刻	◆ 请大家立刻到办公室去。 ◆ 老师一进来，大家立刻不说了。
老	◆ 每天下午他老在图书馆。 ◆ 他老是那么高兴。 ◆ 我早就想去他们家，可是老没时间。

本来	◆ 他本来的样子比现在好看多了。
	◆ 我们几个人本来不是一个班的。
	◆ 他的病没好,本来就不能去。
	◆ 本来么,一个孩子懂什么?

实际	◆ 他的想法很不实际。
	◆ 不能只听他怎么说,要看他的实际行动。
	◆ 他说他去过很多次日本,实际上他只去过一次。

并	◆ 这两个地方并没有很大的区别。
	◆ 他参观了学校,并在教师会上讲了话。

某	◆ 他在某大学工作。
	◆ 他的同事张某病了。
	◆ 有我王某在,你就放心吧!

S INOGRAMS

帮 幫	bāng	to help; a gang of people	

帮会,帮忙,帮手,四人帮

备 備	bèi	to prepare, to complete

备而不用,备课,备用,备注,具备,完备

并	bìng	side by side, and

并非,并进,并举,并立,并且,并行,并重

* 川 two people side by side

弓	gōng	bow (archery)

* 弓 a bow with two curves

汗	hàn	sweat

汗水,出汗,流汗

际 際	jì	limit, border, occasion, inter

边际,国际,无际,一望无际

街	jiē	street

街道,街上,街头,大街

精	jīng	refined, excellent, energy, spirit

精美,精神病,精心,酒精

历 歷 曆	lì	to go through, past, calendar

历代,历法,历来,历年,病历,公历,旧历,来历,年历,日历,阳历

忽	hū	suddenly; to neglect

某	mǒu	certain, some
		某地，某某

派	pài	to send, to dispatch; school of thought, faction
		派别，派出所，派生，派头，学派，正派
		* 𣲑 branch of a river

蛇	shé	snake
		蛇肉
		* 𧈧 snake, enhanced with the crawling animal radical

实 實	shí	solid, true, real, fruit
		实词，实话，实况，实物，实习，实现，实行，实用，实在，果实，老实，落实，其实，事实，现实，写实，真实，子实

舒	shū	to unfold, to stretch, to loosen, to relax
		舒心

似	sì	to be similar to
		似是而非，近似，相似

谈 談	tán	to talk, to chat
		谈话，谈天，谈心，会谈

析	xī	to separate, to analyse
		* 𣂪 to chop up wood

笑	xiào	to laugh
		笑话，发笑，干笑，好笑，可笑，冷笑，取笑
		* 𥬇 a person waving hands under bamboo leaves

忆 憶	yì	to remember

愿 願	yuàn	to wish, to want

愿望，情愿，心愿，祝愿，自愿

助	zhù	to help

助词，助动词，助教，助理

助跑，助手，助听器，助学金，助长

单句

1. 帮助别人做事叫帮忙。
2. 帮助工作的人叫帮手。
3. "一望无际"是一个成语,指很远,眼睛看不到头。
4. 非常用心叫精心。
5. 阳历也叫公历,是一种历法。
6. 旧历是指中国的一种历法。
7. 真实的话叫实话。
8. 汉语中动词、名词、形容词、数词、代词等是实词。
9. "的"、"得"、"地"是助词。
10. "想"、"能"、"要"等是助动词。
11. 实际应用的东西叫实物。
12. 真实的情况叫事实。
13. 相似和近似是同义词。
14. 随便谈话叫谈天。
15. 听起来使人发笑的故事叫笑话。
16. 心中的愿望叫心愿。
17. 情愿和自愿是同义词。
18. 明天中美举行首脑会谈。
19. 我朋友送了我一本精美的日历。
20. 现在很多人对现实不满。
21. 我的愿望是一定会实现的。
22. 他的研究成果已经达到了国际水平。

会话

1 —你的行李准备好了吗?要不要我帮忙?
  —不用了，我的行李都准备好了。

2 —你每天都备课吗?
  —不，其实我一个星期只备一次课。

3 —你觉得王先生怎么样?
  —这个人很老实，并且也很正派。

4 —你现在还是助教吗?
  —不，已经是讲师了，而且还是校长助理。

5 —你怎么买了两个助听器?
  —有一个是备用的。

6 —他得的是什么病?
  —神经病，这是他的病历。

7 —请问，派出所在哪儿?
  —往前走不远就是。

8 —你拿到助学金了吗?
  —拿到了。
  —这下你可舒心了。

9 —今天街上人多不多?
  —太多了，真是人山人海。

Kong Himself: "Pour me a drink."

12

第十二课 《孔乙己》节选〔鲁迅〕

只有孔乙己到店，才可以笑几声，所以至今还记得。……他身材很高大，青白脸色……

他对人说话，总是满口之乎者也，叫人半懂不懂的。……

孔乙己是这样的使人快活，可是没有他，别人也便这么过。……

中秋过后，秋风是一天凉比一天，看看将近初冬；我整天的靠着火……

一天的下半天，没有一个顾客，我正合了眼坐着。忽然间听得一个声音，"温一碗酒"。这声音虽然极低，却很耳熟。……不一会，他喝完酒，便又在旁人的说笑声中，坐着用这手慢慢走去了。

自此以后，又长久没有看见孔乙己。……

我到现在终于没有见—大约孔乙己的确死了。

VOCABULARY

孔乙己	Pn	Kǒng Yǐjǐ	Kong Yiji (Kong Himself)
身材	n	shēncái	stature, figure
青白	Qvb	qīngbái	pale
脸色	n	liǎnsè	complexion
总是	adv	zǒngshì	always
之乎者也	exq	zhīhūzhěyě	pedantic terms, archaisms
快活	Qvb	kuàihuo	happy, joyful
便	adv	biàn	therefore, then, so long as
中秋	n	Zhōngqiū	Mid-Autumn Festival
将近	vb	jiāngjìn	to be close to, nearly, almost
初冬	n	chūdōng	the beginning of winter
整天	Tw	zhěngtiān	the whole day
靠	vb	kào	to lean on, to depend upon, to come up to
顾客	n	gùkè	customer
合	vb	hé	to close
忽然间	adv	hūránjiān	suddenly
温	vb	wēn	to warm up
碗	Mw, n	wǎn	bowl, bowl of…
低	Qvb	dī	low, to be low
耳熟	Qvb	ěrshú	to be familiar to the ear
不一会	loc	bùyíhuì	a little later, in a short while
自此	conj	zìcǐ	from then on
长久	adv	chángjiǔ	a very long time
终于	adv	zhōngyú	finally
大约	adv	dàyuē	approximately
的确	adv	díquè	indeed, really
记得	vb	jìde	to remember

113

只有	◆ 只有他爱人知道他去哪儿了。 ◆ 只有吃这种药,你的病才能好。
总是	◆ 他每天晚上总是来这儿喝茶。 ◆ 他一天到晚总是高高兴兴的。 ◆ 人总是要死的。
叫	◆ 鸡叫过两遍了。 ◆ 小王,老张叫你。 ◆ 他叫了一辆出租汽车。 ◆ 他叫我跟他一起回家。
便	◆ 他一听便明白了。 ◆ 他吃了饭便回家了。
一天比一天	◆ 天气一天比一天冷了。 ◆ 他汉语说得一天比一天好。
碗	◆ 一个碗 ◆ 一碗饭,一碗米,一碗水
终于	◆ 等了他两个小时,他终于来了。 ◆ 住了一个月医院,他的病终于好了。 Unlike 终于, 到底 takes the particle 了 and can have the meaning "after all", especially in a question: 你到底去不去?

大约	◆ 明天大约有五百多人来参观。
	◆ 他大约十七八岁。
	◆ 他大约已经到家了。
的确	◆ 这个电影的确很好。
	◆ 他的确去过那个地方。
	◆ 的确，那时候我是有过这样的想法。

初	chū	beginning

初次,初期,初学,初中,当初,年初,起初,月初,最初

* 㐅彡 a piece of clothing and a knife, the beginning of a cut

此	cǐ	this

此地,此后,此刻,此时,此外,从此,如此,特此,为此,因此,由此可见,至此

耳	ěr	ear

耳边风,耳朵,耳机,耳目,耳语,木耳,亲耳

* 𦥑 an ear

顾 顧	gù	to turn around and look at, to attend to

顾问,顾名思义,不顾,回顾,照顾

合	hé	to close, to unite, to correspond

合不来,合唱,合成,合成词,合得来,合法,合法化,合金,合理,合流,合龙,合情合理,合身,合算,合同,合意,合影,合作,不合,场合,化合物,会合

* 合 a lid and an opening

忽	hū	sudden; to ignore

忽地,忽而,忽冷忽热,忽视

乎	hū	[particle]

不在乎,出乎意外,合乎,几乎,满不在乎,似乎

记 记	jì	to remember, note

记忆,记者,记住,笔记,笔记本,日记,书记,死记,忘记,传记,总书记

靠	kào	to lean on, to depend upon, to count upon, to get near

靠岸,靠不住,靠边,靠得住,靠近,靠山,可靠,依靠

客	kè	visitor, traveller, customer

客车,客店,客饭,客观,客家话,客气,客人,客体,好客,请客,作客

* 客 to stop (a backward foot + an opening) once having arrived under a roof

脸 臉	liǎn	face

不要脸,瓜子脸,花脸

确 確	què	true, real, firmly

确定,确立,确认,确认书,确实,确信,明确,千真万确,正确,准确

熟	shú(shóu)	ripe, cooked, familiar

熟菜,熟人,熟习,成熟,眼熟

碗	wǎn	bowl, a bowl of ... (Mw)

茶碗,饭碗

温	wēn	warm; to heat up, to review

温带，温度，温度计，温故知新，温和，温和 (wēnhuo)，温课，温情，温室，温习，北温带，低温，高温，南温带，气温，体温，体温计，重温旧梦

乙	yǐ	second

约 約	yuē	to make arrangements for; approximately

约定，约会，约请，大约，合约，特约，条约，新约

整	zhěng	complete, correct; to arrange

整风，整个，整理，整年，整体，整天，整整，完整

终 終	zhōng	end

终点站，终究，终了，终年，终日，终身，终生，年终，始终，月终

* ∧ a skein of wire tied at each end and a silk radical

单句

1. 初次就是第一次。
2. 初学就是刚开始学。
3. 当初、起初、最初都是同义词。
4. 一年开始的第一二个月叫年初。
5. "此"是代词,是"这"的意思,"此地"就是这个地方,"此时"就是这个时候。
6. 耳边就是耳朵旁边。
7. 耳语就是小声说话。
8. 几个人在一起照相叫合影。
9. 一会儿冷一会儿热叫忽冷忽热。
10. 记笔记的本子叫笔记本。
11. 请客人或朋友吃饭叫请客。
12. 乐于接待客人叫好客。
13. 客家话是广东一带的一种方言。
14. 脸的样子像瓜子一样叫瓜子脸。
15. 千真万确就是十分正确。
16. 熟人就是认识而且关系很近的人。
17. 喝茶用的碗叫茶碗。
18. 吃饭用的碗叫饭碗。
19. 身体的温度叫体温。
20. 很低的温度叫低温。
21. 汽车或火车的最后一站叫终点站。
22. 从开始到最后叫始终。
23. 这个词用得很准确。
24. 结婚是一个人的终身大事。

25. 他常常做不合法的事,可是他满不在乎。

26. 你这么做合情合理。

27. 他的学习目的不太明确。

28. 他把过去的事情都忘记了。

29. 我的家靠近北京火车站。

30. 他的死确实出乎意外。

31. 十块钱买一个耳机很合算。

会话

1　—你孩子上初中了吗?
　　—还没有,明年开始上初中。

2　—我想找个可靠的人帮我照顾一下我的孩子。
　　—为什么?
　　—因为我是记者,整天不在家。我孩子又太小,很不成熟。

3　—今天的气温是多少度?
　　—三十二度。

4　—假期你想做什么?
　　—我想把上课的笔记整理整理,把学过的课文温习一下。

5　—明天下午开会是真的吗?
　　—没错,我是亲耳听书记说的。

6　—为什么你们选他作班长?
　　—他看问题客观,又很老实,因此我们选他。

7　—你天天写日记吗?
　　—不,大约一个星期写两篇日记。

8　—今天晚上你能来我家吗?
　　—不行,我八点有个约会。

9　—你跟她合得来合不来?
　　—还可以,只是她对我总是那么客气。

10　—你们双方合作得怎么样?
　　—不错,双方都很满意。

13

第十三课　读者来信(一)

'一位'和'一个'

一天，去一家理发店理发。由于店少人多，大家都在门口排队静候服务员呼叫。不同的服务员在招呼顾客时使用不同的量词。有的用'来一位!'，有的用'来一个!'。这'一位'和'一个'，虽然只差一个字，但细细品来，给人的感觉大不相同。前者显得热情，后者则显得冷淡。称'个'还算客气的，不客气的甚至称个子小的顾客为'小个儿的'，称老年人为'老头儿'等等。商业、服务性行业工作人员的一言一行，往往给顾客留下深刻的印象。所以他们应该重视在称呼顾客时的用词。

《北京晚报》

VOCABULARY

读者	n	dúzhě	reader
理发店	n	lǐfàdiàn	hair dresser's, barber's
理发	vb	lǐfà	to have a hair cut
由于	conj	yóuyú	due to, because
排队	vb	páiduì	to queue up
静候	vb	jìnghòu	to wait patiently
服务员	n	fúwùyuán	attendant, employee
呼叫	vb	hūjiào	to call
招呼	vb	zhāohu	to call, to signal
量词	n	liàngcí	measure word
细细	adv	xìxì	in detail, very carefully
品	vb	pǐn	to sample, to savour; quality
前者	pro	qiánzhě	the former
显得	vb	xiǎnde	to appear, to seem
后者	pro	hòuzhě	the latter
则	adv	zé	therefore [indicates result or condition]
冷淡	Qvb	lěngdàn	to be cold, freezing
称	vb	chēng	to call, to name
客气	Qvb	kèqi	polite, to stand on ceremony
甚至	conj	shènzhì	even. . . to the extent of. . .
商业	n	shāngyè	commerce, enterprise
行业	n	hángyè	branch, trade
人员	n	rényuán	staff, personnel
一言一行	exp	yìyányìxíng	every word and action
深刻	Qvb	shēnkè	to be deep
印象	n	yìnxiàng	impression
应该	vb	yīnggāi	must

重视	vb, n	zhòngshi	to attach importance to
称呼	n, vb	chēnghu	to call (by the name of...), to address; name
性		xìng	nature, quality

Use

由于	
	◆ 由于时间关系,我不能再等他了。
	◆ 由于这几天他没有休息,所以他觉得特别累。

则	
	◆ 想看电影的去电影院,不想看的则在家休息。
	◆ 我住的房子冬天则热,夏天则凉。
	◆ 秋天去北京最好,一则天气不冷不热,二则路上和公园里人不多,三则飞机票不太贵。

算	
	◆ 他算题算得很快。
	◆ 今天去参观的人,算上我,一共是十个人。
	◆ 从今天起,你算是大学生了。
	◆ 虽然是冬天了,可是还不算太冷。
	◆ 就算你知道了,又有什么用呢?
	◆ 说话算话,不能说了不算。
	◆ 算了,我们今天不去了。

甚至	
	◆ 他长大了,甚至我都快认不出他了。
	◆ 他在这个地区很出名,不但大人,甚至连六七岁的孩子都认识他。

| 称…为… | ◆ 大家都称他为好好先生。 |
| | ◆ 人们称黄山为天下第一山。 |

等	◆ 火车经过北京、南京、上海等地。
	◆ 他还问了一些别的问题，如语言、人口、天气等等。
	◆ 今年，我学了语文、化学、信息学等三门课。

In the first two examples, 等 has the value of "etc"; however, in the last example it completes an enumeration.

| 应 | ◆ 你是老大，家里的事应多干点儿。 |
| | ◆ 有问题应去请教老师。 |

称 稱	chēng	to name, to call; name
		称号, 称作, 美称, 名称, 统称

淡	dàn	thin, light, tasteless, weak, indifferent
		淡红, 淡水, 淡水鱼, 冷淡

读 讀	dú	to read aloud; to study
		读本, 读书, 读物, 读音, 精读

队 隊	duì	team
		队长, 大队, 带队, 乐队

该 該	gāi	must
		该死, 活该

量	liáng	to measure
		量具
	liàng	quantity, capacity
		大量, 饭量, 分量, 海量, 尽量, 酒量, 能量, 容量, 商量, 少量, 数量, 雨量

* a bag used to measure rice

排	pái	to put in order, to line up; a line
		排比, 排场, 排解, 排他性, 排外, 排长, 排字, 安排, 牛排

品	pǐn	object, quality; to taste, to sample, to savour

品类,品行,品性,品种,次品,礼品,日用品,商品,物品,小品,样品,药品,用品,作品

* 㗊 three mouths, symbol of many objects

深	shēn	deep

深长,深度,深红,深化,深情,深入,深思,深夜,深远,深重

* a torch in the depths of a cave

甚	shèn	very

甚而

视 视	shì	vision

视而不见,视觉,视力,视听,电视,忽视,近视眼,轻视

务 務	wù	service; to be engaged in; must

务农,务实,服务,国务院,家务,事务,特务,医务所,义务

显 顯	xiǎn	to appear, to show, obvious

显明,显目,显然,显示,显现,显眼,显要,明显

性	xìng	nature, sex

性别,性病,性能,本性,感性,个性,惯性,理性,慢性病,男性,女性,阳性

业 業	yè	occupation, profession

业务,成家立业,工业,就业,开业,轻工业,事业,手工业,重工业,专业,作业

印		yìn	seal; to print

印度,印象,重印,打印,排印

* 𝌞 a hand pressing down on a person

应	應	yīng	must

应当,应得,应有

yìng　to comply with, to respond to, to deal with

应声,应承,应用,应用文,反应,呼应,相应

员	員	yuán	member (of an association)

成员,店员,动员,队员,会员,教员,理发员,人
员,学员,研究员,要员

* 𝍕 a circular opening of a container (see 圆)

则	則	zé	rule, regulation; therefore

法则,细则,以身作则,原则,准则

* 𝍣 to use a knife to engrave an inscription on a vase

单句

1. 事物的名字叫名称。
2. 好听的称呼叫美称。
3. 生活在淡水里的鱼叫淡水鱼。
4. 读书有两个意思,一个意思是看书,一个意思是上学。
5. 人们看的书、报、画报等统称为读物。
6. 一个字或一个词的发音也叫读音。
7. 要认真讲解和学习的课文叫精读课文。
8. 一队之长叫队长。
9. 数量很大叫大量,数量很少叫少量。
10. 品类就是品种和类别。
11. 礼品是礼物的同义词。
12. 日常生活中用的商品叫日用品。
13. 对问题想得很深叫深思。
14. 夜里十二点以后叫深夜。
15. 深情就是很深的感情。
16. 忽视就是不重视。
17. 轻视有看不起、小看的意思。
18. 家务就是家里的事务,如做饭等。
19. 男性、女性是人的性别。
20. 印度是一个国家。
21. 应当和应该是同义词。
22. 应得就是应该得到的意思。
23. 在商店里工作的人员叫店员。
24. 在学校中从事教学工作的人员叫教员。
25. 学员一般指在大学、中学、小学以外的学校学习的人。
26. 在研究所从事研究工作的人员叫研究员。

27. 法国是一个工业国。
28. 上海的轻工业很发达。

会话

1　—我酒喝多了，有点儿头疼。
　　—活该！谁让你不听我的话，喝了那么多酒。

2　—关于学什么专业，你最好跟你父母再商量商量。
　　—我们已经深入谈过了，他们同意我的意见。

3　—目前中国得性病的人多不多？
　　—最近几年越来越多。

4　—你看电视怎么离那么近？
　　—我是近视眼，视力不好，离远了看不清楚。

5　—你对这人的印象怎么样？
　　—他看问题很深刻，也很有事业心，就是个性太强。

6　—你要什么菜？
　　—今天我想要个牛排，听说法国牛排很好吃。

7　—老师昨天留的作业，你都会做吗？如果有问题可以问我。
　　—我想尽量先自己做，如果实在做不出来再问你。

8 —你有几个孩子?
   —两个，都已经成家立业了。

9 —你是工会会员吗?
   —是。

10 —这个城市的就业人口有多少?
   —大约有一百多万。

11 —系里的工作你都安排好了吗?
   —差不多了，就是课表还没有打印呢。

12 —他得的是什么病?
   —治了这么长时间都不好，显然是慢性病。

14

第十四课　读者来信(二)

进口洗衣机到哪儿去修?

去年，我买了台进口洗衣机，用了一个月就出了问题。于是，我到卖洗衣机的商店去打听哪里能修。他们说："只管卖，不管修。"后来，我又让人到保定、石家庄、福州找了几家修理部，都说不能修，让我找卖洗衣机的地方。就这样，卖洗衣机的商店不管，修理部门又不修。请问，我该怎么办呢?

《市场报》

'玩具医院'快开张!

我那刚刚三岁的孩子已经有六辆汽车、一架飞机、一台起重机，还有老虎、大象等不少机动玩具，都因出现毛病不能玩儿了。在孩子的强烈要求下，我爱人只好又给他买了一辆新汽车。我是搞经济工作的；据了解，现在城市和农村，孩子们的玩具都是短命货，买回来玩儿不了几天就坏了。这对国家和个人都是很大的浪费。如果各地能开些'玩具医院'就好了。

《市场报》

VOCABULARY

洗衣机	n	xǐyījī	washing machine
修	vb	xiū	to repair
台	Mw	tái	[Mw for machines]
坏	Qvb	huài	bad
管	vb	guǎn	to take care of
保定	Pn	Bǎodìng	Baoding
石家庄	Pn	Shíjiāzhuāng	Shijiazhuang
福州	Pn	Fúzhōu	Fuzhou
修理部	n	xiūlǐbù	repair shop
部门	n	bùmén	department, section
该	vb	gāi	must
玩具	n	wánjù	toy
开张	vb	kāizhāng	to open (a shop etc.)
架	Mw	jià	[Mw for television sets and other objects within a frame]
大象	n	dàxiàng	elephant
机动	adj	jīdòng	motorised
玩儿	vb	wánr	to play
强烈	Qvb	qiángliè	to be strong
搞	vb	gǎo	to do
据	prep	jù	according to
了解	vb	liǎojiě	to understand
经济	n, Qvb	jīngjì	economy; economical
农村	n	nóngcūn	countryside
短命	n	duǎnmìng	short-lived
货	n	huò	merchandise
浪费	n, vb	làngfèi	waste; to waste
各地	n	gèdì	everywhere

| 台 | ◆ 一台洗衣机,一台机器,一台起重机 |

坏	◆ 这是一个坏习惯。
	◆ 我昨天买的肉坏了,不能吃了。
	◆ 这个菜做坏了。
	◆ 这两天把我忙坏了。
	Used as a resultative, 坏 expresses a negative result.

管	◆ 他一个人能管十台机器。
	◆ 我们两个人都工作,没有时间管孩子。
	◆ 在我们这儿买的自行车坏了管修。
	◆ 大家都管他叫老虎。
	In the last example, 管 is an antepositional preposition which introduces the indirect object of the sentence.

该	◆ 下面该你念课文了。
	◆ 我还该你三块五毛二。
	◆ 时间不早,我该走了。
	◆ 他现在来,该多好啊!

| 辆 | ◆ 一辆汽车,一辆自行车,一辆马车 |

| 在……下 | ◆ 在朋友们的帮助下,他买到了火车票。 |
| | ◆ 在其他人的影响下,他同意我们的意见了。 |

| 要求 | ◆ 他的要求有道理。 |
| | ◆ 他要求我明天七点到办公室。 |

只好	♦ 没买到电影票,我们只好不看了。
	♦ 他不来了,我只好一个人去了。
	♦ 小孩儿走不快,我们只好慢点儿。

据	♦ 据医生说,他的病很快会好的。
	♦ 据了解,这个地区有十所大学。

了解	♦ 我对他很了解。
	♦ 我想了解一下事情的经过。

vb 得了 vb 不了	♦ 吃得了/吃不了 去得了/去不了 拿得了/拿不了 完得了/完不了
	♦ 东西太多,我一个人拿不了。 了 acts as a potential complement without having a pre-cise meaning.

保	bǎo	to protect, to guard, to guarantee

保安,保不住,保管,保留,保送,保卫,保温,保育员,多多保重,作保

* a person holding a child in her/his arms

部	bù	part, section, troops, forces

部队,部分,部落,部首,部位,部下,部长,大部分,东部,干部,公安部,工业部,卫生部,西部,小吃部,小卖部

村	cūn	village

村落,村长,村庄,村子,乡村

短	duǎn	short

短处,短工,短篇小说,短语,短期,长短

费 费	fèi	to spend; fees, expenses

费力,费事,费心,费用,经费,路费,小费,学费

福	fú	happiness

福建,福利,福气,幸福,祝福

* a goblet used for offerings (of alcohol)

搞	gǎo	to do, to make

搞对象,搞鬼

各	gè	every

各别,各得其所,各个,各行其是,各有千秋,各
种各样

* ☆ a foot and an opening, to enter into one's home

坏 壞	huài	bad, evil, spoiled, gone bad

坏处,坏分子,坏人

货 貨	huò	merchandise

货车,货机,货色,货物,百货大楼,次货,定货,
国货,黑货

济 濟	jì	to help, to be useful to

接济,无济于事

	jǐ	many, numerous

济济,济济一堂,人才济济

架	jià	frame, rack, shelf; to suport, to prop up; [Mw for radio sets etc.]

架子,笔架,打架,书架,衣架

浪	làng	wave, unrestrained

浪子,风浪,流浪

烈	liè	strong, violent, intense, staunch, upright, stern

烈度,烈风,烈火,烈性酒,强烈,热烈

农 農	nóng	agriculture, peasant

农场,农夫,农活,农具,农历,农民,农人,农
田,农药,农业,农业部,农庄,农作物

台	臺 檯 颱	tái	platform; [Mw for machines and heavy objects] 台北，台风，台湾，电视台，电台，断头台，后台， 讲台，气象台，上台，下台，阳台，站台

玩	wán	to play, to have fun 玩儿命，玩意儿，古玩，好玩儿，开玩笑

洗	xǐ	to wash 洗礼，洗脸

修	xiū	to repair, to decorate, to build 修道院，修建，修路，修养，修业，修正，保修，进 修，进修班

州	zhōu	prefecture, an administrative division 广州，贵州 * 𡿨𡿨𡿨 habitable islands surrounded by water

单句

1. 村子也叫村庄,是农民住的地方。
2. 短语也叫词组。
3. 时间不长叫短期。
4. 花费的钱叫费用。
5. 祝愿别人幸福叫祝福。
6. 各个就是每个。
7. 坏分子就是坏人。
8. 装货物的火车叫货车。
9. 在经济上帮助别人叫接济。
10. 放书的架子叫书架,挂衣服的架子叫衣架。
11. 农业上使用的一种历法叫农历。
12. 农业上使用的工具叫农具。
13. 台北是台湾省的一个城市。
14. 上下火车的地方叫站台。
15. 修建道路叫修路。
16. 广州是中国南方的一个城市。
17. 一路上要多多保重!
18. 小学教师强烈要求提高教师福利。
19. 他们两个人各有千秋。
20. 你可以保留你的意见。
21. 法国向很多国家出口农药。

会话

1　—"吃"这个字的部首是什么?
　　—部首是"口"。

2 —这些古玩儿你能不能帮我保管几天？
　—不行，我们这儿坏人太多。

3 —你弟弟最近怎么老不在家？
　—正在搞对象呢。新认识的这个女朋友在电视台工作，我弟弟
　　很满意。

4 —明年我想去美国进修。
　—谁出路费和学费？
　—都由我自己出，我是自费留学。

5 —听说公安部长要下台了。
　—别开玩笑了。他有后台，下不了台。

6 —这几年大部分农民都富起来了，是吗？
　—有的地区是这样，有的地区大部分农民还很穷。

7 —在中国坐出租汽车给不给小费。
　—一般不给。

8 —北京百货大楼在哪儿？
　—离北京饭店不远。在那儿你能买到各种各样的东西。

9 —在你们这儿买电视能不能保修？
　—能保修一年。

10 —你又跟谁打架了？
　—一个干部。他老在人背后搞鬼，说人的坏话。

11 —你喜欢吃中国饭吗？
　—喜欢吃，但是不喜欢做。做中国饭太费事。

12 —明天海上天气怎么样？

　　—气象台说，明天有台风，风浪很大。

13 —北京有什么好玩儿的地方？

　　—好玩儿的地方可太多了，不知道你喜欢玩儿什么。

15

第十五课　春节

王：明年我想去中国旅行，你说我什么时候去最合适？

李：春节的时候。因为春节是中国最重要的传统节日，春节前后，不论是城市和农村都特别热闹。

王：春节是几月份？

李：中国农历正月初一。明年的春节按阳历算是一月二十八号。

王：听说中国春节的时候，家家要贴春联，'春联'是什么？

李：'春联'也叫对联，是在两条红纸上写上成对的两句话，内容多是表示喜庆的意思。春联都贴在门的两旁。除了贴春联以外，春节时中国人还在门上、墙上、窗户上贴年画和'福'字。

王：据说中国人过春节有'守岁'的习惯，是吗？

李：是的。大年三十晚上，合家吃了团圆饭以后，就点放爆竹，一家人有说有笑，一夜不睡，一直等到新的一年的到来。但是近几年来，北京、上海等大城市，已经不准许放爆竹了。

王：饺子什么时候吃？

李：春节时一般是在大年三十晚上把饺子包好，初一早上吃。吃完饺子，人们就都穿上新衣服出去给人拜年。

王：春节互相见面时说些什么问候的话？

李："给您拜年！过年好！春节好！新年好！"什么的。

恭贺新年

辞旧岁人人欢乐

迎新春家家平安

143

VOCABULARY

春节	Pn	Chūnjié	Spring Festival
旅行	vb, n	lǚxíng	to travel; travel
合适	Qvb	héshì	suitable
节日	n	jiérì	festival
不论…	exp	búlùn	no matter. . .
热闹	Qvb	rènao	lively, noisy, bustling
月份	n	yuèfèn	month
农历	n	nónglì	the lunar calendar
正月	n	zhēngyuè	the first lunar month
初一	n	chūyī	the first day of the month
按	conj	àn	according to
阳历	n	yánglì	the solar calendar
贴	vb	tiē	to stick
春联	n	chūnlián	Spring couplets
对联	n	duìlián	matching couplets, antithetical couplets
纸	n	zhǐ	paper
成对	Qvb	chéngduì	symmetrical
内容	n	nèiróng	contents
喜庆	n	xǐqìng	joyous, jubilant
除了…以外	const	chúle…yǐwài	except
窗户	n	chuānghu	window
年画	n	niánhuà	New Year pictures
福	n	fú	happiness
守岁	vb	shǒusuì	to bring in the new year, stay up all night
合家	n	héjiā	the whole family
团圆	n	tuányuán	reunion

点放	vb	diǎnfàng	to let off, to light (firecrackers)
爆竹	n	bàozhú	firecracker
一直	adv	yìzhí	continuously, all along
穿	vb	chuān	to wear
拜年	vb	bàinián	to pay a new year's visit to
互相	adv	hùxiāng	mutually
问候	vb	wènhòu	to send one's regards, to greet

Use

前后	◆ 我们学校前后都是树。
	◆ 一九八三年前后,他来过法国。
	◆ 开学前后,我们特别忙。
	◆ 我前后给他打了三次电话。

不论……都	◆ 他不论做什么工作,都非常认真。
	◆ 你不论哪一天来都行。

按	◆ 他每天都按时到学校。
	◆ 按理说,他不会不同意的。
	◆ 按一天学一课算, 我们一个月就可以学完了。

家家 n + n	◆ 人人,年年,天天,月月
	◆ 他天天看报。

除了……以外	◆ 除了他以外,别人都看过这个电影。
	◆ 晚上我除了看报以外, 一般不做别的事情。

一直

◆ 一直往前走就是车站。

◆ 这个地方从老人一直到小孩，都对我们非常热情。

◆ 他一直在这个商店工作。

◆ 我一直把他们送到火车站才回来。

互相

◆ 在学习上，我们应该互相帮助。

◆ 他们一直互相通信。

按	àn	according to 按部就班,按期,按时,按语,按照
拜	bài	to greet, to acknowledge 拜会,拜师,拜天地,拜托,礼拜天,礼拜一 * 拜 two hands joined
爆	bào	to explode, to burst 爆发
除	chú	to get rid of; except 除非,除去,解除,开除,排除
穿	chuān	to wear, to cross 穿着,穿越
窗 窗	chuāng	window 窗口 * 窗 a window and a cavity
号 號	hào	mark, number, sign 大号,挂号,记号,句号,口号,老字号,外号,问号,信号 * 号 air being exhaled from the mouth
户	hù	door, family, household 户口,安家落户,家家户户,客户,门户,用户 * 户 a door flap

互	hù	mutual, reciprocal

互利,互助,相互

节 節	jié	joint, division; festival; to save

节目,节气,节育,节约,节制,关节,过节,礼节,
清明节,情节,时节,中秋节

联 聯	lián	to join, to unite

联合国,联欢,联接,联结,联系,联想,关联

* 聯 an ear and silk, the symbol of joining

旅	lǚ	travel

旅店,旅费,旅馆,旅客

* 旅 a regiment of soldiers marching under a flag

内	nèi	inside, interior, internal

内部,内行,内经,内科,内心,内衣,内在,国
内,以内

* 内 to enter into a place

庆 慶	qìng	to celebrate

庆祝,国庆节

适 適	shì	to adapt, to get used to

适当,适合,适口,适应,适用,适中,舒适

守	shǒu	to guard, to watch

守旧,守门,安分守己,把守,保守,看守

* 守 the thumb (symbol of regulations) and a roof

睡		shuì	to sleep
			午睡

贴	貼	tiē	to stick
			贴心

团	團	tuán	group
			团体,团长,代表团,义和团,乐团

圆	圓	yuán	round; circle
			圆满,圆形,方圆

* ![radical] the mouth of a container and a wall radical

直		zhí	straight
			直观,正直,直接

* ![eye] the eye, a direction indicator extending from it

竹		zhú	bamboo
			竹叶,竹子

* ![bamboo] two bamboo stalks with leaves

纸	紙	zhǐ	paper
			纸包不住火,纸钱,纸张,报纸,信纸

单句

1. 按时就是准时的意思,如:他每天按时上班。
2. 按照是根据的同义词。
3. 作者对有关文章或词句所做的说明叫按语。
4. 按照一定的条理去做事情叫按部就班。
5. 礼拜一、礼拜天也叫星期一、星期天。
6. 互助就是互相帮助。
7. 互利就是对双方都有利。
8. 节约的反义词是浪费。
9. 节育就是节制生育。
10. 过节就是欢度节日。
11. 中国每年四月五日是清明节。
12. 中秋节是农历八月十五,这一天月亮又大又圆。
13. 由于某人或某事而想起其他的人或事叫联想。
14. 旅客就是旅行的人。
15. 旅行时所用的费用叫旅费。
16. 旅客住的饭店叫旅店或旅馆。
17. 法国的国庆节是七月十四号。
18. 看守大门叫守门。
19. 中午睡觉叫午睡。
20. 乐团也叫乐队,"乐"是音乐的乐。
21. 竹叶就是竹子的叶子。
22. 明天我们代表团的团长将拜会法国总理。
23. 他在联和国工作。
24. 大会开得很圆满。
25. 出院以后你还要适当休息几天。
26. 他家的房子是圆形的。

1　—这个地方该用句号还是问号？
　　—该用问号。

2　—外号叫"老虎"的那个学生为什么被学校开除了？
　　—因为他老在学校打架。

3　—看内科在哪儿挂号？
　　—在这儿挂号。

4　—在哪儿能买到大号的鞋？
　　—除非到百货大楼去买，才能买到。

5　—今天晚上的电视节目怎么样？
　　—还可以，八点新闻以后有两个美国电影。

6　—你觉得这个女孩儿怎么样？
　　—长得不漂亮，就是穿着有点儿讲究。

7　—你想在这儿安家落户吗？
　　—不想，我对这儿的生活不太适应。

8　—现在国内有电视机的人多不多？
　　—在城市可以说家家户户都有电视机。

9　—你看见我的毛衣和内衣了吗？
　　—我都给洗了。

10 —他为什么不同意学生提出的口号？
　　—这个人的思想太保守。

11 —老王是个怎么样的人？
　　—他很正直，是个安分守己的人。

12 —如果你不在的话，我跟谁联系？
　　—你可以直接和我们经理联系。

Beijing Opera Or a Burst of LAUGHTER

A major art form in China, Beijing opera (this theme is approached in Lesson 16) is very different from Western opera, much more so than its name would suggest. It is a total show which combines theatre, music, song, martial arts, ballet and gestural art. The orchestra has no conductor, the composer is generally unknown, the role of the music is to accompany the play and the direction is the arrangement of theatrical conventions, at the heart of which lies the concept that any innovations or "reinterpretation of the work" would be perceived as improper. As for the set, it is almost absent and must be suggested; for example, a chair could suggest an obstacle or a bed, a tribunal might be represented by a brush or an inkpot etc...

Beijing opera is an art form where conventions concerning hand gesture, make-up, glance and step are prescribed in such minute detail that different types of characters can be stylised: the 生 shēng, male characters; the 旦 dàn, female characters (including the 青衣 qīngyī "black dress", the role of a decent woman and the 花旦 huādàn the role of a pretty, flirtatious and bold woman), the 花脸 huāliǎn "painted faces", the role of a warrior, and the 丑 chǒu, the clowns.

Laughter is one of the codes heavily used in the theatre, a use which extends from cultural phenomena. The Chinese language itself has drawn some extremely fine distinctions, using nearly 80 words to describe different types of laughter. In the theatre each type of character is assigned a particular type of laugh:

■ The laugh of the painted faces must be "ample".

■ The laugh of the black dress, "peaceful and sweet".

■ The laugh of the clown, "bewildered and strained".

■ The laugh of the flirtatious woman, "clear and charming".

There are 27 types of laughter in Beijing opera, each with its specified amplitude, pitch and the number of laughs, only a tiny minority of which express mere happiness.

■ 冷笑 lěngxiào (cold laugh), reveals an internal torment which is released in this way.

■ 气笑 qìxiào (humorous laugh), indicates malice that cannot be expressed in any other way.

■ 故笑 gùxiào (constrained laugh), more steady than the 强笑 qiǎngxiào (forced laugh).

■ 惧笑 jùxiào (relieved laugh), the moment of a fear being lifted.

■ 僵笑 jiāngxiào (set laugh).

■ 妒笑 dùxiào (jealous laugh), must end on a resounding note.

■ 呆笑 dāixiào (inane laugh), sudden bursts eventually drawing together.

■ 骄笑 jiāoxiào (proud laugh), released slowly, the end being prolonged and sustained.

■ 假笑 jiǎxiào (false laugh), the laugh of a person who is not happy but who laughs so that others will hear.

■ 苦笑 kǔxiào (bitter laugh), often used by those who plays the role of poor scholars who maintain a sense of dignity by forcing themselves to keep up their spirits despite their difficult situation. In this way it only serves to suggest sadness because "if they cry shortly after speaking, they thus loose their wisdom and virtue".

16

第十六课　京剧

张：你了解中国的京剧吗？

李：我看过不少次京剧，而且也读过不少有关京剧的书，可以说对京剧有些了解。

张：你认为京剧在表演形式上有什么独到的地方？

李：我认为是'程式化'。京剧中演员的舞台动作，上马下马、上楼下楼、开门关门、喝酒吃饭、写字看书、走路、睡觉、哭笑等都有一定的格式。

张：是这样。由于有这种规范性的舞台动作，京剧舞台上几乎不用布景，布景就在演员身上，观众可以通过演员的动作来了解剧情的空间环境和时间。

李：这种'程式化'还表现在京剧演员的化装和演出服装上。不同性别、不同年纪、不同身分、不同职业的人，化装也不同。所穿的衣服都有固定的式样。

张：我很喜欢京剧的服装，京剧服装非常具有民族特色。

李：在演唱方面也是一样。是文人、是武生，一听就知道。因为不同的角色，在唱法上也有一定的风格。

VOCABULARY

Presentation

京剧	n	jīngjù	Beijing opera
表演	vb, n	biǎoyǎn	to perform, to act; a performance
形式	n	xíngshì	form, shape
独到	adj	dúdào	original
程式	n	chéngshì	form, pattern
程式化	n	chéngshìhuà	stylization
演员	n	yǎnyuán	actor, actress
舞台	n	wǔtái	stage
动作	n	dòngzuò	gesture
格式	n	géshì	form, model
规范	Qvb	guīfàn	norm, standard; to conform
几乎	adv	jīhū	almost, nearly
布景	n	bùjǐng	set, setting, scene
观众	n	guānzhòng	audience
通过	vb	tōngguò	by means of, through. . .
剧情	n	jùqíng	plot (of a play)
空间	n	kōngjiān	space
环境	n	huánjìng	environment, context
化装	n	huàzhuāng	make-up
演出	n, vb	yǎnchū	performance; to perform, to put on a show
服装	n	fúzhuāng	costume
年纪	n	niánjì	age
职业	n	zhíyè	profession
固定	Qvb	gùdìng	to be fixed, determined
式样	n	shìyàng	style, type, model

民族	n	mínzú	race, ethnic group	
演唱	n, vb	yǎnchàng	singing; to sing (in a performance)	
武生	n	wǔshēng	role of a warrior	
角色	n	juésè	role	
风格	n	fēnggé	style	

Use

几乎	◆ 他几乎天天去书店。 ◆ 今天来的人我几乎都认识。
通过	◆ 前边正在修路，汽车不能通过。 ◆ 我的论文已经通过了。 ◆ 通过朋友介绍，我认识了那位作家。
来	◆ 我来说两句。 ◆ 他用这种方法来学中文。
表现	◆ 他在各方面的表现都很好。 ◆ 孔子思想的影响表现在很多方面。 ◆ 他爱在别人面前表现自己。
固定	◆ 我们每天工作的时间是固定的，从早上八点到下午六点。 ◆ 我想在这儿固定一个人，他的工作是接电话。
在……方面	◆ 他的主要成就在文学方面。 ◆ 这个国家在很多方面还很落后。

布		bù	cloth, material; to spread, to deploy

布店,布丁,布告,布鞋,分布,公布

* 𠃌 cloth and a hand holding a stick

程		chéng	measure, rule, journey, distance

程度,工程,工程师,过程,教程,课程,历程,路程,旅程,日程

独 獨		dú	only, unique

独立,独立自主,独身,独生女,独生子,独特,独一无二,独子

范 範		fàn	model

示范,师范学校,师范学院

格		gé	standard, pattern, case

格格不入,格外,格言,表格,别具一格,合格,品格,人格,体格,性格

固		gù	solid, stubborn, by nature

固然,固体,固有

规 規		guī	rule, regulation; to plan

规程,规定,规范,规格,规则,常规,法规,教规,圆规,正规

环 環		huán	ring; to encircle

环抱,耳环,花环,连环画

纪 纪 jì   to put down in writing; discipline

纪念,纪念品,纪要,纪元,世纪,中世纪

* 紀 string and the silk radical, to untangle silk threads

角   jiǎo   horn, corner, angle

角度,角落,牛角,三角形,口角

  jué   role, character

口角,名角儿,主角儿

* 角 the horn of an animal

境   jìng   boundary, border, region

境况,边境,出境,处境,国境,入境,意境

* 境 "end" (of a speech: a tongue and a graphic symbol) and the earth

---

剧 劇 jù   theatre, opera

剧本,剧场,剧团,剧院,川剧,歌剧,话剧,文剧,喜剧,越剧

空   kōng   empty, hollow

空话,空军,空气,空前,空想,空中客车,架空,落空

  kòng   free time; to leave empty

空白,空子,留空,有空儿

式	shì	form, formula

式样,方式,各式各样,公式,旧式,西式,新式,
正式,中式

武	wǔ	military, soldier

武打,武汉,武剧,武器,武术,武装

* 步 the foot (movement) and halberd

舞	wǔ	dance

舞会,舞剧,飞舞,歌舞

演	yǎn	to act, to perform in public

演讲,演说,重演,合演,开演,主演

职 職	zhí	employment, function

职称,职工,职位,职务,职员,革职,就职

众 衆	zhòng	crowd

众多,众所周知,出众,大众,大众化,听众

* 㐺 three people

族	zú	race, clan, ethnic group

白族,汉族,回族,家族,满族,种族,种族主义

* 㫃 arrows under a banner

单句

1. 卖布的商店叫布店。
2. 布丁是一种点心。
3. 旅行的过程叫路程。
4. 只生育一个孩子，是女孩儿叫独生女，是男孩儿叫独生子。
5. 独一无二是一个成语，意思是只有一个，没有第二个。
6. 示范就是做给别人看。
7. 固有就是本来就有。
8. 圆规是画图的一种工具。
9. 用花做的圆环叫花环。
10. 给人留作纪念的东西叫纪念品。
11. 主要的角色叫主角儿。
12. 国境就是一个国家的边境。
13. 出入一个国家的边境叫出境和入境。
14. 所处的境况叫处境。
15. 剧场和剧院是同义词，都是指表演和观看话剧或舞剧的地方。
16. 川剧的川是四川的川，川剧就是四川剧。越剧在上海一带很流行。
17. 留下空白不写东西叫留空。
18. 设法就是想办法。想方设法就是想尽一切办法。
19. 新式就是新的式样。中式就是中国的式样。西式就是西方的式样。
20. 各式各样指的是各种式样。

21. 主要是武打的京剧叫武剧。
22. 武汉是中国的一个城市。
23. 演讲和演说是同义词。
24. 众多指人很多。
25. 众所周知是成语，意思是人人都知道。
26. 汉族是中国人口最多的一个民族。白族、回族、满族等是少数民族。

1 —你将来想当工程师吗？
   —不想当，我想当老师，我现在在师范学院学习。

2 —据说中国人都会武术，是吗？
   —哪儿的事，不可能。

3 —明天晚上你有空儿吗？
   —有空儿。

4 —我们一块儿去看场话剧，好吗？
   —可以。什么话剧？哪个剧团演的？
   —《北京人》，是北京话剧团演的。
   —好，一言为定。明天我在剧场门口等你。

5 —你看学校的布告了吗？
   —看了，学校公布了今年大学的所有课程和一些新的规定。

6 —我觉得喜欢过独身生活的人性格都有点问题。
   —不一定，我认为只不过是生活方式不同而已。

7　—这是一个什么工程?

　　—据说要在这儿建设一所现代医院，设备都是从外国进口
　　　的。

8　—明年我想写两个电影剧本和一部长篇小说。

　　—我希望你的设想不要落空。

9　—你知道明天的日程安排吗?

　　—知道，上下午都去参观，晚上有舞会。

10　—法国向很多国家出口武器吗?

　　—是的。

11　—这本连环画怎么样?

　　—不错，别具一格。

12　—为什么法国人喜欢到农村去度假?

　　—因为那儿安静，空气又好。

13　—职称和职务是不是一回事?

　　—不是，我的职务是校长助理，我的职称是讲师。

14　—你们学校有多少职工?

　　—三百六十人。

17

第十七课　怎样写中文信

中文信的格式分五部分：第一部分是对收信人的称呼；第二部分是信开头对收信人的问候；第三部分是信的主要内容；第四部分是最后对收信人的致意和祝愿；第五部分是写信人的名字和写信日期。

给家人写信时一般使用在家中的称呼，而且可以在称呼前加'亲爱的'等形容词，如：爸爸、妈妈、大哥、亲爱的文平。注意中文的'亲爱的'一词不能用于一般的朋友。

给同事或朋友写信时可使用平时你们之间的称呼，如老王、小张、立阳。

给行政官员或商界人士写信时，应该先称呼他们的职务，然后是姓名。如果收信人是男的要在姓名后加先生或同志，如果收信人是女的可称女士或小姐。如：北京大学校长王力先生。

中文信开头一般要写一两句问候语，如：你好！好久没收到你的来信了！你最近怎么样？等等。

中文信在最后一般要使用一个表示致意或祝愿的词语。一般公文信常用'此致敬礼'四个字。'此致'写在信纸右边，'敬礼'写在左边。给家人或朋友写信时常用一些表示祝愿的话，如：祝你万事如意！祝你身体健康！一切顺利！

写信人的名字要写在信的右下角，名字旁边或下面写上写信的日期，有时也可写上写信的地点。注意中文信在信纸的左上角和右上角什么都不要写，这点和英、法文信不同。

下面是中文信封的书写格式：

100083

北京语言文化大学汉语速
成学院

田立阳　　　先生

上海南京路二十六号
邮政编码：200000

收信人地点

收信人姓名

寄信人地点

VOCABULARY

Presentation

开头	n	kāitóu	beginning
致意	vb	zhìyì	to give one's regards to
祝愿	n, vb	zhùyuàn	wish; to wish
爸爸	n	bàba	dad
妈妈	n	māma	mum
亲切	Qvb	qīnqiè	cordial, kind
行政	n	xíngzhèng	administration
官员	n	guānyuán	official
商界	n	shāngjiè	business world
人士	n	rénshì	personage, public figure
职务	n	zhíwù	employment, function
加	vb	jiā	to add
同志	n	tóngzhì	comrade
女士	n	nǚshì	madam
小姐	n	xiǎojiě	Miss
王力	Pn	Wáng Lì	Wang Li
问候语	n	wènhòuyǔ	greetings
此致	exp	cǐzhì	to extend (greetings); to pay (one's respects)
敬礼	n	jìnglǐ	greetings; (to pay one's) respects
健康	Qvb	jiànkāng	healthy
顺利	Qvb	shùnlì	favourable, successful
左上角	n	zuǒshàngjiǎo	top left corner
右上角	n	yòushàngjiǎo	top right corner
英文	n	Yīngwén	English
信封	n	xìnfēng	envelope

vb + 于	◆ 用于,生于,大于,小于
	◆ 他生于一九六五年。
	◆ 中国大于日本。

应该	◆ 有病不能上课,应该请假。
	◆ 他不认识那个地方,应该你去。
	◆ 他是八点钟离开家的,现在应该到了。

然后	◆ 我们先到北京,然后再去南京、上海。
	◆ 你们先看一下这篇文章,然后回答这几个问题。

int···都···	◆ 他什么地方都去过。
	◆ 你什么时候来都可以。
	◆ 他今天什么东西都没买。
	◆ 这个字,谁都会写。
	◆ 哪儿都有。
	This construction changes the interrogative into an indefinite: 什么 becomes "whatever" and 哪儿 "anywhere".

爸	bà	dad

封	fēng	seal, envelope, [Mw for letters]

封底, 封地, 封建, 封建主义, 封面, 反封建, 原封不动

* 丰寸 to plant trees to mark out a fief

官	guān	official

官方, 官话, 官气, 当官, 法官, 感官, 器官, 清官, 文官, 武官, 五官, 做官

* 宀 a roof sheltering something (people? arms? a symbol of power?): seat of administration

加	jiā	to add

加班, 加车, 加法, 加工, 加号, 加快, 加强, 加热, 加入, 加上, 加深, 加以, 参加, 更加, 强加

健	jiàn	robust, healthy

健美, 健全, 保健

姐	jiě	elder sister

姐姐, 表姐

界	jiè	world, limit

界说, 边界, 境界, 世界, 世界语, 体育界, 外界, 文艺界, 学术界, 眼界, 租界

* 田 + 介: "field" and "to separate"

敬	jìng	to respect	

敬爱, 敬而远之, 敬老院, 敬意, 敬祝

康	kāng	good health	

康乐

力	lì	energy, force, strength	

力量, 力气, 力求, 力图, 力学, 吃力, 出力, 费力, 活力, 极力, 记忆力, 尽力, 马力, 能力, 人力, 视力, 体力, 听力, 主力

* ⼒ the ploughshare of a plough

妈 媽	mā	mama, mum	

切	qiē	to cut, to slice	

切除, 切断, 切开

	qiè	corresponding to; eager; be sure to	

切合, 切记, 切身, 确切, 贴切, 一切

士	shì	scholar, soldier	

道士, 烈士, 女士, 骑士, 学士

* ♟ a phallic symbol

顺 順	shùn	flowing, favourable; to conform to	

顺便, 顺从, 顺当, 顺耳, 顺口, 顺路, 顺手, 顺水, 顺心, 顺眼, 顺着, 笔顺, 不顺, 通顺, 一路顺风

* 川 + 页 : a river and "head"

英	yīng	hero, flower	

英国, 英国人, 英明, 英语

右	yòu	right

右边，右面，右派，极右派

* 𠮠 the right hand and a symbolic object

政	zhèng	government, politics

政见，政教分离，政客，政论，政体，政治，政治家，当政，内政，专政

* 政 "to adjust" with the help of a stick

致	zhì	to transmit, to pass; fine, delicate

致电，致敬，致使，致意，标致，别致，大致，一致，以致

* 至 + 攵 "to reach" and a hand holding a stick

志	zhì	aspiration, will, local history

志气，志趣，志士，志向，志愿，标志，方志，意志

左	zuǒ	left

左边，左派，左右，极左派

* 左 the left hand holding a set square

单句

1. 反对封建主义叫反封建。
2. 官话也叫国语。
3. 当官和做官是同义词。
4. 感官就是感觉器官，如眼睛、鼻子等。
5. 健美就是健康而美丽。
6. 边界也叫边境。
7. 敬老院也叫养老院。
8. 康乐就是健康快乐。
9. 力量和力气是同义词。
10. 力学是自然科学里的一门学科。
11. 视觉的能力叫视力，听觉的能力叫听力。
12. 记忆事物的能力叫记忆力。
13. 确切有准确、贴切的意思，如：这个词用得很确切。
14. 顺当是口语词，是顺利的意思。
15. 看着舒服叫顺眼，听着舒服叫顺耳。
16. 政见就是政治见解。
17. 政论文是一种文体。
18. 向某人打电报叫致电。
19. 致敬和致意是同义词，意思是向某人表示敬意。
20. 大致就是差不多的意思。
21. 这个句子不太通顺。
22. 你这个字笔顺写得不对。
23. 祝你一路顺风！
24. 这本书的封面很好看。
25. 他现在是大使馆的武官。

26. 这次会见加深了我们之间的了解。
27. 最近他有很多不顺心的事。

会话

1 —你参加明天的晚会吗?
　—参加，据说有很多文艺界的名人要来。

2 —你们明天休息吗?
　—不休息，我们加班，大约五点半左右下班。

3 —同志，顺着这条路走可以到火车站吗?
　—不行，您应该走右边那条路。

4 —你来英国干什么?
　—想开开眼界，顺便看望几个体育界的老朋友。

5 —王女士这个人怎么样?
　—长得很标志，但是对人总是敬而远之。

6 —你们两个人的意见一致不一致?
　—不一致，他同意极右派的看法。

7 —你想当政治家吗?
　—不想当，政治家一般都想做官，可是我不想当官。

8 —你能看英文报纸吗?
　—我的英文水平不高，看得很吃力。

9 —听说你姐姐很有志气。
   —是的，虽然她生活上很困难，可是从没向家里要过一分
      钱。

10 —你爸爸做什么工作?
    —他是法官，在法院工作。

11 —你想找一个什么样的男人?
    —有骑士风度的。

18

第十八课 以听觉为主还是以视觉为主？

现代心理学研究证实，人在用眼睛和耳朵接受信息时，有人是以视觉为主，有人是以听觉为主。判断一个人主要是以什么方式接受信息，这对于了解一个人的特性以及如何对这个人进行培养和教育是十分重要的。你想了解你自己吗？请回答以下几个问题：

一、你在看电视时，同时还常干点其他事吗？如：打毛衣、和别人谈话、干零碎活儿。

二、你看电视时喜欢对电视节目进行评论和发表议论吗？

三、你喜欢一个人单独进行跑步、骑自行车等体育活动，还是喜欢参加集体性的球类运动？

四、你喜欢看小说呢还是喜欢看理论性的文章呢？

五、你善于认路吗？

六、你上中学的时候是数学好还是外语好？

七、你初学中文时和别的同学比较起来，你是声调好呢还是汉字写得好？

八、音乐和美术你更喜欢哪个？

九、你请客人来你家时你很容易画一张来你家的路线图吗？

十、你集中精神思考问题的时候，你容易受周围动静的干扰吗？

十一、你容易不容易记住一个人的衣服或眼睛是什么颜色？

VOCABULARY

以…为…	const	yǐ…wéi…	to regard as, to take as
听觉	n	tīngjué	hearing
视觉	n	shìjué	seeing
证实	vb	zhèngshí	to prove
耳朵	n	ěrduo	ear
接受	vb	jiēshòu	to accept, to receive
判断	vb	pànduàn	to determine
对于	prep	duìyú	regarding. . .,as for. . .
特性	n	tèxìng	characteristic
以及	conj	yǐjí	as well as
如何	int	rúhé	how
培养	vb	péiyǎng	to train, to cultivate
以下	loc	yǐxià	below, under; the following
电视	n	diànshì	television
打毛衣	exp	dǎmáoyī	to knit
零碎活儿	n	língsuìhuór	odd jobs
节目	n	jiémù	programme
评论	n	pínglùn	commentary
发表	vb	fābiǎo	to publish
议论	n, vb	yìlùn	discussion; to discuss
单独	adj	dāndú	alone, independent
跑步	vb	pǎobù	to run, to jog
体育	n	tǐyù	physical education, sport
参加	vb	cānjiā	to participate
集体	n	jítǐ	collective, group

球	n	qiú	ball games, sports
运动	n, vb	yùndòng	movement, sport; to move
善于	vb	shànyú	to be good at
数学	n	shùxué	mathematics
比较	v, adv	bǐjiào	to compare; relatively
声调	n	shēngdiào	tone (of a Chinese character)
容易	Qvb	róngyì	easy
路线	n	lùxiàn	route, itinerary
集中	vb, Qvb	jízhōng	to concentrate; concentrated
思考	vb	sīkǎo	to reflect, to ponder
周围	n	zhōuwéi	environment, surroundings
动静	n	dòngjìng	sound (of something), activity
干扰	vb, n	gānrǎo	to annoy, to trouble; interference
颜色	n	yánsè	colour

Use

以…为…	◆ 他们国家的人以吃肉为主。 ◆ 这个商店卖的东西以法国货为最多。
对于	◆ 对于他们的习惯,我还不太了解。 ◆ 对于这个问题,我不同意你的意见。 ◆ 这是学生们对于教学的意见。
以及	◆ 这个商店卖衣服、家用电器,以及各种日用品。 ◆ 什么时候去,以及怎么去、去多长时间,都要商量。

| 如何 | ◆ 你这么办,我不知如何是好。 |
| | ◆ 无论如何你要去医院。 |

| 以下 | ◆ 我就说这些,以下由老王来讲。 |
| | ◆ 这座楼房,三层以下住的都是外国人。 |

比较	◆ 你把这两篇文章比较一下,就知道哪篇好了。
	◆ 他们用的是比较的方法。
	◆ 从这儿走比较近。
	◆ 他比较喜欢吃四川菜。

| 更 | ◆ 他法语说得比过去更好了。 |
| | ◆ 比较起来,我更喜欢这张画。 |

受	◆ 孩子应该受教育。
	◆ 他喜欢看书,是受他父亲的影响。
	◆ 听了他的话,大家都很受感动。

vb + 住	◆ 你记住他的名字了吗?
	◆ 这么大的东西,你一只手拿得住吗?
	◆ 天气热了,毛衣穿不住了。
	This resultative conveys the idea of being fixed in a certain state.

步	bù	to walk, step	

步行，步子，初步，地步，脚步，进步，起步，却步，让步

* 𭭈 two feet

单 單	dān	single, odd, simple, thin; sheet, bill, list	

单程，单词，单打，单方，单个儿，单号，单间，单身汉，单位，单衣，单一，单元，单子，菜单，传单，床单，名单

shàn — a surname

调 調	diào	to transfer; accent, melody	

调动，调度，调号，调虎离山，调换，调子，笔调，步调，单调，强调，语调

tiáo — to mix, to suit well, to mediate

调和，调节，调解，调皮，调情，调整，空调

及	jí	to reach; and	

及格，及时，及时雨，及早，遍及，来不及，来得及，力所能及

* 𭤃 a hand catching somebody

集	jí	to gather; market, collection, volume	

集成，集合，集会，集体，集团，上集，诗集，收集，下集

* three birds gathering in a tree

较 較	jiào	relatively	

较量

| 考 | kǎo | to sit an examination, to investigate |
| | | 考察，考古，考究，考取，考生，考上，考题，报考，参考 |

| 判 | pàn | to judge, to evaluate |
| | | 判别，判处，判定，判决，判决书，判明是非，谈判 |

| 培 | péi | to bank up with earth, to foster, to cultivate |
| | | 培育 |

| 评 評 | píng | to evaluate, to criticise, to comment, to review |
| | | 评比，评定，评分，评论家，评判，评语，短评，书评，影评 |

| 球 | qiú | ball, sphere |
| | | 球场，球票，打球，地球，排球，皮球，气球，手球 |

| 扰 擾 | rǎo | to trouble, to annoy |
| | | 打扰 |

| 善 | shàn | good, to be good at, kind; friendly |
| | | 善心，善意 |

| 碎 | suì | to break, to smash; in pieces |
| | | 打碎，切碎 |

围 圍	wéi	to encircle, to surround

围墙，包围，解围

* 圍 a foot on either side of a place and borders

线 綫	xiàn	thread, line

线路，线条，单行线，电线，火线，界线，
毛线，前线，无线电

* silk and 戋 (derogatory element)

颜 顏	yán	colour, face, countenance

五颜六色，喜笑颜开

议 議	yì	to discuss, to debate; opinion, view

议会，议会制，议题，议员，不可思议，会
议，建议

易	yì	easy; change

《易经》，来之不易，平易近人

* 易 a chameleon

运 運	yùn	to transport, to employ; fortune, fate

运动会，运动员，运河，运气，运送，运
行，运用，海运，空运，命运，托运，幸运

证 證	zhèng	proof, (ID)papers; to demonstrate that...

证据，证明，证人，证书，出入证，工作
证，考证，论证，学生证，作证

* 言＋正："word" ＋ "straight"

1. 走着去叫步行。
2. 步子就是人的脚步。
3. 开始走叫起步，如：车子起步了。
4. 单和双是反义词，单个儿就是一个，单方就是一方。
5. 一、三、五、七、九是单号，二、四、六、八、十是双号。
6. 没有结婚的男子叫单身汉。
7. 饭馆里写着菜名的单子叫菜单。
8. 写着人的名字的单子叫名单。
9. 调皮有不听话的意思。
10. 到处都有叫遍及。
11. 很多人集合在一起开会叫集会。
12. 考上和考取是同义词。
13. 文字不长的评论叫短评。
14. 对一本书和一部电影的评论叫书评和影评。
15. 评定某人或某事的几句话叫评语。
16. 五颜六色意思是颜色很多，各种各样的颜色都有。
17. 会议要议论的题目叫议题。
18. 一个东西得来得不容易叫来之不易。
19. 《易经》是中国一本古书的名字。
20. 运气有幸运的意思。
21. 用飞机来运送东西叫空运。
22. 能为某人或某事作证的人叫证人。
23. 这儿的生活很单调。
24. 有了病应该及早去医院。
25. 中美两国首脑举行谈判。

26. 他的语音语调很好。
27. 研究这个问题时，你可以参考这本书。
28. 他想调换一下工作。

会话

1 —您在哪个单位工作？您有工作证吗？
　　—我现在不工作，我是学生。这是我的学生证。

2 —你喜欢打排球吗？
　　—喜欢打，更喜欢看排球。我刚买了一张明天晚上的球票。

3 —今年报考大学的人数多不多？考题难不难？
　　—很多，考题比去年难一点儿。

4 —你的中文考得怎么样？
　　—不怎么样，考了十分，刚刚及格。

5 —你看我考什么专业合适？
　　—我建议你考无线电专业。

6 —为什么你最近汉语学习进步得这么快？
　　—我现在是一个人住，没有人打扰我。一天我可以记五十多
　　　个单词。

7 —为什么中国菜里的肉都切得很碎？
　　—可能跟中国人吃饭用筷子有关系。

8 —你今天买了些什么东西？
　　—一个床单、一点儿毛线和一本诗集。

9　—都十一月了，你怎么还穿单衣呀？
　　—你不知道我是运动员吗？我不怕冷。

10　—你认识那位议员吗？
　　—认识，他非常平易近人。

11　—你有什么爱好？
　　—我喜欢收集各国的明信片。

19

第十九课　阴阳

关：'阴阳'这个词是什么意思?

包：'阴阳'是中国古代思想中比较重要的一个概念。'阴阳'一词最早出现在《易经》中,原来指自然现象:向着太阳叫阳,背着太阳叫阴。后来,中国古代的一些思想家用'阴阳'这一词来指自然界中一切不可分的、相互对立而又可以互相转换的现象。

关：你说得不够具体,能不能给我举一些具体的例子?

包：比如:大自然的天和地、白天和黑夜;人的男和女、生和死、活动和休息都是阴阳现象。

关：'阴阳'这个概念看来很有道理。

包：是的,所以中国历史上的'阴阳五行学说'(注:'五行'指金、木、水、火、土)对中国古代科学技术和医学的发展产生了积极的影响。

关：中医理论中怎样应用'阴阳'这个概念呢?

包：中医认为人生病的时候,就是阴阳不合,有时候需要补阴,有时候需要壮阳。

关：汉语词语中,有些词语的组合方式是不是也受'阴阳'概念的影响?比如:大小、多少、长短、天地、冷暖、动静、开关等等。

包：这方面我没有研究,我想有可能。另外,中国画和西方油画不同,为什么有的中国画只用黑白两种颜色?为什么中国菜,在鱼和蛋白上放一点儿绿色的菜?这是不是也受阴阳概念的影响,都可以研究。总之,中国古代的阴阳思想对中国各个方面都有影响。因此要试图研究中国的历史、文化、艺术以及中国人的衣食住行,非要先弄清楚'阴阳'这个概念不可。

VOCABULARY

阴	n	yīn	Yin
概念	n	gàiniàn	concept
《易经》	Pn	Yìjīng	*The Book of Changes*
向着	vb	xiàngzhe	facing, towards
背着	vb	bèizhe	hidden from, with one's back to
自然界	n	zìránjiè	nature
相互	adv	xiānghù	mutual, reciprocal
转换	vb, n	zhuǎnhuàn	to change; transition
不够	Qvb	búgòu	insufficient, not enough
具体	Qvb	jùtǐ	concrete, precise
举	vb	jǔ	to lift
例子	n	lìzi	example
历史	n	lìshǐ	history
注	n	zhù	note, N. B.
土	n	tǔ	earth
技术	n	jìshù	technique
发展	vb	fāzhǎn	to develop; development
产生	vb	chǎnshēng	to produce
积极	Qvb	jījí	active, positive
不合	Qvb	bùhé	not to conform to, to be unsuited to
需要	vb, n	xūyào	to need; need
补阴	vb	bǔyīn	to "enrich" the Yin
壮阳	vb	zhuàngyáng	to "strengthen" the Yang
组合	n, vb	zǔhé	combination; to group together
暖	Qvb	nuǎn	mild, temperate, warm
另外	adj, adv	lìngwài	other, on the other hand
油画	n	yóuhuà	oil painting

蛋白	n	dànbái	egg white
试图	vb	shìtú	to try to
衣食 住行	exp	yīshízhùxíng	food, clothing, shelter and transportation (the basic necessities of life)
弄	vb	nòng	to handle, to do, to play with, to leave something in a certain state
非… 不可	const	fēi…bùkě	must, have to

Use

一切
- ◆ 这儿的一切都安排好了。
- ◆ 要不怕一切困难。

够
- ◆ 你带的钱够不够?
- ◆ 你的发音不够标准。
- ◆ 一个面包你够吃吗?
- ◆ 这些书够我看一个月的。
- ◆ 我还没睡够,让我再睡一会儿。
- ◆ 我今天买了很多水果,让你吃个够。

具体
- ◆ 事情的经过,他讲得很具体。
- ◆ 你要具体了解一下。
- ◆ 他做什么具体工作?

应用
- ◆ 对于理论,不但要理解,更重要的是要会应用。
- ◆ 这是在农业上的应用。

另外	◆ 你们几个人先骑自行车走,另外的人坐汽车走。 ◆ 我拿了一本,另外一本不知谁拿走了。 ◆ 这儿没有座位了,我们另外找个地方吧!
一点儿	◆ 我会说一点儿中文。 ◆ 我想去买一点儿吃的东西。 ◆ 他一点儿都没听懂。 ◆ 今天比昨天冷一点儿。
因此	◆ 我跟他在一起工作了许多年,因此对他很了解。 ◆ 老师病了,因此我们今天不上课了。
非 ... 不可	◆ 今年夏天我非去中国不可。 ◆ 我非买到那本书不可。

补 補	bǔ	to mend, to repair, to fill, to supply, to enrich

补考，补课，补品，补贴，补习，补药，补语，补助，程度补语，结果补语，可能补语，取长补短，时量补语

产 産	chǎn	to produce, to bear children; product

产地，产妇，产假，产科，产量，产品，产物，产业，不动产，共产主义，国产，流产，难产，生产，生产力，特产，土产，无产者，早产

蛋	dàn	egg

蛋黄，坏蛋，鸡蛋，皮蛋，完蛋，王八蛋

概	gài	general, approximate

概况，概论，概要，大概，气概，一概

够	gòu	sufficient; to suffice

够本，够了，够朋友，够受的，能够

积 積	jī	to amass, to accumulate, to continue

积极性，积木，积少成多，面积，容积，体积

技	jì	skill, ability, trick

技工，技能，技术性，技术员，技艺，科技，口技，特技

例	lì	example

例假，例句，例如，例题，例外，例证，比例，成例，定例，举例，前例，事例，条例

另	lìng	other, another, separation
		另眼相看

弄	nòng	to do, to leave something in a certain state
		弄假成真，卖弄，玩弄
		* 𡘋 to play with jade

暖	nuǎn	warm, mild
		暖和，暖气，春暖花开，温暖

食	shí	food
		食品，食品店，食用，食欲，食物，冷食，面食，日食，月食，主食
		* 𩙿 a container filled with food and its lid

史	shǐ	history
		史诗，史实，史书，史无前例，史学
		* 史 a hand holding a writing instrument

试 试	shì	to try
		试点，试题，试用，笔试，考试，口试

土	tǔ	earth
		土布，土产，土地，土耳其，土法，土方，土工，土话，土货，土块，土里土气，土木工程，土生土长，土星，土性，土音，土语，出土，国土
		* 土 a mound of earth

需	xū	to need	
		需求	

阴 陰	yīn	Yin, moon, shade, north side; cloudy, hidden

阴电，阴极，阴间，阴历，阴天，阴文，阴性
* the mound radical and the moon

油	yóu	oil

油菜，油田，油条，花生油，加油，加油站，石油，香油

展	zhǎn	to develop, to deploy

展出，展开，展品，展示，展现，画展，进展，开展

转 轉	zhuǎn	to transmit, to pass on

转车，转达，转告，转给，转化，转换期，转机，转交，转让，转身，转眼，掉转，好转，回转，周转

	zhuàn	to turn, to revolve

转动，转向，转转

壮 壯	zhuàng	strong

壮大，壮举，壮丽，壮年，壮观，强壮

单 句

1. 把没有学的课补上叫补课。
2. 具有地方特色的产品叫特产。
3. 物品出产的地方叫产地。
4. 能够就是能的意思，两个词都是能愿动词。
5. 积木是一种玩具。
6. 技工就是技术工人。
7. 科技就是科学和技术。
8. 独特的技术叫特技。
9. 举例来说明问题的句子叫例句。
10. 例如和比如是同义词。
11. 女人来月经也叫来例假。
12. 吃的东西叫食品，食物是食品的同义词。
13. 卖食品的商店叫食品店。
14. 用面做的食物叫面食，如：饺子、面条等。
15. 农村人工生产的一种布叫土布。
16. 当地的特产也叫土产，多指农产品。
17. 小地区使用的方言叫土语或土话。
18. 土耳其是一个国家的名字。
19. 法语的名词、形容词有阴性和阳性之分，汉语没有。
20. 把一方的话转告给另一方叫转达。
21. "转眼"一词形容时间过得很快，如：冬天过去，转眼又是
    春天了。
22. 壮丽就是壮观美丽。
23. 四十岁左右叫壮年。

1　—老师，您能不能帮我把"他吃完了。"这个句子分析一下？
　　—可以。"他"是主语，"吃"是动词，"完"是补语。
　　—"完"是什么补语？
　　—是结果补语，表示动作的结果。

2　—你考试考得怎么样？
　　—口试考得还可以，笔试考得不怎么样，可能要补考。笔试
　　的试题太难了。

3　—我这儿有香油、花生油、鸡蛋、油菜和肉。你想吃什么就
　　做什么。
　　—今天天气太热，没有食欲，只想吃点儿面条。

4　—大夫，产妇吃补药好不好？
　　—产妇最好什么药都不吃，可以多吃点儿鸡蛋和水果。

5　—中国的石油工业怎么样？
　　—中国有不少油田，生产技术也很先进，石油产量一年比一
　　年高。

6　—你们那儿技术员和工人的比例是多少？
　　—一比六。

7　—中国的面积有多大？
　　—中国差不多相当于十七个法国那么大。

8　　—小王知道你流产了，送来了二十块钱，让我给你买点儿
　　　补品。
　　　—小王真够朋友。

9　　—不知道哪个王八蛋把我刚买的油条给吃了！
　　　—大概是那个土里土气的乡下人。

10　—这个画展你看过吗？
　　　—看过，没什么意思，展出的都是现代作品。

11　—你认为中国最大的问题是什么？
　　　—生产力不发达。
　　　—怎么发展生产力呢？
　　　—应该提高工人们工作的积极性。

12　—你想什么时候去英国旅行？
　　　—等英国经济好转以后，找一个春暖花开的时候去。

20

第二十课　中医

王：这两年你去哪儿了？怎么一直没见到你？

李：我去中国留学了。

王：你学的是什么专业？

李：我学的是中医，是在北京中医学院学的。

王：你以前不是学过西医吗？怎么又学中医呢？

李：我觉得有些病，用咱们西医的方法治疗效果不如中医好。

王：听说中医的理论缺乏科学性，里面有许多迷信的东西。

李：不能那么说。中医已有几千年的历史，而且能治那么多的病，里面一定有科学的道理。只是没有用现代的方法总结出来。

王：你认为中医在对病的诊断和治疗上有什么特点？

李：我认为第一是它的整体观念。中医认为人体是一个有机的整体，人体与外界自然环境有着密切的关系。中医在分析一个人的病情时总是从全身来考虑，不是'头疼医头，脚疼医脚'。这有点儿像现代系统论的理论。

王：是的。中国人几千年以前就具有这种认识论，很了不起。在治疗方面呢？

李：在治疗方面，中医讲究辨证论治。这方面比较复杂，不是一两句话能讲清楚的。要想真正了解中医的理论，要先读点儿中国古代思想的书。

王：你觉得吃中药比吃西药好吗？

李：我觉得吃中药比吃西药好。我牙疼的时候，就喜欢吃中药止痛。因为中药里面生物成分多，化学成分少，所以有人说吃中草药副作用小。只是中药味儿，西方人有点儿不太适应。

王：目前，你还在继续研究中医吗？

李：是的。

VOCABULARY

留学	vb	liúxué	to study abroad
专业	n	zhuānyè	major, speciality
咱们	pro	zánmen	we, us (inclusive)
治疗	n	zhìliáo	treatment, cure
效果	n	xiàoguǒ	effect, result
缺乏	vb	quēfá	to lack
许多	adj	xǔduō	many, plentiful
治	vb	zhì	to treat
总结	n, vb	zǒngjié	to sum up, to summarise
诊断	n, vb	zhěnduàn	diagnosis; to diagnose
整体	n	zhěngtǐ	whole, entire
观念	n	guānniàn	sense, idea, concept
有机	adj	yǒujī	organic
与	prep	yǔ	and, with
外界	n	wàijiè	the external world
密切	Qvb	mìqiè	to be close, intimate
分割	vb	fēngē	to cut up, to break up
全	adj, adv	quán	total; entirely
考虑	vb	kǎolǜ	to reflect, to ponder
医	n, vb	yī	doctor, medicine; to cure, to treat
系统论	n	xìtǒnglùn	global approach
认识论	n	rènshilùn	theory of knowledge, epistemology
了不起	Qvb	liǎobùqǐ	extraordinary, wonderful, amazing
讲究	vb, Qvb	jiǎngjiu	to pay special attention to; to be particular about
辨证论治	exp	biànzhènglùnzhì	diagnosis and treatment (a global approach which examines the patient's general condition as well as their symptoms)

复杂	Qvb	fùzá	complex
牙	n	yá	tooth
止痛	vb	zhǐtòng	to relieve pain
草药	n	cǎoyào	medicinal herbs
副作用	n	fùzuòyòng	side effects
味	n	wèi	taste
继续	vb	jìxù	to continue

Use

如	
	◆ 他工作总是这样，几十年如一日。
	◆ 事情不如他们想像的那么复杂。
	◆ 到我们学校坐汽车不如骑自行车快。
	◆ 论书法，谁也不如他。
	◆ 他的身体一天不如一天。
	◆ 这个商店不如那个大。

V + 出来	
	◆ 树林里跑出来一只老虎。
	◆ 他从书包里拿出一本书来。
	◆ 我们走出饭馆来的时候，已经是晚上十点了。
	◆ 办法我们已经研究出来了。
	◆ 他有点儿不高兴，我已经看出来了。

与	
	◆ 中国与法国建立了外交关系。

全	◆ 这个图书馆有关历史的书很全。
	◆ 这是全中国人民的愿望。
	◆ 我把他说的话全都记下来了。
	◆ 我全听懂了。
	◆ 不论干什么工作，他全都很认真。

继续	◆ 后一个过程是前一个过程的继续。
	◆ 我继续在大学学习一年。
	◆ 我希望你的研究工作能继续下去。

| 咱们 | ◆ 咱们一起去吧！ |
| | Unlike 我们，咱们 is mainly used in spoken form and includes the person being spoken to. |

辨		biàn	to discuss, to debate 辨(辩)明，辨认，辨(辩)正，辨(辩)证，分辨
草		cǎo	grass 草包，草草了事，草书，草图，草写，草药，草原，草约，草字头，起草，行草
乏		fá	to lack; tired 乏味儿，不乏其人
副		fù	vice-(e. g. vice-president etc.), secondary, auxiliary 副部长，副产品，副词，副会长，副食，副手，副书记，副业，副院长，副总理
复	復 複	fù	to return, to recover 复本，复发，复工，复古，复合词，复合元音，复活，复活节，复旧，复句，复课，复习，复写，复信，复姓，复印，复原，复员，报复，重复，答复，反复，文艺复兴，修复
疗	療	liáo	to care for, to treat 疗法，疗养，疗养院，电疗，医疗
虑	慮	lǜ	to ponder, to reflect;anxious 处心积虑，顾虑，过虑，千虑一得，深思熟虑，思虑，疑虑
密		mì	thick, intimate, secret 密电，密度，密封，密集，密件，密谈，保密，告密，机密，精密，亲密

全	quán	completely, totally	

全部，全程，全国，全集，全面，全能，全球，全天候，全体，全文，全心全意，安全，百科全书，健全，齐全，完全

缺	quē	to be short of, to lack; incomplete	

缺点，缺货，缺口，缺少

* 𦈎 a "vase" and a derogatory graphic element (chipped jade)

味	wèi	taste, flavour	

味道，味精，味觉，风味儿，海味，口味，美味，气味，趣味，调味，无味，意味

效	xiào	effect, to immitate, to devote	

效法，效力，效能，效用，成效，见效，无效，有效

许 許	xǔ	to allow, maybe	

许久，许可，不许，或许，容许，少许，也许，准许

续 續	xù	continuous; to continue, to join onto	

续假，连续

牙	yá	tooth	

牙科，牙医，补牙，象牙

* 𠃌 two teeth closing together

与 與	yǔ	and , with	

与众不同

| 杂 雜 | zá | miscellaneous, sundry; to mix |
| | | 杂感，杂货，杂技，杂文，杂志，打杂 |

| 咱 | zán | we (inclusive) |
| | | * 口 + 自 : "mouth" + "oneself" |

| 诊 診 | zhěn | to examine (a patient) |
| | | 诊断书，诊所，诊治，出诊，会诊，门诊，确诊，听诊器 |

止	zhǐ	to stop, to prevent
		止步，止境，不止，为止，学无止境，制止
		* ㄩ a foot

单句

1. 草字头是一个部首。

2. 用草做的鞋叫草鞋。

3. 乏味儿就是没有趣味。

4. 不乏其人是一个成语，意思是不缺少这样的人。

5. 复古和复旧是近义词，"古"指古代，"旧"指过去。

6. 由两个以上单句组成的句子叫复句。

7. 复信就是回信。

8. 修复就是通过修理使某物复原。

9. 疗法就是治疗方法。

10. 反复而深入地思考叫深思熟虑。

11. 亲密指两个人的关系亲近而密切。

12. 很缺少的货物叫缺货。

13. 缺点是优点的反义词。

14. 气体的味道叫气味。

15. 效法就是跟别人学，别人怎么做，你就怎么做。

16. 没有效能叫无效。

17. 许可、容许、准许都是同义词，意思是同意某人去做某事。

18. 少许就是一点儿。

19. 也许是可能的意思。

20. 象牙就是大象的牙。

21. 学无止境是一个成语，意思是学习没有到头的时候。

22. 止步的意思是不能往前走了。

1 —"我们走马上。" 这个句子为什么错了？
　—你把副词放在动词后边了。汉语的副词要放在动词前边。

2 —你的病确诊了吗？
　—确诊了。今天内科大夫和外科大夫会诊，说我是旧病复发。你看，这是诊断书。

3 —这个菜的味道不错，是什么风味儿？
　—广东风味儿，我放了一点儿味精。

4 —明天牙科诊所开不开门？我想去补牙。
　—明天是复活节，全国都放假，诊所一定关门。

5 —有关中医辨证论治的那篇文章发表在哪本杂志上？
　—《中医》杂志。我已经复印了一份，你看复印的吧。

6 —今天晚上我们都去看杂技，你去吗？
　—也许去，不一定。

7 —做什么事儿都要辨明是非。
　—我反复考虑了几天，那件事我是做错了。

8 —这个地方的农民都搞什么副业？
　—做点儿小买卖，卖点儿杂货什么的。

9　—中国人为什么把油呀，肉呀，鱼呀什么的叫副食？
　　—因为中国人把米面叫主食，他们认为这些是每天吃的主要
　　　食物。

10　—你向副院长提的要求，他答复你了吗？
　　—到目前为止，他还没有给我答复。

11　—你出院以后马上就上班吗？
　　—不，我想找个疗养院再疗养一个时期。

12　—你吃这种药见效不见效？
　　—我已经连续吃了一个月了，效果不明显。

13　—你的工具书真不少，够齐全的了！
　　—不，还缺少一本大百科全书。

CIVILISATION

Introduced Words

Words ignore borders. We find imported, transplanted and transformed words in all languages. The Chinese language, however, is a world of meanings and as such has been a very unfavourable terrain for phonetic transcriptions, thus, purely phonetic transcriptions have more often than not given way to words that convey meaning, e. g. délǔfēng (telephone) has been replaced by diànhuà (electric speech), démókèlāxī (democracy) to mínzhǔ (the people's rule) and pālìmén (parliament) to yìyuàn (council of debates).

When a phonetic transcription is in operation it is usually the case that the words thus created will still show signs of this tendency to rely on meaning. Such is the case with wéitāmìng (to protect one's life) for vitamin, kěkǒukělè (tasty and pleasing) for Coca-Cola, yǐndé (quote and obtain) for index, kǔdiédǎ (to hit hard many times) for coup d'Etat and àisībùnándú (to love what is not difficult to read) for Esperanto.

These words from external sources have their own history, their own course.

UNTIL THE IVth CENTURY A. D.

In accordance with this era's fashion of an essentially phonetic transcription, there are words from this period which came from the Barbarian peoples of the North (to whom the Chinese owe xīngxīng orangutang, and luòtuo camel) and from Persian, Sanskrit and Greek (shīzi, lion and pútao, raisin).

FROM THE IVth TO THE XIIth CENTURY A. D.

During this period Chinese was enriched by words coming mainly from Sanskrit. The mode of translating according to meaning imposed itself gradually, thus favouring the spread of Buddhism. Words like fútú, later fó came from the word Buddha, tǎ (pagoda) came from a contraction of stupa, yèchā (demon) from yaksa and mòlì (jasmine) from mallika. However other words were formed semantically, e. g. tiāntáng (Heavenly palace) for "paradise", dìyù (earthly prison) for "hell", yīnguǒ (relationship of cause and effect), xìnyǎng "faith", guòqù, xiànzài and wèilái for "past, present and future" and píngděng for "equality", etc.

FROM THE XIIIth TO THE XIXth CENTURY A. D.

Despite the domination of the Yuan (1279 – 1368) and the Qing (1644 – 1911) few Mongolian and Manchu words became integrated into Chinese during this era. Under the Ming (1368 – 1644), however, Chinese was enriched by a considerable number of words coming from Western languages and in particular from the translations of scientific works by Jesuit missionaries. Appearing during this period: zìxíngchē, "bicycle"; bǐlì, "proportion"; luòrìjiā (from logica), "logic"; chǐlún, "gearwheel"; jǐhé, "geometry"; égènuòmǐjiā, "economy", etc.

THE CONTEMPORARY PERIOD

Since the Opium War, Beijing, Shanghai and Guandong have become translation centres and the translation of foreign works has entered into an unprecedented era of prosperity.

It is more interesting than ever to examine the creation of words, be that semantic or phonetic, as a way of revealing possible areas that are "lacking" in the Chinese language or equally as part of the material and cultural environment that the Chinese language has not reflected:

gélángmǎ "grammar", (in 1898!)later replaced by yǔfǎ (language law); jièshuō (the words that form a boundary, i. e. that categorise) later dìngyì (established meaning), "definition"; niúyóu (cow oil) later huángyóu (yellow oil), "butter", etc.

In terms of quantity, the creation of new words from Japanese is also very important. Nevertheless , the actual origins of these words themselves come from three very distinct procedures:

– In order to translate notions that have come across from Western languages, Japanese uses words from ancient Chinese and gives them a new meaning. Such is the case for "society", shèhuì; "economy", jīngjì; "metaphysics", xíng´érshàngxué; "conscience", yìshì; . . . ism, zhǔyì ,etc.

– Japanese uses sinograms to convey the meaning of a word: chuántǒng, "tradition"; qǐyè, "enterprise"; wénhuà, "culture", etc.

– Actual Japanese words transcribed into Chinese: shǒuxù, "formalities "; jījí, "positive"; xiāojí, "negative", etc.

21

第二十一课　月牙儿 (老舍)

叫我最难过的是我慢慢地学会了恨妈妈。可是每当我恨她的时候，我不知不觉地便想起她背着我上坟的光景。想到了这个，我不能恨她了。我又非恨她不可。我的心像—还是像那个月牙儿，只能亮那么一会儿，而黑暗是无限的。妈妈的屋里常有男人来了，她不再躲避着我。他们的眼像狗似地看着我。

在很短的期间，我忽然明白了许多事。我知道我得保护自己，我觉出我身上好像有什么可贵的地方，我闻得出我已有一种什么味道，是我自己害羞，多感。我身上有了些力量，可以保护自己。

我愿爱妈妈，这时候我有好些必要问妈妈的事；可是正在这个时候，我得躲着她，我得恨她；要不然我自己便不存在了。当我睡不着的时节，我很冷静地思索，妈妈是可原谅的。她得顾我们俩的嘴。可是这个又使我要拒绝再吃她给我的饭菜。我的心就这么忽冷忽热，像冬天的风，休息一会儿，刮得更要猛；我静候着我的怒气冲来，没法儿止住。

VOCABULARY

月牙儿	n	yuèyár	crescent moon
难过	Qvb	nánguò	sad
恨	vb	hèn	to hate
不知不觉	exp	bùzhībùjué	unwittingly, inconsciously
背	vb	bēi	to carry on one's back
坟	n	fén	grave
光景	n	guāngjǐng	scene
像	vb	xiàng	to resemble, to be like
亮	vb, Qvb	liàng	to shine; bright
黑暗	n	hēi'àn	darkness, obscurity
无限	adj	wúxiàn	infinite
躲避	vb	duǒbì	to avoid
狗	n	gǒu	dog
像…似的	const	xiàng... shìde	like...
保护	vb	bǎohù	to protect
害羞	Qvb	hàixiū	shy
多感	adj	duōgǎn	sensitive
力量	n	lìliàng	strength, force
必要	n	bìyào	necessity
躲	vb	duǒ	to avoid, to hide
要不然	conj	yàoburán	otherwise
存在	vb, n	cúnzài	to exist; existence
时节	n	shíjié	moment, time
冷静	Qvb	lěngjìng	to be calm, undisturbed
思索	vb	sīsuǒ	to reflect, to meditate
原谅	vb	yuánliàng	to forgive

顾	vb	gù	to worry about
嘴	n	zuǐ	mouth
拒绝	vb	jùjué	to refuse
忽…忽…	const	hū…hū	now… now…
刮	vb	guā	to blow (of the wind)
猛	Qvb	měng	to be violent
怒气	n	nùqì	anger
冲	vb	chōng	to charge, to attack
止住	vb	zhǐzhù	to contain, to control, to stop

Use

不知不觉	◆ 他不知不觉地睡着了。 ◆ 我不知不觉地想起了许多过去的事。
一会儿	◆ 你先等一会儿,他一会儿就来。 ◆ 刚才我看了一会儿电视。
像…似地(的)	◆ 他长得像老虎似的。 ◆ 他像风似地跑了进来。
得	◆ 你得快点儿,要不然就晚了。 ◆ 这个问题,我还得考虑考虑。 ◆ 这个工作至少得三个人。 ◆ 你一定要多穿点衣服,要不然得生病。
要不然	◆ 你先吃点儿药,要不然就马上去医院。 ◆ 你要想见他,最好现在去,要不然他一会儿就回家了。
忽…忽…	◆ 忽大忽小,忽近忽远,忽多忽少,忽好忽坏 ◆ 他们说话的声音忽大忽小。

暗	àn	dark, secret

暗暗，暗淡，暗地里，暗含着，暗害，暗号，
暗杀，暗示，暗室，暗算，暗无天日，暗想，
暗笑，暗指，暗中，明来暗往，阴暗

避	bì	to avoid

避风，避开，避难所，避雨，避重就轻，回避

必	bì	must, to have to ; certainly

必不可少，必得，必定，必然，必然性，必修
课，必需，必需品，必由之路，不必，何必，
务必，物极必反，言必有据，有求必应

冲 衝	chōng	to charge, to rush, to clash, to rinse, to wash, to develop (film)

冲茶，冲淡，冲动，冲天，冲突，冲洗

存	cún	to exist, to conserve

存车处，存放，存货，存钱，存心，存衣处，
存在主义，保存，并存，封存，积存，寄
存，现存，万古长存

躲	duǒ	to hide, to avoid, to shelter from

躲开，躲雨

坟 墳	fén	grave

坟地

狗	gǒu	dog

狗腿子，海狗，走狗

刮 颳	guā	to shave, to blow (of the wind)	

刮风，刮脸

恨	hèn	to hate

恨不得，怀恨，可恨

护 護	hù	to help, to protect

护城河，护理，护理人员，护士，护送，护卫，护照，爱护，看护

拒	jù	to refuse, to resist

来者不拒

绝 絕	jué	to break, to anihilate; extreme

绝笔，绝大多数，绝代，绝对，绝对多数，绝境，绝密，绝命书，绝食，绝育，断绝，回绝，谢绝

*　　a person cutting thread

谅 諒	liàng	to forgive, to pardon, to presume

谅解，体谅

猛	měng	violent, cruel, sudden

猛然

怒	nù	anger

怒火，怒冲冲，怒视，发怒

索	suǒ	rope; to search, to demand

索道，索取，索性，思索，线索

*　　a knotted rope under a roof

屋	wū	house, room
		屋子，房屋，里屋

限	xiàn	limit; to limit
		限定，限度，限量，限期，限于，限制，界限，期限，无限，有限

像	xiàng	image, portrait; to resemble
		像话，画像，不像话，不像样子，人像，石像

羞	xiū	shame
		羞答答，怕羞

嘴	zuǐ	mouth
		嘴脸，张嘴

单句

1. 笑的时候不让别人看见叫暗笑。
2. 回避主要的问题只谈次要的事情叫避重就轻。
3. 一定要经过的路叫必由之路。
4. 事物发展到了极点一定要走向它的反面叫物极必反。
5. 何必就是用反问的语气表示不必，如：不买东西，何必带钱呢？
6. 某些公共场所存放衣服的地方叫存衣处。
7. 存货就是指积存的货物。
8. 看护就是看管和护理的意思。
9. 人工修的围着城墙起保护城市作用的河叫护城河。
10. 来者不拒是一个成语，意思是对什么人来都不拒绝。
11. 人死以前最后所写的文字或所作的字画叫绝笔。
12. 没有出路的境地叫绝境。
13. 答复对方表示拒绝叫回绝。
14. 怒气冲冲就是非常生气的样子。
15. 怒视就是非常生气地用眼睛看着别人。
16. 索取就是向别人要东西。
17. 里边的屋子叫里屋。
18. 限定日期叫限期。
19. 没有限度叫无限。
20. 人的画像叫人像。
21. 羞答答就是害羞的样子。
22. 张开嘴叫张嘴。

会话

1　—你知道哪儿有存车处吗?我想把自行车存起来。
　　—往前走不远，就有一个存车处。

2　—你现在已经存了多少钱了?
　　—我没有必要告诉你。

3　—你拿到护照了吗?
　　—我都等了半年了，还没有拿到。我真恨不得马上能拿到护
　　　照。

4　—你喜欢当护士吗?
　　—谈不上喜欢。每天护理病人，我已经习惯了。

5　—听说今天有不少学生绝食了，是吗?
　　—是的，绝大多数的学生都参加了。

6　—你为什么让你爱人做绝育手术呀?
　　—她已经做了几次人工流产了，老做人工流产对她身体不
　　　好。

7　—你们有几门必修课?
　　—三门必修课，两门选修课。

8　—下雨了，咱们找个地方躲躲雨吧?
　　—不必了，马上就到我家了。

9 —你最恨什么人？

　　—在暗地里说别人坏话的人。你呢？

　　—我觉得给人当走狗最可恨。

10 —你有理，为什么不为自己辩白呀？

　　—他当时很冲动，不是讲理的时候。

11 —美国总统是被谁暗害的？

　　—据说是被一个神经病人。

12 —在法国理发刮不刮脸？

　　—不刮脸，这和中国不一样。

13 —听说北京春天常常刮风，是吗？

　　—是的。

14 —你认为存在主义的出现是必然的吗？

　　—是必然的，这是时代的产物。

15 —去中国，你看我带点儿什么东西？

　　—我看买点儿生活必需品就够了。

22

第二十二课　广告

求婚广告

　　本人，男，三十五岁，中等身材，小学教员，月收入五百二十元，有房三间。爱好文学、美术，喜欢看电影。愿找一位二十到三十五岁之间，长相漂亮，身材不低于一米六零，最好也作教育工作的女性。来信请寄：四川省成都市育才小学周志军收。

寻人广告

　　王春花，女，十五岁，高一米五九，神经病人，穿绿上衣，黑布鞋。如发现请通知东城区金鱼胡同派出所。

商业广告

　　上海造船厂推出新产品全自动电话总机。该机采用电脑技术，设计先进，功能齐全，性能可靠。该机可容九门、二十四门内部自动电话，全自动交换，不用任何管理人员，交直流两用，使用方法与市内电话相同，适用于公司、机关、工厂、医院、学校等单位。本产品保修一年。为了满足广大用户要求，本厂特设为用户上门服务项目。

产品规格及价格：九门 ... 2300 元(台)
　　　　　　　　　二十四门 ... 5450 元(台)
地点：上海市南京路十三号
电话：43215160　　电报：206316
传真：43223026　　联系人：王增云

EC 经济周刊

第32期

第五版 市场观察 第六版 企业风景 第七版 经济论坛

每周一出版

应大力加强对停车问题的

最近几年，我国城市机动车年均增长速度在15%以上，停车场建设却差距较大。以北京为例，目前全市机动车保有量已超过112万辆，每日还有几十万辆外地车进京，但公共停车场车位仅有2万多个，面积74万平方米。

由于停车位严重短缺，致使机动车占路停放，严重影响了道路……行。在深圳，一条7米宽的道路，两边却往往被占作停……通过。据广州市对该市33条道路的停车……面积的40%。大量的机动车……绿地。

建造停车泊位，或缩小停车场的面积，或干脆不建。

停车场的政策管理体制混乱，再加上对非法……加剧了停车供需矛盾。据广州市的调查，目前该……理有关的政府机构近20个，包括一些居委会也……者稍有不慎"得罪一方"，就会直接影响停车库……许多城市都把路上停车作为解决停车场地不足……国外大城市路上停车也很普遍，但中国城市……

……部门预测，我国2……

教育工作者的正确选择

本报评论员

在教师节前夕，我们向……大读者推荐刘让贤这位扎根……业默默奉献的优秀教师的典型……教师学习的楷模。

刘让贤是一位普普通通的……献的土乡山村的教育事业，几……斗、无私奉献，做出了出色的成……品质深深打动了千千万万人的……的爱戴。

刘让贤身上教书育人的闪……人的，是他甘守清贫、为了教育……精神。刘让贤曾经说过，人生的……不是索取，有人说我是有钱不会……孩子们，我甘愿当这样的"傻子"……清贫，但教师的追求是富有的，……时的，精神上的富有才是永恒的……神上的富有者！

青海属于西部贫困地区，经……滞后，有人认为这里条件艰苦、……所作为。但是，面对山区的贫困、……通的人民教师、共产党员，刘让……没有怨天尤人，而是以一个开拓……一滴小事做起，踏踏实实地、创造……了显著成绩。刘让贤同志的事迹……个道理，只有从地面起飞，才能……与宏观环境、现实条件有很大关……有条件创造条……

"烟草专卖法实施条例"施行

打私打假执法手段更为明确

《中华人民共和国烟草专卖法实施条例》于一九九七年七月三日，经国务院审批同意，由李鹏总理以中华人民共和国国务院令（第223号）发布实施。这是继一九九二年《中华人民共和国烟草专卖法》颁布实施之后，烟草行业的又一件大事，标志着由《烟草专卖法》所确立的烟草专卖法律制度得以进一步巩固和完善。

该条例共分十一章七十条，从烟草专卖许可证管理；烟叶的种植、收购和调拨；烟草制品的生产、销售、运输；卷烟纸、滤嘴棒、烟用丝束、烟草专用机械的生产和销售等方面将《烟草专卖法》所确立的烟草专卖许可证制度、准运证制度，以及烟草专卖品的生产、经营等管理制度进一步具体化。在法律责任方面明确规定了对违法行为的处罚幅度。同时还明确了烟草专卖行政主管部门的执法手段，大大提高和增强了《烟草专卖法》的可操作性。

据上海市烟草专卖局副局长顾钧凯称，《烟草专卖法实施条例》特别是针对东南沿海及部分地区走私烟和制售假冒卷烟相当严重的实际情况，对烟草专卖行政主管部门规定了相应的职责。因此该条例的实施对于打击非法经营，保护合法经营，尤其是进一步打击卷烟走私、贩私和制售假冒商标卷烟，维护国家和广大消费者利益，具有十分重要的现实意义。

查市场 端窝点 堵源头

上海市卷烟市场得到有效治理

本报记者 ……

去年6月25日，当解放军战士手持几十支火焰喷射枪，将堆集在上海市青浦县一地的4万2千余条假冒卷烟焚毁一尽时，主持这次销毁假烟现场大会的上海市副市长蒋以任和烟草专卖局局长董浩林进行了全市治理烟草市场的总动员，时至今日，走私烟、假冒烟泛滥的局面得到了有效控制。

从上海市烟草专卖局得到的两组数据可反映出这个情况。1996年，上海市共查处卷烟违法案件5974起，查获假冒卷烟63420条，走私烟267345条，今年上半年查处这类案件6553起，查获假冒烟46579条、走私烟59350条。其中可观察到不仅执法力度加强，市场走私烟明显下降。另据调查，目前主要商业街区、市场基本无假冒烟、走私烟，大饭店、大宾馆均守法经营卷烟。

据悉，上海市烟草专卖局根据法定职权，依靠公安、工商等执法部门，已设定了一套"查市场、端窝点、堵源头"的卷烟市场治理方案。该局已组建了以日常检查辅以突击检查的专业执法队伍。市局有检查大队，各区县有检查中队，全市卷烟批发网点已设立烟草专卖监督站59个，烟草专卖管理已形成网络，覆盖全市各个角落。

上海共有陆上道口15个，分别与浙江、江苏相通，而浙江嘉善、江苏花桥两个非法卷烟市场紧临上海。为彻底堵住陆上源头，上海市烟草专卖局于去年与上海市陆上运输管理处签定了协议书，向青浦、嘉定、金山、宝山四个区县的进出境道口派驻烟草专卖管理人员。

去年，上海市烟草专卖局向社会公布了举报电话，实行24小时接收举报制度，仅半年就收到群众举报电话159次，……及制假……地区运……的窝点……员以……工厂……红……厂……万……

法制……

烟草专……对执行《烟……的情况进行……反《烟草专……件，并会同……草专卖品的……行为……

国门缉私

——全国海关……

4月8日结束的《中华国门——全国海关反走私展览》以700余幅图片、近400件实物和8件模型，展示了近10年来全国海关反走私工作取得显著成绩：查获走私案件9.2万余宗，案值277.6亿元；查获违规案件65.8万余宗，案值246.5亿元。这一串串数字后面，是一个个惊心动魄的故事……

怒海轻骑擒私枭

走私，起源于海上，也疯狂于海上。

1995年10月，"顺发006"号铁甲船运载价值1500万元的外国香烟穿行南海水域时，海口海关缉私艇鸣枪警告并跳帮未果，6400匹马力的走私船放出浓烟掩护逃窜。缉私队员在艇首被撞裂1米多的情况下，第5次强行跳帮终于成功，缉私队员们包围驾驶舱，枪弹齐发，最终克敌制胜。

走私手段的诡谲多变，同样给海关缉私带来艰难。"子"、"母"船进行私货过驳，从事先约定，到临时指定；从我领海转移到公海；运送私货从船舱藏匿，发展到水下拖带；甚至还用"间谍"手段对付海关行动。

1993年4月，一走私团伙派人住进鹭江宾馆，对厦门海关缉私艇昼夜监视。海关将计就计，遣双艇扰乱对方视线，第三艇深夜出击，一举擒获狡诈的走私分子。

暴利和暴力，往往是孪生的。走私分子对海关的查缉，从原先的闻风逃窜，发展为武力抗拒，气焰十分嚣张。据统计，仅仅在1994年至1995年，就发生暴力抗拒缉私的案件15起！展白……上，在深圳大鹏湾将我4名……海，并夺去……

……为乙类货，因为……法利润。

"夹藏"，在1……驶座位、油箱、隔……制的夹层。

随着外向型经……型贸易方式令人目……分子视为"暗渡陈仓……口时，以少报多。该……工的进口货，给你来个……自倒卖，或将应该返销……密内销。1994年5月，……料加工名义进口价值人……500套及显示器332台，……了对付海关核销，竟以重……充电脑复出口！更稀奇的……化工公司将自来水注满容器……来料加工成品"二乙苯烯"……十分艰难，但是，"有人发明，……侦探福尔摩斯的名言，就是……看出破绽，继而斩断走私"黑手"……

阳光下的罪恶和黑夜中的……假"出招，使反走私战线更是充……假单证、假印章，这些由……品，令海关的……

V OCABULARY

广告		n	guǎnggào	advertisement, advertising
求婚		v-o	qiúhūn	request for marriage, marriage proposal
收入		n	shōurù	income
长相		n	zhǎngxiàng	appearance, looks
省		n	shěng	province
成都		Pn	Chéngdū	Chengdu (city)
育才		Pn	Yùcái	Yucai [given name]
周志军		Pn	Zhōu Zhìjūn	Zhou Zhijun [a name]
寻		vb	xún	to search, to look for
神经		n	shénjīng	nerves
东城区		n	dōngchéngqū	eastern district
胡同		n	hútòng	alley, lane
派出所		n	pàichūsuǒ	local police station
造船厂		n	zàochuánchǎng	shipyard, dockyard
推出		vb	tuīchū	to promote
总机		n	zǒngjī	telephone exchange
该		pro	gāi	the afore mentioned
采用		vb	cǎiyòng	to adopt, to use , to employ
设计		n, vb	shèjì	design; to plan
功能		n	gōngnéng	function, use
齐全		Qvb	qíquán	complete
容		vb	róng	to contain
内部		n	nèibù	internal, inside
交换		vb	jiāohuàn	to exchange
任何		pro	rènhé	any. . . whatever. . .
管理		vb	guǎnlǐ	to manage, to run (a company etc.)
适用		vb	shìyòng	to suit, to be applicable

公司	n	gōngsī	company
机关	n	jīguān	administrative organisation
满足	vb	mǎnzú	to satisfy
用户	n	yònghù	client, customer
设	vb	shè	to work out, to establish
项目	n	xiàngmù	item
规格	n	guīgé	norm, model
价格	n	jiàgé	price
保修	vb	bǎoxiū	guarantee, warranty
传真	n	chuánzhēn	facsimile, fax
联系人	n	liánxìrén	person to contact
王增云	Pn	Wáng Zēngyún	Wang Zengyun (a name)

Use

愿	◆ 你愿干什么就干什么。 ◆ 我愿安静一点儿。 ◆ 你愿他来我们家吗?
通知	◆ 我已经通知他们了。 ◆ 学校通知我们明天开学。 ◆ 你昨天不是通知说那个会不开了吗?
任何	◆ 今天我们不安排任何活动。 ◆ 没有校长的同意,任何人都不能进去。 ◆ 任何困难他都不怕。
vb + 于	◆ 适用于,用于,生于,建于,出身于; 这座楼建于一九八三年。

采		cǎi	to collect, to pick

采集，采取，开采

* 𝒳 a hand picking fruit from a tree

厂 廠	chǎng	factory

厂家，厂商，厂长，厂子，化工厂，制片厂

船	chuán	boat

船夫，船员，船长，船只

功	gōng	work, merit

功夫，功过，功课，功利，功效，功用，成功，记功，立功，马到成功，气功，一得之功，用功

胡	hú	meddled, recklessly; beard

胡话，胡来，胡闹，胡说，胡说八道，胡言，胡子，二胡

计 計	jì	plan, strategy

计较，计量，计数器，计算，计算机，百年大计，会计(kuàijì)，生计，体温计，温度计，心计

价 價	jià	price

价目，价钱，标价，差价，代价，定价，高价，评价，原价，物价

交　jiāo　to hand over, to deliver; relationship; mutual

交班，交错，交道，交给，交换，交际，交流，交谈，交通，交响乐，交易，交易所，建交，外交，性交

*　交　a person with his legs crossed

军 軍　jūn　army

军队，军服，军官，军国主义，军号，军情，军区，军人，军事，军校，军医，军用，狗头军师，海军，红军，将军，解放军，进军，空军

*　軍　chariots placed in a circle around a camp

任　rèn　in charge of, to give free rein to

任教，任命，任期，任务，任意，调任，接任，连任，听任，信任，主任

省　shěng　to save (money); province

省得，省掉，省份，省会，省钱，省心，节省，外省

*　省　an eye looking in many directions (see 省 xǐng)

司　sī　to direct; service, department

司法，司机，打官司

*　司　to give an order; a mouth and a hand pointing upward

设 設　shè　to set up, to establish, to work out; given

设备，设法，设立，设身处地，设想，安设，建设，开设，想方设法

推	tuī	to push, to promote	

推动，推断，推广，推进，推举，推理，推论，推却，推让，推算，推土机，推托，推想，推行，推选，类推

项 項	xiàng	nape, item, sum (of money)

事项

鞋	xié	shoes

鞋带儿，鞋跟，便鞋，草鞋，凉鞋，雨鞋

寻 尋	xún	to look for

寻常，寻根究底，寻求，寻找

云 雲	yún	clouds

云层，云集，云南

*　　　twirling clouds

造	zào	to construct, to make, to create

造成，造反，造价，造就，造句，造林，造作，构造，人造，制造

增	zēng	to increase, to grow

增产，增光，增加，增进，增强，增长

足	zú	foot, sufficient

足够，足球，足以，不足道，不足为奇，立足，十足，无足轻重，自给自足

*　　　the foot and a symbol (the knee?)

单句

1. 工厂方面叫厂方。
2. 制作电影片的工厂叫制片厂。
3. 在船上工作的人员叫船员。
4. 二胡是中国的一种民间乐器。
5. 价钱是价格的意思。
6. 商品上写着的价格叫标价。
7. 原来的价格叫原价。
8. 和别人谈话叫交谈。
9. 建交就是建立外交关系。
10. 男女发生性关系叫性交。
11. 军人穿的服装叫军服。
12. 军情就是军事情报。
13. 培养军官的学校叫军校。
14. 任教就是当教员。
15. 任意就是想怎么干就怎么干。
16. 云南是中国的一个省份。
17. 成都是四川的省会。
18. 节省钱叫省钱。
19. 推断、推算、推想是同义词。
20. 寻常就是平常的意思。
21. 与众不同是一个成语，意思是和大多数人都不一样。
22. 造就有培养的意思。

1 —今天的功课你都做完了吗?
　—"回答问题"做完了，"造句"还没有做完。

2 —你孩子学习用功吗?
　—比较用功，各门功课都不错。我和我爱人都很省心。

3 —听说气功能治病，你会气功吗?
　—是的，气功可以健身。我会气功。

4 —现在北京的物价怎么样?东西还那么贵吗?
　—和去年相比日用品的价格又提高了，一双凉鞋卖二十多
　块。

5 —你觉得北京的交通方便不方便?
　—太不方便了，坐公共汽车的人太多。我觉得骑自行车最方
　便。

6 —你是军人吗?
　—是的，我是军医，在北京军区医院工作。

7 —为什么教研室主任把这个任务交给你?
　—他知道我办事认真，他信任我。

8 —你会使用电子计算机吗?
　—会，我家有两台计算机。使用计算机可以节省很多时间。

9 —你现在是谁的司机?
　—是厂长的司机，给厂长开车。

10　—听说你是球迷，为了看足球可以不吃饭。
　　—胡说，哪儿能不吃饭呀！

11　—中国能制造军用飞机吗？
　　—早就能制造了。

12　—中国和法国是什么时候建立外交关系的？
　　—大概是六十年代初。

13　—对这个问题应该辨证地分析。
　　—我同意！

14　—怎么院长任命这么个人当研究室主任？
　　—不足为奇，这个人爱打小报告。

15　—你们化工厂今年增产了吗？
　　—和去年同期相比增产了百分之二十。

16　—你们想采取什么方法来推广这种新技术？
　　—我们想举办一个学习班，培养一些技术员。

第二十三课　鲁迅

　　鲁迅是中国现代著名的文学家和思想家，绍兴人，生于一八八一年九月二十五日，原名周树人。鲁迅是他的笔名。鲁迅出身于破落的封建士大夫家庭。小时在家乡上过旧式的学校，读过四书五经之类的书。一八九八年他到南京上学，受到了'科学'、'民主'以及'进化论'思想的影响。一九〇二年他去日本留学。起初，他先学医学，想走医学救国的道路。后来，发现医学对于落后的中国并不是一件紧要的事，最重要的是要改变中国民众的精神。于是，他改而从事文学活动。一九〇九年鲁迅回国，先后在绍兴、北京、广州等地工作，当过教员、中学校长、教育部官员、大学教师和中文系系主任。与此同时，他开始不断在《新青年》等许多杂志上发表文学作品。自一九二七年起，鲁迅定居上海，专心从事文学创作。

　　鲁迅在文学上的主要成就是他的白话小说和杂文。鲁迅白话小说的特点是不仅具有鲜明的反封建色彩，而且写作手法独特。因此他的白话小说在'五四'时期影响很大。鲁迅生前还写了大量的杂文。他的杂文反映了他在各个历史时期对社会事件和某些学术问题的看法和态度，其写作技巧曾受到人们的高度评价。

　　鲁迅除了白话小说和杂文以外，还写了一些有关文学史方面的学术著作。

　　一九三六年十月十九日，由于劳累过度，鲁迅在上海因病去世。

VOCABULARY

鲁迅	Pn	Lǔ Xùn	Lu Xun
绍兴	Pn	Shàoxīng	Shaoxing
周树人	Pn	Zhōu Shùrén	Zhou Shuren
出身	n	chūshēn	family background, class origin
破落	Qvb	pòluò	in decline
封建	Qvb	fēngjiàn	feudal
士大夫	n	shìdàfu	mandarin, scholar
家庭	n	jiātíng	family
家乡	n	jiāxiāng	birthplace, hometown
旧式	n	jiùshì	old style, ancient style
四书	Pn	sìshū	the Four Books
五经	Pn	wǔjīng	the Five Classics
民主	n, Qvb	mínzhǔ	democracy; democratic
进化论	n	jìnhuàlùn	evolutionism
起初	n	qǐchū	in the beginning
救	vb	jiù	to save, to rescue
并不	neg	bìngbù	actually not
件	Mw	jiàn	[Mw for events]
紧要	Qvb	jǐnyào	urgent
改变	vb	gǎibiàn	to change, to transform
民众	n	mínzhòng	the people
改	vb	gǎi	to change
从事	vb	cóngshì	to be engaged in, to take up
广州	Pn	Guǎngzhōu	Guangzhou (Canton)
主任	n	zhǔrèn	master, leader, director
与此同时	exp	yǔcǐtóngshí	at the same time
杂志	n	zázhì	magazine, journal

作品	n	zuòpǐn	work (of art)
自…起	const	zì…qǐ	from…
定居	vb	dìngjū	to settle dowm
专心	vb	zhuānxīn	to give one's full attention to
创作	vb	chuàngzuò	creation
成就	n	chéngjiù	success
白话	n	báihuà	vernacular
杂文	n	záwén	essay
鲜明	Qvb	xiānmíng	clear, obvious
色彩	n	sècǎi	colour, tint
写作	vb	xiězuò	writing
手法	n	shǒufǎ	technique, style
社会	n	shèhuì	society
事件	n	shìjiàn	event, affair
学术	n	xuéshù	sphere of learning, sciencc of learning
技巧	n	jìqiǎo	skill, art
评价	vb	píngjià	to appraise, to evaluate; appreciation
劳累	Qvb	láolèi	tired, run down, over worked
过度	Qvb	guòdù	excessive, undue
去世	vb	qùshì	to die, to pass away

* **The Four Books of the Confucian school:**

《论语》	Lúnyǔ	*Analects of Confucius*
《中庸》	Zhōngyōng	*The Doctrine of the Mean*
《大学》	Dàxué	*The Great Learning*
《孟子》	Mèngzǐ	*Mencius*

* * **The Five Classics:**

《易经》	Yìjīng	*The Book of Changes*
《诗经》	Shījīng	*The Book of Songs*
《书经》	Shūjīng	*The Book of History*
《礼记》	Lǐjì	*The Book of Rites*
《春秋》	Chūnqiū	*The Spring and Autumn Annals*

起初	◆ 他起初在小学工作，后来在大学工作。 ◆ 我起初不认识他，后来通过你的介绍认识他了。
先后	◆ 我先后去过美国、日本、法国等许多国家。 ◆ 做事情应该有个先后。
并	◆ 你说的这件事，我并不知道。 ◆ 他见了王老师，并把这件事告诉了他。
件	◆ 一件事，一件衣服，一件上衣
与此同时	◆ 为了找工作，他给很多公司打了电话。与此同时，他还给不少朋友写了信。 ◆ 在中国期间他主要在北京大学学习，与此同时，他还为一家报社写文章。
自 . . . 起	◆ 自明天起学校开始放假。 ◆ 他自六岁起就开始学画画儿。
不仅 . . . 而且	◆ 他不仅会说汉语，而且还会说日语、英语。 ◆ 昨天的会不仅学生都去了，而且所有的老师也都去了。

变 變	biàn	change

变成，变调，变动，变法，变革，变更，变化，变换，变色，变色龙，变相，变种，事变，谈虎色变，演变，政变，转变

彩	cǎi	multicoloured

彩电，彩票，彩色，挂彩，光彩，喝彩，精彩

曾	céng	[indicates past action]

曾经，不曾

创 創	chuàng	to create

创办，创建，创见，创举，创立，创设，创始人，创新，创业，创造，创造性，首创

改	gǎi	to change, to correct

改掉，改动，改革，改革派，改观，改过，改行，改换，改进，改期，改善，改天，改天换地，改正，改组，土改，修改

* 𣪕 a hand holding a stick and a child

件	jiàn	[Mw for events, habits]; article

机件，计件，零件，密件，事件，条件，文件，无条件，物件，信件，原件，证件

紧 緊	jǐn	tight

紧接，紧密，紧张，不要紧，加紧，要紧

救	jiù	to save

救护，救火，救济，救命，救星，补救，不可救药，见死不救，坐视不救

居	jū	to reside, to be in a certain place

居功，居留证，居民，居然，居住，安居乐业，故居，旧居，同居

劳 劳	láo	labour, merit

劳保，劳动，劳动节，劳动力，劳动者，劳工，功劳

* 勞 two torches and "force"

鲁 鲁	lǔ	[Fn]

鲁班

破	pò	to break, to destroy

破产，破除，破格，破坏，破旧立新，破例，破碎，冲破，打破，看破，识破，突破

巧	qiǎo	clever, cunning; opportunely

巧合，花言巧语，正巧

社	shè	association, society

社会地位，社会关系，社会科学，社会制度，社会主义，社交，社论，报社，公社，合作社，旅社，旅行社

* 社 to worship the god of soil

| 庭 | | tíng | room, hall, tribunal |
| | | | 庭院，法庭 |

| 鲜 | 鮮 | xiān | fresh, tasty |
| | | | 鲜红，鲜花，鲜美，海鲜，新鲜 |

| 迅 | | xùn | fast, rapid |
| | | | 迅猛 |

单句

1. 声调有变化叫变调。
2. 变更就是改变和变动的意思。
3. 同时存在叫并存。
4. 彩电就是彩色电视。
5. 创见就是独到的见解。
6. 创立就是初次建立。
7. 创业就是创办事业。
8. 改动是有变动的意思，如：这篇文章我只改动了两个字。
9. 改进就是改变旧有的情况，使有所进步。
10. 改期就是改变日期。
11. 把不对的改为正确的叫改正。
12. 土改指中国解放初期在农村进行的土地改革。
13. 机密的文件叫密件。
14. 证件就是证明某人身分、经历等的文件，如：学生证、工作证等。
15. 要紧就是重要的意思。
16. 救济就是用钱物帮助生活上有困难的人。
17. 故居就是以前住的房屋。
18. 男女没有结婚，但是生活在一起叫同居。
19. 破旧立新指破除旧的创立新的。
20. 破例就是打破惯例。
21. 历史事实叫史实。
22. 出世和问世是同义词，都是出生的意思。
23. 房屋前的院子叫庭院。
24. 鲜红就是鲜明的红色。
25. 鲜美指饭菜和瓜果的味道好。

1 —北京的居民家家都有彩电吗？
　　—近几年，因为进行经济改革，人民生活水平有了很大的改善，有彩电的家庭越来越多了。

2 —五一劳动节的电视节目精彩不精彩？
　　—非常精彩。

3 —改革开放以后，人民的思想和观念变化大不大？
　　—变化很大，人们对社会主义有了新的认识。

4 —你现在还在大学教历史吗？
　　—我已经改行了，不当老师了。我现在在一家旅行社工作。

5 —你来得正巧，我今天买了点儿海鲜，中午就在我这儿吃饭吧！
　　—一会儿我还要去送文件，改天再来。

6 —你听新闻了吗？哪国发生了政变？
　　—是一个非洲国家。政变后很多商店受到破坏。

7 —你觉得报社的工作紧张不紧张？
　　—很紧张。有时候为了写一篇社论，晚上常常要加班。

8 —你知道《世界报》是谁创办的吗？
　　—不知道，只知道这是法国发行量较大的一份报纸。

9 —你拿到你的居留证了吗？
　　—还没有，我还缺一个文件。

10 —你为什么要去法庭？
   —我要给我朋友作证，证明他和杀人事件无关。

11 —这条鱼怎么样？
   —很新鲜，并且不太贵。买两条吧！

12 —你认识那位干部？
   —认识，他过去是公社的书记，曾经参加过土改。

13 —这儿怎么变成了一家饭馆了？以前不是一家公司吗？
   —那家公司早就破产了。

24

第二十四课　新闻报道

　　新华社北京 4 月 5 日电：中美两国首脑昨天在北京举行会谈。双方就两国共同关心的国际问题交换了意见。双方对目前中东发生的流血事件表示极大的关切。参加会谈的还有中国党和政府的有关领导人。会谈后，美国总统还将访问上海和南京两大城市并参观两所大学和一座化工厂。

　　据新华社南京 10 月 2 日电：中国最大的一所灯具厂最近在南京建成。

　　中新社台北 6 月 10 日电：今年第三季度，台湾工业和农业产值和去年同期相比增长百分之三。农业获得近十年来最好收成。

　　美联社旧金山 8 日电：美国政府计划集资在当地修建一个农业虫害防治中心，其中有数十个现代化试验室将由私人公司资助。某些国际基金组织对这一计划也非常关注。

　　人民日报报道：一支由中国研究人员和学者组成的小分队将去非洲进行考察。

VOCABULARY

汉字		词性	拼音	英文
新闻		n	xīnwén	the news
报道		n	bàodào	report
新华社		Pn	Xīnhuáshè	Xinhua News Agency
电	脑	n	diàn	telegram, cable
首	脑	n	shǒunǎo	leader (of State)
举	行	vb	jǔxíng	to hold (a meeting, etc.)
会	谈	n	huìtán	talks
国	际	n	guójì	international
目	前	Tw	mùqián	now, at present
流	血	v-o	liúxuè	to bleed
关	切	n	guānqiè	concern
党		n	dǎng	(political) party
政	府	n	zhèngfǔ	government
领	导	n, vb	lǐngdǎo	leader; to lead
总	统	n	zǒngtǒng	president (of a republic)
访	问	v, n	fǎngwèn	to visit; visit
化	工厂	n	huàgōngchǎng	chemical factory
灯	具厂	n	dēngjùchǎng	lamp factory
建	成	vb	jiànchéng	to finish building/constructing
中	新社	Pn	Zhōngxīnshè	China News Service
台	北	Pn	Táiběi	Taibei (Taipei)
季	度	n	jìdù	quarter (of a year), season
台	湾	Pn	Táiwān	Taiwan
工	业	n	gōngyè	industry
农	业	n	nóngyè	agriculture
产	值	n	chǎnzhí	output value
同	期	n	tóngqī	the same period

相比	vb	xiāngbǐ	to compare
增长	vb	zēngzhǎng	to increase, to augment
获得	vb	huòdé	to obtain
收成	n	shōuchéng	harvest
美联社	Pn	Měiliánshè	Associated Press Agency
计划	n, vb	jìhuà	plan; to plan
集资	vb	jízī	to raise funds
当地	n	dāngdì	local
修建	vb	xiūjiàn	to construct
虫害	n	chónghài	insect pest
防治	vb	fángzhì	to prevent and treat
其中	prep	qízhōng	among
试验室	n	shìyànshì	laboratory
私人	n	sīrén	private
资助	vb, n	zīzhù	to subsidise; financial aid
基金	n	jījīn	funds
组织	n, vb	zǔzhi	organisation; to organise
关注	n, vb	guānzhù	to follow with interest, to pay close attention to
支	Mw	zhī	[Mw for pens, troops. . .]
小分队	n	xiǎofēnduì	small team
非洲	Pn	Fēizhōu	Africa
考察	vb	kǎochá	to inspect, to examine

Use

就	
	◆ 你等一会儿,他马上就回来。
	◆ 饭一会儿就好了。
	◆ 十年前我就认识他了。
	◆ 吃完饭他就回家了。
	◆ 他一看见我就哭了起来。
	◆ 他就是我的老师。

◆ 我就不信我学不会汉语。

◆ 他们家就两口人。

◆ 昨天就他一个人没来，别的人都来了。

◆ 就汉语来说，他的水平比你的高多了。

◆ 我就他研究的问题，提了几点意见。

◆ 他就着灯亮儿看书。

极	◆ 他车开得极快。
	◆ 我极不愿意他用我的东西。
	◆ 国家极需要从国外进口这种汽车。
	◆ 你住在这儿极不安全。

| 所 | ◆ 一所大学，一所医院，一所房子 |

| 座 | ◆ 一座山，一座化工厂，一座楼 |

| 并 | ◆ 我找到他并把事情都跟他讲了。 |
| | ◆ 这件事我并不知道。 |

| Vb＋成 | ◆ 建成，写成，说成，变成，画成 |
| | ◆ 你把四月三号说成四月五号了。 |

近	◆ 他家离学校很近。
	◆ 他近两年来身体一直不好。
	◆ 参加会的近三千人。

| 其中 | ◆ 我们班有四十个学生，其中有一半是女生。 |
| | ◆ 这篇文章我已经看了，其中有几个词我不懂。 |

| 支 | ◆ 一支笔，一支军队 |

将	◆ 火车将要进站了。
	◆ 这将是我们遇到的最大困难。
	◆ 你买的面包将够吃。

虫 蠱	chóng	insect

虫子，害虫，寄生虫

* ⌇ a venenous snake

党 黨	dǎng	party

党报，党纪，党派，党性，党员，党章，共产党，国民党，劳动党，民主党，社会党，死党，政党

导 導	dǎo	to lead

导电，导火线，导论，导热，导线，导师，导言，导演，传导，教导，指导

灯 燈	dēng	lamp, light, lantern

灯光，灯火，灯头，电灯，红灯，绿灯，台灯，油灯

防	fáng	to prevent, to protect

防备，防风林，防护，防火，防空，防守，防水，防卫，防线，防止，防治，边防，国防部

访 訪	fǎng	to visit, to interview

访友，拜访，采访，走访

府	fǔ	government office, prefecture, residence

总统府

华 華	huá	magnificent, splendid, best; China

华北，华表，华而不实，华丽，华人，华语，才华，中华人民共和国

划 劃	huá	to row a boat, to scratch; it pays to
		划不来，划船，划得来，划算
	huà	to delimit, to differentiate
		划分，划清，划时代，规划，区划

| 获 獲 | huò | to obtain, to acquire |
| | | 获取，不劳而获，收获 |

* 𤩹 a hand grabbing a bird and "animal with claws"

| 基 | jī | base, foundation |
| | | 基本，基本功，基本上，基层，基地，基点，基调，基建，基因 |

| 季 | jì | season |
| | | 季度，季风，季节，春季，四季，夏季，雨季 |

| 领 領 | lǐng | neck, outline; to lead, to receive, to understand |
| | | 领带，领队，领海，领会，领教，领空，领路，领情，领取，领事，领事馆，领受，领水，领头，领土，领先，领子，本领，带领，首领 |

| 私 | sī | private, secret |
| | | 私产，私房，私货，私交，私利，私立，私情，私生活，私生子，私事，私心，私有，私有制，私自，大公无私，自私，走私 |

* 禾 + 厶 : "cereal" and "private"

血		xuè	blood

血管，血统，血小板，白血病，红血球，流血

* 𥁕 a sacrificial vase with a symbolic mark representing blood

---

验	驗	yàn	to examine, to check

验光，验货，验收，验算，验血，验证，化验，考验，试验，先验

支		zhī	branch; to support; [Mw for pens, troops. . .]

支部，支出，支架，支解，支流，支票，支取，支使，支书，分支，开支

* 支 a hand holding a twig

织	織	zhī	to weave

织布，织女星，毛织品，毛织物

值		zhí	value; to be worth, to be on duty

值班，值当，值得，值钱，值日，比值，不值一提，产值，价值

资	資	zī	riches, qualification

资本，资本家，资本主义，资产，资方，资格，资金，资历，工资，合资，师资

单句

1. 有害的虫子叫害虫。
2. 共产党、民主党是两个不同的政党。
3. 一个政党办的，并且代表这一政党的政治观点的报纸叫党报。
4. 导电、导热就是传导电流和热能。
5. 高等学校和研究机关中指导人学习、写作论文的人叫导师。
6. 教导就是教育和指导。
7. 电灯的光叫灯光。
8. 放在台子或桌子上的电灯叫台灯。
9. 防卫就是防护和保卫。
10. 拜访、走访都有访问的意思。
11. 一个国家总统办公的地方叫总统府。
12. 华语就是汉语。
13. 华北是中国北方的一个地区。
14. 美丽而有光彩叫华丽。
15. 划不来就是不值得的意思。
16. 不劳而获是一个成语，意思是不通过劳动而能有所收获。
17. 基建就是基本建设。
18. 基因是生物学上的一个概念。
19. 私人所有叫私有。
20. 个人的事是私事。
21. 私人之间的交情叫私交。
22. 为自己打算的念头叫私心。
23. 没有结婚的男女所生的子女叫私生子。
24. 支部书记叫支书。
25. 两数相比所得的值叫比值。
26. 资格和经历叫资历。

会话

1　—你们领队是党员吗？
　　—那还用说，基层干部差不多都是党员。

2　—带红色领带的那位先生是谁？
　　—是法国著名的电影导演，他曾导演过很多部电影。

3　—过马路的时候要注意红绿灯！
　　—知道，我又不是小孩儿了。

4　—为什么今天很多记者都采访美国国防部部长？
　　—因为明天他将访问中华人民共和国。

5　—你们这个地区的华人子弟都上什么学校？
　　—差不多都上私立学校。

6　—你喜欢划船吗？
　　—很喜欢，基本上每个星期天我都跟我的孩子去划船。

7　—一年四季你最喜欢哪个季节？
　　—我最喜欢春季。

8　—这个月的工资你领了吗？
　　—已经领了。

9　—你验血了吗？
　　—验了，这是化验报告，白血球有点儿高。

10 —现在我没有现金，我用支票可以吗？
    —不行，价值一百元以下的商品我们不收支票。

11 —建一座小的化工厂需要多少资金好？
    —至少需要五千万美金。

12 —你觉得私有制好还是公有制好？
    —两种制度都有优点，也都有缺点，这个问题很难说清楚。

13 —你们领队这个人怎么样？
    —这个人很自私，私心太重。

14 —为什么过海关每个人都要把行李打开？
    —这叫验关，为了防止走私。

25

第二十五课　北京土话

王：最近你看了些什么书？

马：前一阶段较忙，没看什么书。这几天有了点儿时间，正在看一本中文小说。

王：你二年级还没上完就能看小说了，真不简单！什么小说？

马：书名叫《天桥的把势，光说不练》，是位北京作家写的。这是我第一次看中文小说。我是想试试，看看能不能看懂一点儿。结果我发现有好些词都没学过。有的词在词典里也查不到。我正想问你呢。'拉晚儿'这个词是什么意思？

王：这不是普通话里的词，这是北京土话。过去人力车夫晚上拉客人叫'拉晚儿'。

马：哦！'消停、爷们儿、铁了心'这些词是不是也是北京土话？

王：是。'消停'普通话说'安静'，比如说："你让我安静一会儿吧！"用北京土话说："你让我消停一会儿吧！"。'爷们儿'是指男人，比如说："这儿都是爷们儿，没有女的。"'铁了心'是下定了决心的意思。

马：北京土话里的好多词都和普通话不一样吗?

王：有不少。人们常说的'小子'普通话叫'男孩儿'，'一丁点儿'普通话说'一点儿'，'今儿、明儿、昨儿'普通话说'今天、明天、昨天'。

马：北京土话里的词，现在北京人还用吗?

王：有些还用，有些已经不用了。刚才我说的一些词还在用，像'心里美，老头儿乐'，这样的词人们也在用。但是像'拉晚儿、委冬儿、局着、取灯儿'这样的词人们已经不用了。

马：你要是不急的话，我还想问你几个句子。你看：
"谁知他是这么块料!"
"我看他们两个人半斤八两。"
"谁知他骨子里怎么想的!"
"到了这个肯节儿上，你怎么还不说话?"
"要是拿到市场上卖，苦死也能卖上五六十块。"

王：这里的'料、半斤八两、骨子里、肯节儿、苦死'都是北京土话。我建议你到书店去买本《北京土语词典》，这些词，那本词典里都有。

Map of Beijing

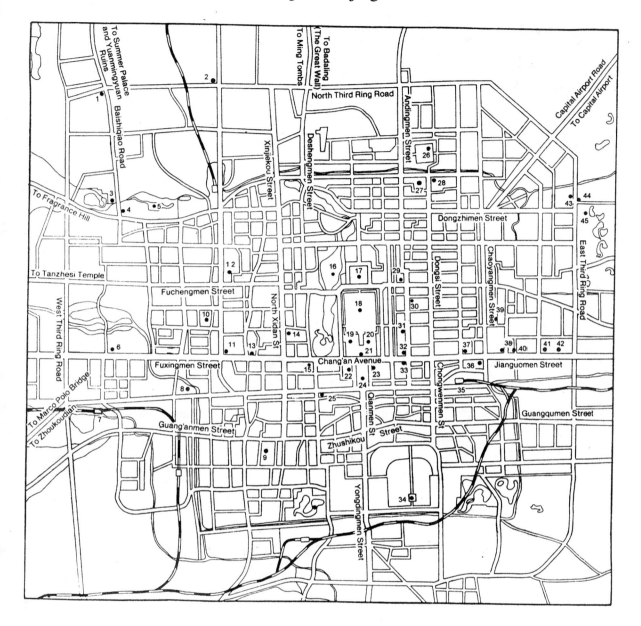

1. Friendship Hotel
2. Great Bell Temple
3. National Library of China
4. Capital Gymnasium
5. Beijing Zoo
6. Military Museum
7. Beijing West Railway Station
8. White Cloud Taoist Temple
9. Niujie Libai Mosque
10. Yuetan Park (Altar of the Moon)
11. China Arts and Crafts Gallery
12. Lu Xun Museum
13. Culture Palace for Nationalities
14. Xidan Shopping Centre
15. Beijing Concert Hall
16. Beihai Park

17. Jingshan Park (Coal Hill)
18. Palace Museum (Forbidden City)
19. Zhongshan Park
20. Working People's Cutural Palace
21. Tian'anmen Square
22. Great Hall of the People
23. History Museum
24. Chairman Mao Memorial Hall
25. Laoshe Teahouse
26. Ditan Park (Altar of the Earth)
27. Confucian Temple
28. Harmony and Peace Lamasery
29. China Art Gallery
30. Capital Theatre
31. Wangfujing Department Store
32. Beijing Hotel

33. China international Travel Service
34. Tiantan Park (Temple of Heaven)
35. Beijing Railway Station
36. Ancient Observatory
37. International Mansion
38. China International Trust & Investment Corporation Building
39. Ritan Park (Altar of the Sun)
40. Friendship Store
41. Jianguo Hotel
42. Beijing-Toronto Hotel
43. Kunlun Hotel
44. Great Wall Sheraton Hotel
45. Agricultural Museum

VOCABULARY

阶段	n	jiēduàn	period
年级	n	niánjí	year (of study)
简单	Qvb	jiǎndān	simple
天桥	Pn	Tiānqiáo	Heavenly Bridge
把势	n	bǎshi	martial arts master
光	adv	guāng	solely, only
练	vb	liàn	to practise
试	vb	shì	to try
结果	n	jiéguǒ	result; finally
词典	n	cídiǎn	dictionary
查	vb	chá	to check, to examine
普通话	n	pǔtōnghuà	*putonghua* (standard pronunciation)
下决心	v-o	xiàjuéxīn	to make up one's mind, to make a decision
心里美	n	xīnlǐměi	a type of turnip with green peel and purple-red flesh
老头儿乐	n	lǎotóurlè	back scratcher
委冬儿	exp	wěidōngr	to stay idly at home during the winter
局着	exp	júzhe	to be embarrased by somebody's presence
取灯儿	exp	qǔdēngr	matches
急	Qvb	jí	in a hurry
料	n	liào	(to have the) makings/stuff
半斤八两	exp	bànjīnbāliǎng	tweedledum and tweedledee, six of one and half-a-dozen of the other
骨子里	exp	gǔzilǐ	in one's heart of hearts (to the bone)
肯节儿	exp	kènjiér	crucial moment
苦死	exp	kǔsi	at worst
建议	vb, n	jiànyì	to suggest, to propose; proposition

天桥的把势,光说不练　　　exp　　　to be all talk

什么	◆ 你干什么呢？
	◆ 你买什么东西了？
	◆ 我没去什么地方。
	◆ 您想吃什么就吃什么。
	◆ 他什么都不吃。
光	◆ 我光喝酒不吃饭。
	◆ 这种纸很光。
	◆ 他光着身子，没穿衣服。
	◆ 他们把酒都喝光了。
安静	◆ 你住的地方很安静。
	◆ 我想安静一会儿。
谁	◆ 谁喜欢你！
	◆ 谁知他想干什么！
要是	◆ 要是你去，我也去。
	◆ 你要是同意的话，我还想看一遍。
怎么	◆ 你怎么去中国？ 坐飞机还是坐火车？
	◆ 你怎么没去上课？
	◆ 老师怎么讲我都不懂。
	◆ 你想怎么做就怎么做。
半斤八两	◆ 这两个人半斤八两。
	◆ 他和那个人半斤八两。
五六十块	◆ 两三个，四五个，五六个，七八个，八九个
建议	◆ 他的建议很好。
	◆ 我建议你吃吃这种药。

251

查	chá	to check, to examine
		查办，查点，查对，查封，查看，查考，查收，查问，查证，调查

典	diǎn	code, standard, ceremony
		典范，典故，典礼，大典，古典，经典，字典
		* 丗 writing tablet placed on a stand

段	duàn	section, piece
		段落，唱段，片段，手段，选段

骨	gǔ	bone
		骨头，骨干，骨架，骨节，骨科，骨气，骨肉，骨子里，排骨
		* 骨 a bone and flesh

急	jí	anxious, worried, irritated, fast, urgent
		急电，急件，急救，急剧，急忙，争切，急性病，急行军，急性子，急需，急用，急于，急诊室，当务之急，告急，紧急，着急

级 級	jí	level, rank, grade
		级别，等级，高级，留级，上级，升级，特级，下级，中级

简 簡	jiǎn	simple, brief; letter
		简报，简便，简称，简单化，简短，简化，简历，简练，简明，简体字，简写，简要，简易，简直

阶 階	jiē	steps, stairs
		阶层，阶级，台阶

斤	jīn	a pound
		斤斤计较,公斤
		* 尺 an axe

局	jú	a game (of chess), office, situation
		局部,局面,当局,电话局,公安局,教育局,结局,卫生局

决	jué	to decide, to execute, to breach
		决定,决断,决口,决议,处决,解决
		* water and chipped jade: a gap in a dam

肯	kěn	to be willing to
		中肯

苦	kǔ	bitter, painful
		苦处,苦笑,苦干,苦心,苦瓜,吃苦,苦力,劳苦,苦难,受苦,苦头,痛苦,苦味

拉	lā	to pull, to play an instrument with a bow
		拉丁文,拉拉队,拉丁字母,拉买卖,拉肚子,拉关系,拉货

练 練	liàn	to exercise, to train
		练功,练习,练习本,练习题,练字,教练,老练,熟练

料	liào	to expect, to predict; material, grain
		料酒,料理,料想,料子,不出所料,不料,布料,材料,出乎意料,出人意料,毛料,木料,史料,原料,资料,作料
		* 米 + 斗:"rice" and "a measure for grain", to measure

普		pǔ	vast, universal, common

普遍,普查,普及,普通话,普选

* 晉 (glyph) the sun shining on everyone (two people)

桥 橋	qiáo	bridge

桥头,大桥,木桥,铁桥

取	qǔ	to take, to obtain, to aim at

取材, 取长补短, 取代, 取得, 取而代之, 取经,
取决, 取暖, 取巧, 取笑, 采取, 考取, 可取, 领
取, 提取, 听取

* 取 (glyph) to remove the ear from a prisoner, once a sign of capture

---

势 勢	shì	power, momentum, appearance

势必, 势力, 势能, 得势, 局势, 声势, 守势, 手
势, 形势, 优势

铁 鐵	tiě	iron

铁板, 铁板一块, 铁道, 铁道部, 铁饭碗, 铁路,
铁器, 铁水, 铁证, 地铁

停	tíng	to stop

停车, 停车场, 停当, 停放, 停工, 停火, 停留,
停业, 停职, 停止

委	wěi	to entrust, to shift; indirect

委派, 委任, 委托, 委员, 委员会, 市委

* 委 (glyph) a (cereal) stalk bent over and a woman kneeling down

---

消	xiāo	to disappear, to remove, to pass time

消除, 消防队, 消费, 消费品, 消费者, 消化, 消
极, 消息, 取消

爷 爺	yé	grandfather (respectful title given to an old man)

爷爷, 老大爷, 老爷, 少爷

单句

1. 观察事物存在的情况叫查看。
2. 段落指一篇文章根据内容划分成的部分。
3. 骨头的关节叫骨节。
4. 需要马上传送的电报叫急电。
5. 要马上发送的紧急的文件叫急件。
6. 急救指对得急性病或受重伤的病人进行紧急的救治。
7. 急忙指心里着急，行动加快。
8. 性子很急的人叫急性子。
9. 急需就是紧急需要。
10. 级别就是等级的区别。
11. 阶层指在同一个阶级中因经济地位不同而分成的层次。
12. 局部指一部分，不是全体。
13. 最后的结果叫结局。
14. 苦的味道叫苦味。
15. 用车来运送货物叫拉货。
16. 拉丁文所使用的字母叫拉丁字母。
17. 办理或处理也叫料理，如：料理家务。
18. 练字就是练习写字。
19. 停止工作叫停工。
20. 委托就是把事情交给别人去办。
21. 委员会的成员叫委员。
22. 简体字也叫简化字。
23. 停汽车的地方叫停车场。

会话

1 —这种材料市场上缺不缺？
  —我已经作过市场调查，目前市场上不缺。

2 —对一个孩子来说，小学、中学、大学，哪个阶段的学习最重要？
  —人们普遍认为小学阶段的学习最重要。

3 —老马是不是你们卫生局的骨干？
  —是。他工作很认真，也很老练。

4 —不要着急，着急也没有用。
  —怎么能不着急呢，他这是第三次留级了。

5 —你现在上几年级？
  —大学二年级，明年该上三年级了。

6 —为什么对什么问题都要进行阶级分析？
  —因为人生活在一个有阶级的社会里。

7 —明天你去公安局干什么？
  —我去办居留证。

8 —这件西服是什么料子的？
  —是毛料的。

9 —你做菜放不放料酒？
  —做肉和做鱼的时候，我喜欢放一点儿料酒。

10　—昨天老师留的练习你都做了吗？
　　—都做了，但是不知道对不对。

11　—上海人会说普通话吗？
　　—大多数上海人会说普通话。

12　—请问，这儿能不能停放自行车？
　　—不行，这儿离铁道太近。

13　—你有没有北京的消息？
　　—有啊，北京正在进行人口普查。

14　—你觉得这两种布料，那种更好一点儿？
　　—我看半斤八两，差不多。

15　—这次去中国旅行，你们在北京停留几天？
　　—我们想停留三天。

16　—你今天买了些什么东西？
　　—三斤排骨、一斤苦瓜、几个练习本和一本《新华字
　　　典》。

17　—你看了昨天的简报了吗？
　　—看了，各个地方的形势普遍都不太好。

Table of 900 Characters in Complex Form

	A	B	C	D	E	F	G	H	I	J	K	L	M	N	O	P	Q	R	S	T	U	V	W	X	Y	Z	A'	B'	C'	D'
1	啊	愛	安	暗	按	八	把	爸	吧	白	百	拜	班	般	板	半	辦	幫	包	保	抱	報	爆	杯	北	被	背	備	本	鼻
2	比	筆	避	必	邊	便	遍	辨	變	標	表	別	病	并	補	不	部	布	步	才	材	采	彩	菜	參	草	層	曾	茶	察
3	查	差	產	長	常	場	廠	唱	車	徹	稱	成	城	承	程	吃	衝	蟲	出	初	除	楚	處	川	穿	傳	船	窗	床	創
4	春	詞	此	次	從	村	存	錯	答	達	打	大	帶	待	代	單	但	淡	蛋	當	黨	導	到	道	的	得	燈	等	低	底
5	地	第	弟	點	典	電	店	掉	調	丁	定	冬	東	懂	動	都	讀	獨	度	短	斷	段	對	隊	多	朵	躲	餓	兒	而
6	耳	二	發	乏	法	反	飯	範	方	房	防	訪	放	非	飛	費	分	墳	份	風	封	夫	服	福	府	父	副	複	富	婦
7	該	改	概	敢	感	乾	剛	鋼	高	搞	告	哥	歌	革	隔	格	個	給	跟	根	更	工	公	功	共	狗	夠	構	姑	古
8	骨	故	顧	固	瓜	刮	掛	怪	關	觀	官	館	管	慣	光	廣	規	鬼	貴	國	果	過	還	孩	海	害	含	漢	好	號
9	喝	河	和	何	合	黑	很	恨	紅	后	候	呼	忽	乎	湖	胡	虎	戶	互	護	花	華	劃	畫	化	話	懷	壞	歡	環
10	換	黃	回	會	婚	活	火	或	貨	獲	機	雞	積	基	極	及	集	級	急	幾	己	寄	繼	際	記	濟	紀	技	計	季
11	家	加	假	架	價	間	簡	見	建	健	件	江	將	講	交	餃	腳	角	叫	教	較	接	街	階	結	節	解	姐	介	界
12	今	金	斤	僅	緊	近	進	盡	京	經	精	晴	景	靜	境	究	九	酒	久	就	舊	救	居	局	舉	句	具	據	劇	拒
13	覺	絕	決	軍	開	看	康	考	靠	科	可	課	刻	客	肯	空	孔	口	苦	哭	快	筷	塊	況	困	拉	來	浪	勞	老
14	樂	了	累	類	冷	離	李	里	理	禮	立	麗	利	歷	力	例	連	聯	臉	練	涼	兩	輛	亮	量	諒	療	料	烈	林
15	零	○	領	另	龍	留	流	六	樓	路	旅	綠	慮	論	落	媽	馬	嗎	買	賣	滿	慢	忙	毛	么	沒	美	每	門	們
16	猛	夢	迷	米	密	面	民	名	明	命	某	母	木	目	拿	哪	那	男	南	難	腦	鬧	呢	內	能	你	年	念	娘	鳥
17	您	牛	農	弄	怒	女	暖	怕	排	派	判	旁	跑	培	朋	皮	篇	片	票	品	平	評	漂	破	普	七	期	騎	其	奇
18	齊	起	氣	汽	器	千	前	錢	強	牆	橋	巧	切	且	親	輕	青	清	情	請	慶	窮	秋	求	球	區	取	去	趣	全
19	缺	卻	確	然	讓	擾	熱	人	認	任	日	容	肉	如	入	三	色	殺	山	善	商	傷	上	少	紹	蛇	設	社	誰	身
20	深	什	神	甚	生	聲	升	省	師	詩	十	時	識	實	食	始	使	史	是	事	市	室	示	似	視	適	式	士	試	世
21	勢	收	手	守	首	受	書	舒	熟	數	術	樹	雙	水	睡	順	說	思	司	私	死	四	送	拆	算	雖	隨	歲	碎	所
22	索	他	她	它	臺	太	態	談	特	疼	提	題	體	替	天	田	條	鐵	聽	庭	停	通	同	統	頭	突	圖	土	團	推
23	托	外	完	玩	晚	碗	萬	王	往	忘	望	為	圍	委	位	衛	味	溫	文	聞	問	我	屋	無	五	午	武	舞	物	務
24	西	息	希	析	習	喜	洗	細	係	下	嚇	夏	先	鮮	顯	現	幾	限	香	鄉	相	想	響	象	向	像	項	消	小	校
25	笑	效	些	鞋	寫	謝	新	心	信	星	行	形	醒	姓	興	幸	性	休	修	需	許	續	選	學	雪	血	尋	牙	呀	言
26	研	顏	眼	演	驗	陽	羊	養	樣	要	藥	爺	也	夜	葉	業	一	醫	衣	依	疑	以	已	意	義	藝	憶	易	議	因
27	音	陰	印	應	英	影	硬	映	用	優	由	油	有	友	又	右	魚	于	語	雨	與	遇	育	欲	元	園	原	員	圓	遠
28	院	願	約	月	越	雲	運	雜	在	再	咱	早	造	則	怎	增	展	站	張	丈	章	招	找	照	者	這	着	真	診	正
29	整	政	證	知	之	支	織	直	職	值	祇	指	紙	止	至	制	治	致	志	中	鍾	終	種	重	眾	周	洲	州	竹	主
30	住	祝	注	著	助	專	轉	莊	裝	壯	準	資	子	仔	字	自	總	走	租	族	足	組	嘴	最	昨	左	作	做	坐	座

Notes:

1. Some sinograms have only one form – they were originally in a simple form.

2. The following sinograms have different complex forms:

復,複=复　　乾,幹=干　　歷,曆=历　　鐘,鍾=钟

臺,檯,颱=台　係,繫=系　雙,衹=只

TEXTS
IN
COMPLEX
CHARACTERS

第一課　畫龍點睛

　　傳說古代有一位畫家在牆上畫了四條龍，每條龍畫得都很好，像真的一樣，可是都沒有畫眼睛。人們看了都覺得特別奇怪，問他為什麼不畫眼睛。畫家很自信地說：“要是我畫上眼睛，龍馬上就會飛起來。”人們都不相信，要求他把龍眼睛畫上去。他說：“我只畫一條。”畫家提起筆來在一條龍上畫了眼睛。畫家剛一畫完，立刻下起大雨來。這時，那條有眼睛的龍突然動了起來。過了一會兒，這條龍離開了牆，飛到天上去了。那幾條沒有眼睛的龍還留在牆上。

　　這個成語常常指寫文章或說話的時候用一兩句重要的話，把意思說得更清楚。如：這句話起到了‘畫龍點睛’的作用。

第二課　中國文字

王：你認為漢語和其它語言的最大區別是什麼?

馬：我認為是文字。因為只有漢字是表意文字，其它文字都是表音文字。

王：那日文呢?

馬：日文中使用了兩千多個漢字，同時日文還使用假名，假名只表音不表意，所以不能說日文也是表意文字。

王：一個漢字就是一個詞嗎?

馬：不一定。有的詞是一個漢字，有的詞是由幾個漢字組成的。

王：常用漢字有多少?

馬：有三千多。由這三千多漢字可以構成幾萬個詞。用字構詞，這是漢語的一個特點。

王：有人說漢字是一種落後的文字，你同意這種看法嗎?

馬：我不同意。我認為漢字有很多優點，漢字的優點會越來越被人們認識到。現在有一些科學家說，西方人學習漢字可能對大腦有好處。

王：是嗎?那學漢語就太有意義了!

馬：我對漢字感興趣還有一個原因。

王：什麼原因?

馬：我覺得漢字是一種藝術。你看，這是昨天我朋友送我的一份禮物。

王：幾個毛筆字。

馬：對!這是中國的書法，多好看!

3

第三課　中國人的習慣

王：你來中國已經幾個月了，你覺得哪些事情使你感到有點兒奇怪？

馬：一次我去看一個老朋友，我們已經五年多沒見面了。我送給他一張畫。為了買這張畫，我差不多花了一天時間，不知跑了多少家商店，可是當我送給他時，他怎麼連看都不看！

王：這是中國人的習慣。中國人接受禮物後，往往不馬上打開看，只是向送禮的人表示感謝。他們覺得當着人的面打開看，不太好。

馬：原來是這樣！還有我對中國朋友在見到我時問的一些問題有時不理解。他們常問我一些很具體的事。比如你吃飯了嗎？你去哪兒呀？

王：這是在向你打招呼。中國人之間見面時很少說"你好！"、"你身體好嗎？"。在吃飯前後，你的朋友遇到你，問你吃飯了沒有，就是在向你打招呼。

馬：那在路上遇到我呢？

王：可能會說"去哪兒了？"、"進城呀？"什麼的。

馬：那中國人打招呼的用語就太多了！

王：是呀！多極了！

馬：據說中國人孩子對父母不說"謝謝！"，是嗎？

王：是的！對愛人也不說。你們西方人太愛說"謝謝！"了。

馬：這太有意思了！我真想寫一本書，叫《論中國人的習慣》。

第四課　怕不怕鬼?

王：你怕不怕鬼?

馬：我不怕，我不相信有鬼。

王：那麼，你家門上掛着一塊紅木板，這是怎麼一回事?

馬：一個算命的告訴我，鬼怕紅色，門口掛塊紅木板，鬼就不敢來。

王：這都是迷信說法，根本沒那麼回事!我是個徹底的無神論者。

馬：那你家為什麼有那麼多樂器、鬧鐘之類的東西?

王：聽說鬼怕聲音，一有聲音，鬼就嚇跑了。

馬：這有什麼根據呢?這不也是迷信嗎?

王：我也說不清楚，總覺得有這些東西心裏才放心。

馬：總之，我不信鬼，可是不知怎的，經常注意人背後有沒有影子!

王：我也不信鬼，可是一見到漂亮的女人，就懷疑她會不會是鬼!

5

第五課　　中國人的名字(一)

王：我想向您請教幾個有關中國人起名字的問題。聽説你是個中國通!

馬：不敢當，不敢當!什麽問題?

王：據説中國人的名字都具有一定的含義，是嗎?

馬：是的!姓一般是繼承父親的，名字却是由家人或者請朋友起的。

王：中國人的名字都表示哪些含義?換句話説孩子的父母怎樣給孩子起名呢?

馬：我發現中國人的名字所表示的含義有這樣幾類：一類是表達了父母對子女的期望；一類是表示子女出生的地點；一類是和子女出生的時間或時代有關係。

王：中國人一般對子女都抱有什麽期望呢?

馬：期望可太多了!你看這幾個名字：李成才、張富貴、王國强。成才就是成為有才能的人；富貴就是將來成為高貴而富有的人；國强就是國家富强，父母希望國家富强。

王：看來有的名字不僅表達了父母對子女的期望，還表達了對國家的期望。

馬：是的!人們往往把對國家的希望寄托在孩子身上。

王：我從報上隨便選一個中國人的名字，你都能講出它的含義嗎?

馬：要看情况。有的可以，有的要問他本人才知道。

第六課 中國人的名字(二)

王：給男孩兒起名和給女孩兒起名有什麼不同？

馬：剛才講的三個名字一般是給男孩兒起的，給女孩兒起名中國人常愛用一些美麗的字眼如：何文靜、夏麗花、周小香。

王：也就是說他們希望女孩兒將來長得漂亮。

馬：是呀！人之常情嗎！

王：我有一個中國朋友叫田京生，這麼說他可能是在中國首都生的。

馬：很有可能。

王：你能不能給我介紹幾個和時間、時代有關係的名字？

馬：李春光這個名字就表示這個孩子是春天生的。王雪這個名字表示這個孩子出生時可能正在下雪。林建國這個名字一看就知道這個孩子是一九四九年生的。

王：那麼文化革命中出生的孩子一定愛用紅衛、立新之類的詞了。

馬：可不是嗎！

王：看來中國人的名字很有時代特色。

馬：仔細研究的話還會發現中國城裏人和鄉下人，北京人和上海人，知識分子和一般市民在起名上都有些差別。

王：是嗎？這太有意思了，真能寫篇論文了！

第七課　有用和無用之間

莊子是中國古代的思想家。莊子的思想對中國傳統文化和思想影響很大。至今人們還在不斷研究他的思想。下面這個故事反映了莊子所抱的處世態度和做人標準。

有一天，莊子和他的學生到樹林裏去，看見有的樹被砍了，有的沒有被砍。他的學生問他：

"為什麼有的樹沒有被砍呢?"

莊子回答說：

"因為這些樹不成材，没有用。"

他們從樹林裏出來，來到一位朋友家。這位朋友養了兩隻鳥，一隻會叫，一隻不會叫。為了招待莊子和他的學生，這位朋友就讓人把那隻不會叫的鳥殺了去做菜。這時，莊子的學生又問莊子：

"為什麼要殺不會叫的那隻呢?"

莊子說：

"因為它不會叫，没有用。"

學生聽了不解地問：

"有用的樹被砍掉，而無用的鳥却被殺。那麼，一個人是有才有用好呢?還是無才無用好?"

莊子說：

"兩者都不好，最好是處于有才和無才、有用和無用之間。"

8

第八課　比老虎還利害

　　孔子是中國古代的大教育家和思想家。《論語》是他的弟子記錄他言行的著作。孔子的思想過去被看成是中國的正統思想。盡管孔子已經死了二千多年了，可是孔子的思想還影響着中國人的行為。

　　有一天，孔子和他的弟子到齊國去，從一座大山旁邊經過，看到一位婦女在路旁哭，而且哭得很傷心。于是，孔子就讓他的弟子上前去問這位婦女，看看發生了什麼事。

　　孔子的弟子問那位婦女：

　　"您為什麼哭得這麼傷心啊？一定是遇到了什麼不幸吧？"

　　那位婦女答道：

　　"是呀！我們這個地方有老虎，前幾天老虎吃了我公公。昨天我丈夫和我兒子又被老虎吃了。我怎麼能不傷心呢？"

　　孔子的弟子感到很奇怪，又問：

　　"你們明知道這兒有老虎，但為什麼不離開這個地方，到別的地方去住呢？"

　　婦女答道：

　　"雖然這裏有老虎，但是沒有專制統治。"

　　孔子的弟子把這位婦女說的話告訴了孔子，孔子對他的弟子們說：

　　"你們聽到了嗎？專制統治比老虎還利害呀！"

第九課　古詩三首

〔王安石〕

京口瓜洲一水間
鍾山祇隔數重山
春風又綠江南岸
明月何時照我還

〔李白〕

床前明月光
疑是地上霜
舉頭望明月
低頭思故鄉

〔王之渙〕

白日依山盡
黃河入海流
欲窮千里目
更上一層樓

10

第十課　走馬觀花

人們傳説，從前有個叫貴亮的年輕人，他的腳有毛病，走路很困難。可是，他却想找一個長得好看的愛人，于是就讓他的朋友何漢替他介紹一個姑娘。正好，有個名叫葉青的姑娘，鼻子有些毛病，也要何漢給她找個滿意的情人。何漢想：讓她和貴亮結婚，不是很好嗎？

有一天，何漢讓貴亮騎着馬從葉青家門前走過，又叫葉青手裏拿着一朵花，站在家門口，裝作聞花的樣子。

葉青看到貴亮騎在馬上，樣子好看極了，心裏非常喜歡。貴亮也愛上了這個很好看的聞花姑娘。

結婚那天，兩人又見了面，説起"走馬觀花"的情景，雙方這時才明白為什麼一個騎馬，一個聞花。

現在人們常用這個成語來形容，一個人參觀一個地方，很快地看了一遍，但沒有仔細觀察。

第十一課　杯弓蛇影

　　古時候，有個人叫樂廣。他很喜歡幫助人，也很會用道理說服人。樂廣有個好朋友，和他住在同一條街上。兩個人常常在一起喝酒、談天。可是後來，那個朋友有一個多月沒到樂廣家來了。樂廣就派人去了解情況。派去的人回來說，那個朋友病了。原來上一次他在樂廣家喝酒，看見酒杯裏有一條小蛇。可是酒已經喝下去了，有什麼辦法呢！他當時心裏很不舒服，回到家裏就病了。

　　樂廣聽了，覺得很奇怪，酒杯裏怎麼會有小蛇呢？他走到上一次喝酒的地方，仔仔細細地看了一遍，忽然看見牆上掛着一張弓，他立刻明白了。于是，他又派人去請那個朋友來喝酒，而且還說他能治好他的病。

　　那個朋友開始很不願意來，最後他還是來了。樂廣已經準備好了酒菜，讓他朋友還坐在老地方。那個朋友本來就很不放心，他往酒杯裏一看，啊！那條小蛇還在酒杯裏呢！他嚇得出了一身冷汗。樂廣指着牆上的弓笑着說："酒杯裏沒有什麼蛇，這是牆上弓的影子。"

　　他把牆上的弓拿下來，酒杯裏的小蛇立刻不見了。他朋友這才明白是怎麼一回事，病也就好了。

　　這個成語用來形容有人懷疑這個、懷疑那個，實際上并沒有那麼一回事。

　　西方人看了這個成語故事之後，可能會覺得這和現代精神分析學所使用的方法類似。精神分析醫生在給某一個病人治病時，往往要這個人回憶他過去所經歷的事情。

12

第十二課 《孔乙己》

只有孔乙己到店，才可以笑幾聲，所以至今還記得。……他身材很高大，青白臉色……

他對人說話，總是滿口之乎者也，叫人半懂不懂的。……

孔乙己是這樣的使人快活，可是沒有他，別人也便這麼過……

中秋過後，秋風是一天涼比一天，看看將近初冬；我整天的靠着火……

一天的下半天，沒有一個顧客，我正合了眼坐着。忽然間聽得一個聲音，"溫一碗酒"。這聲音雖然極低，却很耳熟。……不一會，他喝完酒，便又在旁人的說笑聲中，坐着用這手慢慢走去了。

自此以後，又長久沒有看見孔乙己。……

我到現在終于沒有見——大約孔乙己的確死了。

13

第十三課　讀者來信(一)

'一位' 和 '一個'

一天，去一家理髮店理髮。由于店少人多，大家都在門口排隊靜候服務員呼叫。不同的服務員在招呼顧客時使用不同的量詞。有的用'來一位!'，有的用'來一個!'。這'一位'和'一個'，雖然祇差一個字，但細細品來，給人的感覺大不相同。前者顯得熱情，後者則顯得冷淡。稱'個'還算客氣的，不客氣的甚至稱個子小的顧客為'小個兒的'，稱老年人為'老頭兒'等等。商業、服務性行業工作人員的一言一行，往往給顧客留下深刻的印象。所以他們應該重視在稱呼顧客時的用詞。

《北京晚報》

14

第十四課　讀者來信(二)

進口洗衣機到哪兒去修?

去年，我買了臺進口洗衣機，用了一個月就出了問題。于是，我到賣洗衣機的商店去打聽哪裏能修。他們說："只管賣，不管修。"後來，我又讓人到保定、石家莊、福州找了幾家修理部，都說不能修，讓我找賣洗衣機的地方。就這樣，賣洗衣機的商店不管，修理部門又不修。請問，我該怎麼辦呢?

《市場報》

'玩具醫院'快開張!

我那剛剛三歲的孩子已經有六輛汽車、一架飛機、一臺起重機，還有老虎、大象等不少機動玩具，都因出現毛病不能玩兒了。在孩子的強烈要求下，我愛人祇好又給他買了一輛新汽車。我是搞經濟工作的；據了解，現在城市和農村，孩子們的玩具都是短命貨，買回來玩兒不了幾天就壞了。這對國家和個人都是很大的浪費。如果各地能開些'玩具醫院'就好了。

《市場報》

15

第十五課　春節

王：明年我想去中國旅行，你說我什麼時候去最合適?

李：春節的時候。因為春節是中國最重要的傳統節日，春節前後，不論是城市和農村都特別熱鬧。

王：春節是幾月份?

李：中國農曆正月初一。明年的春節按陽曆算是一月二十八號。

王：聽說中國春節的時候，家家要貼春聯，'春聯'是什麼?

李：'春聯'也叫對聯，是在兩條紅紙上寫上成對的兩句話，內容多是表示喜慶的意思。春聯都貼在門的兩旁。除了貼春聯以外，春節時中國人還在門上、牆上、窗戶上貼年畫和'福'字。

王：據說中國人過春節有'守歲'的習慣，是嗎?

李：是的。大年三十晚上，合家吃了團圓飯以後，就點放爆竹，一家人有說有笑，一夜不睡，一直等到新的一年的到來。

王：餃子什麼時候吃?

李：春節時一般是在大年三十晚上把餃子包好，初一早上吃。吃完餃子，人們就都穿上新衣服出去給人拜年。

王：春節互相見面時說些什麼問候的話?

李："給您拜年!過年好!春節好!新年好!"什麼的。

16

第十六課　京劇

張：你了解中國的京劇嗎？

李：我看過不少次京劇，而且也讀過不少有關京劇的
　　書，可以說對京劇有些了解。

張：你認為京劇在表演形式上有什麼獨到的地方？

李：我認為是‘程式化’。京劇中演員的舞臺動作，上
　　馬下馬、上樓下樓、開門關門、喝酒吃飯、寫字看
　　書、走路睡覺、哭笑等都有一定的格式。

張：是這樣。由于有這種規範性的舞臺動作，京劇舞臺
　　上幾乎不用布景，布景就在演員身上，觀眾可以通
　　過演員的動作來了解劇情的空間環境和時間。

李：這種‘程式化’還表現在京劇演員的化裝和演出服
　　裝上。不同性別、不同年紀、不同身分、不同職業
　　的人，化裝也不同。所穿的衣服都有固定的式樣。

張：我很喜歡京劇的服裝，京劇服裝非常具有民族特
　　色。

李：在演唱方面也是一樣。是文人、是武生，一聽就知
　　道。因為不同的角色，在唱法上也有一定的風格。

第十七課　怎樣寫中文信

　　中文信的格式分五部分：第一部分是對收信人的稱呼；第二部分是信開頭對收信人的問候；第三部分是信的主要內容；第四部分是最後對收信人的致意和祝願；第五部分是寫信人的名字和寫信日期。

　　給家人寫信時一般使用在家中的稱呼，而且可以在稱呼前加‘親愛的’等形容詞，如：爸爸、媽媽、大哥、親愛的文平。注意中文的‘親愛的’一詞不能用于對一般的朋友。

　　給同事或朋友寫信時可使用平時你們之間的稱呼，如老王、小張、立陽。

　　給行政官員或商界人士寫信時，應該先稱呼他們的職務，然後是姓名。如果收信人是男的要在姓名後加先生或同志，如果收信人是女的可稱女士或小姐。如：北京大學校長王力先生。

　　中文信開頭一般要寫一兩句問候語，如：你好！好久沒收到你的來信了！你最近怎麼樣？等等。

　　中文信在最後一般要使用一個表示致意或祝願的詞語。一般公文信常用‘此致敬禮’四個字。‘此致’寫在信紙右邊，‘敬禮’寫在左邊。給家人或朋友寫信時常用一些表示祝願的話，如：祝你萬事如意！祝你身體健康！一切順利！

　　寫信人的名字要寫在信的右下角，名字旁邊或下面寫上寫信的日期，有時也可寫上寫信的地點。注意中文信在信紙的左上角和右上角什麼都不要寫，這點和英、法文信不同。

18

第十八課　以聽覺為主還是以視覺為主？

　　現代心理學研究證實，人在用眼睛和耳朵接受信息時，有人是以視覺為主，有人是以聽覺為主。判斷一個人主要是以什麽方式接受信息，這對于了解一個人的特性以及如何對這個人進行培養和教育是十分重要的。你想了解你自己嗎？請回答以下幾個問題：

　　一、你在看電視時，同時還常幹點其他事嗎？如：打毛衣、和別人談話、幹零碎活兒。

　　二、你看電視時喜歡對電視節目進行評論和發表議論嗎？

　　三、你喜歡一個人單獨進行跑步、騎自行車等體育活動，還是喜歡參加集體性的球類運動？

　　四、你喜歡看小說呢還是喜歡看理論性的文章呢？

　　五、你善于認路嗎？

　　六、你上中學的時候是數學好還是外語好？

　　七、你初學中文時和別的同學比較起來，你是聲調好呢還是漢字寫得好？

　　八、音樂和美術你更喜歡哪個？

　　九、你請客人來你家時你很容易畫一張來你家的路綫圖嗎？

　　十、你集中精神思考問題的時候，你容易受周圍動靜的干擾嗎？

　　十一、你容易不容易記住一個人的衣服或眼睛是什麽顏色？

19

第十九課　陰陽

關：'陰陽'這個詞是什麼意思？

包：'陰陽'是中國古代思想中比較重要的一個概念
'陰陽'一詞最早出現在《易經》中，原來指自然
現象：向着太陽叫陽，背着太陽叫陰。後來，中國
古代的一些思想家用'陰陽'這一詞來指自然界中
一切不可分的、相互對立而又可以互相轉換的現
象。

關：你説得不夠具體，能不能給我舉一些具體的例子？

包：比如：大自然的天和地、白天和黑夜人的男和女、
生和死、活動和休息都是陰陽現象。

關：'陰陽'這個概念看來很有道理。

包：是的，所以中國歷史上的'陰陽五行學説'（注：
'五行'指金、木、水、火、土)對中國古代科學
技術和醫學的發展產生了積極的影響。

關：中醫理論中怎樣應用'陰陽'這個概念呢？

包：中醫認為人生病的時候，就是陰陽不合，有時候需
要補陰，有時候需要壯陽。

關：漢語詞語中，有些詞語的組合方式是不是也受'陰
陽'概念的影響？比如：大小、多少、長短、天
地、冷暖、動靜、開關等等。

包：這方面我沒有研究，我想有可能。另外，中國畫和

西方油畫不同，為什麼有的中國畫祇用黑白兩種顏色？為什麼中國菜，在魚和蛋白上放一點兒綠色的菜？這是不是也受陰陽概念的影響，都可以研究。總之，中國古代的陰陽思想對中國各個方面都有影響。因此要試圖研究中國的歷史、文化、藝術以及中國人的衣食住行，非要先弄清楚‘陰陽’這個概念不可。

20

第二十課　中醫

王：這兩年你去哪兒了？怎麼一直沒見到你？

李：我去中國留學了。

王：你學的是什麼專業？

李：我學的是中醫，是在北京中醫學院學的。

王：你以前不是學過西醫嗎？怎麼又學中醫呢？

李：我覺得有些病，用咱們西醫的方法治療效果不如中醫好。

王：聽說中醫的理論缺乏科學性，裏面有許多迷信的東西。

李：不能那麼說。中醫已有幾千年的歷史，而且能治那麼多的病，裏面一定有科學的道理。祇是沒有用現代的方法總結出來。

王：你認為中醫在對病的診斷和治療上有什麼特點？

李：我認為第一是它的整體觀念。中醫認為人體是一個有機的整體，人體與外界自然環境有着密切的關係。中醫在分析一個人的病情時總是從全身來考慮，不是‘頭疼醫頭，腳疼醫腳’。這有點兒像現代系統論的理論。

王：是的。中國人幾千年以前就具有這種認識論，很了不起。在治療方面呢？

李：在治療方面，中醫講究辨證論治。這方面比較複雜，不是一兩句話能講清楚的。要想真正了解中醫的理論，要先讀點兒中國古代思想的書。

王：你覺得吃中藥比吃西藥好嗎？

李：我覺得吃中藥比吃西藥好。我牙疼的時候，就喜歡吃中藥止痛。因為中藥裏面生物成分多，化學成分少，所以有人說吃中草藥副作用小。只是中藥味兒，西方人有點兒不太適應。

王：目前，你還在繼續研究中醫嗎？

李：是的。

21

第二十一課　月牙兒〔老舍〕

　　叫我最難過的是我慢慢地學會了恨媽媽。可是每當我恨她的時候，我不知不覺地便想起她背着我上墳的光景。想到了這個，我不能恨她了。我又非恨她不可。我的心像──還是像那個月牙兒，只能亮那麼一會兒，而黑暗是無限的。媽媽的屋裏常有男人來了，她不再躲避着我。他們的眼像狗似地看着我。

　　在很短的期間，我忽然明白了許多事。我知道我得保護自己，我覺出我身上好像有什麼可貴的地方，我聞得出我已有一種什麼味道，是我自己害羞，多感。我身上有了些力量，可以保護自己。

　　我願愛媽媽，這時候我有好些必要問媽媽的事；可是正在這個時候，我得躲着她，我得恨她；要不然我自己便不存在了。當我睡不着的時節，我很冷静地思索，媽媽是可原諒的。她得顧我們倆的嘴。可是這個又使我要拒絕再吃她給我的飯菜。我的心就這麼忽冷忽熱，像冬天的風，休息一會兒，颳得更要猛；我静候着我的怒氣衝來，没法兒止住。

22

第二十二課　廣告

求婚廣告

本人，男，三十五歲，中等身材，小學教員，月收入五百二十元，有房三間。愛好文學、美術，喜歡看電影。願找一位二十到三十五歲之間，長相漂亮，身材不低於一米六零，最好也作教育工作的女性。來信請寄：四川省成都市育才小學周志軍收。

尋人廣告

王春花，女，十五歲，高一米五九，神經病人，穿綠上衣，黑布鞋。如發現請通知東城區金魚胡同派出所。

商業廣告

上海造船廠推出新産品全自動電話總機。該機采用電腦技術，設計先進，功能齊全，性能可靠。該機可容九門、二十四門内部自動電話，全自動交換，不用任何管理人員，交直流兩用，使用方法與市内電話相同，適用于公司、機關、工廠、醫院、學校等單位。本産品保修一年。為了滿足廣大用户要求，本廠特設為用户上門服務項目。

產品規格及價格：九門 ... 2300 元(臺)

二十四門 ... 5450 元(臺)

地點：上海市南京路十三號

電話：43215160　電報：206316　傳真：43223026

聯繫人：王增雲

23

第二十三課　魯迅

　　魯迅是中國現代著名的文學家和思想家，紹興人，生于一八八一年九月二十五日，原名周樹人。魯迅是他的筆名。魯迅出身于破落的封建士大夫家庭。小時在家鄉上過舊式的學校，讀過四書五經之類的書。一八九八年他到南京上學，受到了'科學'、'民主'以及'進化論'思想的影響。一九〇二年他去日本留學。起初，他先學醫學，想走醫學救國的道路。後來，發現醫學對于落後的中國并不是一件緊要的事，最重要的是要改變中國民衆的精神。于是，他改而從事文學活動。一九〇九年魯迅回國，先後在紹興、北京、廣州等地工作，當過教員、中學校長、教育部官員、大學教師和中文系系主任。與此同時，他開始不斷在《新青年》等許多雜誌上發表文學作品。自一九二七年起，魯迅定居上海，專心從事文學創作。

　　魯迅在文學上的主要成就是他的白話小説和雜文。魯迅白話小説的特點是不僅具有鮮明的反封建色彩，而且寫作手法獨特。因此他的白話小説在'五四'時期影響很大。魯迅生前還寫了大量的雜文。他的雜文反映了他在各個歷史時期對社會事件和某些學術問題的看法和態度，其寫作技巧曾受到人們的高度評價。

　　魯迅除了白話小説和雜文以外，還寫了一些有關文學史方面的學術著作。

　　一九三六年十月十九日，由于勞累過度，魯迅在上海因病去世。

第二十四課　新聞報道

新華社北京 4 月 5 日電：中美兩國首腦昨天在北京舉行會談。雙方就兩國共同關心的國際問題交換了意見。雙方對目前中東發生的流血事件表示極大的關切。參加會談的還有中國黨和政府的有關領導人。會談後，美國總統還將訪問上海和南京兩大城市并參觀兩所大學和一座化工廠。

據新華社南京 10 月 2 日電：中國最大的一所燈具廠最近在南京建成。

中新社臺北 6 月 10 日電：今年第三季度，臺灣工業和農業產值和去年同期相比增長百分之三。農業獲得近十年來最好收成。

美聯社舊金山 8 日電：美國政府計劃集資在當地修建一個農業蟲害防治中心，其中有數十個現代化試驗室將由私人公司資助。某些國際基金組織對這一計劃也非常關注。

人民日報報道：一支由中國研究人員和學者組成的小分隊將去非洲進行考察。

第二十五課　北京土話

王：最近你看了些什麽書？

馬：前一階段較忙，没看什么書。這幾天有了點兒時間，正在看一本中文小説。

王：你二年級還没上完就能看小説了，真不簡單！什麽小説？

馬：書名叫《天橋的把勢，光説不練》，是位北京作家寫的。這是我第一次看中文小説。我是想試試，看看能不能看懂一點兒。結果我發現有好些詞都没學過。有的詞在詞典里也查不到。我正想問你呢。‘拉晚兒’這個詞是什麽意思？

王：這不是普通話裏的詞，這是北京土話。過去人力車夫晚上拉客人叫‘拉晚兒’。

馬：哦！‘消停、爺們兒、鐵了心’這些詞是不是也是北京土話？

王：是。‘消停’普通話説‘安静’，比如説：“你讓我安静一會兒吧！”用北京土話説：“你讓我消停一會兒吧！”。‘爺們兒’是指男人，比如説：“這兒都是爺們兒，没有女的。”‘鐵了心’是下定了決心的意思。

馬：北京土話裏的好多詞都和普通話不一樣嗎？

王：有不少。人們常說的'小子'普通話叫'男孩兒'，'一丁點兒'普通話說'一點兒'，'今兒、明兒、昨兒'普通話說'今天、明天、昨天'。

馬：北京土話裏的詞，現在北京人還用嗎？

王：有些還用，有些已經不用了。剛才我說的一些詞還在用，像'心裏美，老頭兒樂'，這樣的詞人們也在用。但是像'拉晚兒、委冬兒、局着、取燈兒'這樣的詞人們已經不用了。

馬：你要是不急的話，我還想問你幾個句子。你看：

"誰知他是這麼塊料！"

"我看他們兩個人半斤八兩。"

"誰知他骨子裏怎麼想的！"

"到了這個肯節兒上，你怎麼還不說話？"

"要是拿到市場上賣，苦死也能賣上五六十塊。"

王：這裏的'料、半斤八兩、骨子裏、肯節兒、苦死'都是北京土話。我建議你到書店去買本《北京土語詞典》，這些詞，那本詞典裏都有。

VOCABULARY

A

爱国主义	àiguózhǔyì	patriotism	2
爱国主义者	àiguózhǔyìzhě	patriot	4
爱护	àihù	to cherish, to treasure	21
爱情	àiqíng	love	3
安分守己	ānfènshǒujǐ	to know one's place	15
安家落户	ānjiāluòhù	to make a home, to settle down	15
安静	ānjìng	quiet, peaceful	6
安排	ānpái	to arrange, to plan	13
安设	ānshè	to install, to set up	16
安装	ānzhuāng	to install, to erect	10
岸	àn	shore, bank (of river etc.)	9
岸边	ànbiān	edge, bank (of river etc.)	9
按	àn	according to	15
按部就班	ànbùjiùbān	to keep to conventional ways	15
按期	ànqī	on schedule, on time	15
按时	ànshí	on time	15
按语	ànyǔ	note, comment	15
按照	ànzhào	according to	15
暗	àn	dark, hidden	21
暗淡	àndàn	dark	21
暗地里	àndìli	secretly, on the sly	21
暗含着	ànhánzhe	to imply	21
暗害	ànhài	to kill secretly, stab in the back	21
暗杀	ànshā	to assassinate	21
暗示	ànshì	to drop a hint, to suggest	21
暗室	ànshì	dark room	21
暗算	ànsuàn	to plot against	21
暗无天日	ànwútiānrì	complete darkness, total absence of justice	21
暗想	ànxiǎng	to think in one's heart	21
暗指	ànzhǐ	to allude to	21
暗中	ànzhōng	in the dark, secretly	21

B

爸	bà	dad	17
爸爸	bàba	dad	17
把势	bǎshi	martial arts specialist	25
把守	bǎshǒu	to guard, to defend	15
白话	báihuà	vernacular	23
白色	báisè	white	4
白眼	báiyǎn	a supercilious look, disdainful	1
白族	báizú	the Bai minority	16
百分之一	bǎifēnzhīyī	one percent	3
百花齐放	bǎihuāqífàng	Let a hundred flowers blossom.	8
百货大楼	bǎihuòdàlóu	department store	14
百科全书	bǎikēquánshū	encyclopaedia	20
百年大计	bǎiniándàjì	a vital and lasting project	22
百思不解	bǎisībùjiě	remain perplexed despite great thought	3
百闻不如一见	bǎiwénbùrú yíjiàn	Seeing is believing! (better to see for oneself than to hear from others)	10
拜	bài	to greet, to make a courtesy call	15
拜访	bàifǎng	to pay a visit, to call on	24
拜会	bàihuì	to pay an official call	15
拜年	bàinián	to pay New Year's call	15
拜师	bàishī	to accept someone as one's teacher	15
拜天地	bàitiāndì	bow to Heaven and Earth as part of wedding ceremony	15
拜托	bàituō	to ask someone to do sth.	15
般	bān	type, sort	5
板	bǎn	plank	4
板板六十四	bǎnbǎnliùshísì	stubborn, rigid	4
板子	bǎnzi	plank	4
办理	bànlǐ	to handle, to conduct, to transact	3
办事处	bànshìchù	office	2
半斤八两	bànjīnbāliǎng	tweedledum and tweedledee	25
帮	bāng	to help; gang	11
帮会	bānghuì	secret society	11
帮忙	bāngmáng	to lend a hand	11
帮手	bāngshǒu	a helping hand, helper	11
帮助	bāngzhù	to help	11
包含	bāohán	to contain, to embody	5
保	bǎo	to protect, to guarantee	14
保安	bǎo'ān	to ensure (public) security	14
保不住	bǎobúzhù	most likely, may well be	14

初次	chūcì	the first time	12
初冬	chūdōng	the beginning of winter	12
初期	chūqī	initial stage, early days	12
初学	chūxué	to begin to learn	12
初一	chūyī	the first day of a lunar month	15
初中	chūzhōng	junior middle school	12
除	chú	to get rid of; except, besides	15
除非	chúfēi	only if, only when	15
除了…以外	chúle…yǐwài	except	15
除去	chúqù	except	15
楚	Chǔ	the Chu Kingdom	1
楚国	Chǔguó	the Chu Kingdom	1
处	chǔ/chù	place, part; to get along with	2
处分	chǔfèn	to punish	2
处境	chǔjìng	unfavourable situation, plight	16
处决	chǔjué	to put to death, to execute	25
处理	chǔlǐ	to handle, to deal with	3
处女	chǔnǚ	virgin	2
处女作	chǔnǚzuò	maiden work, first work	2
处事	chǔshì	to conduct affairs	2
处世	chǔshì	to conduct onself in society	7
处心积虑	chǔxīnjīlǜ	to scheme, to plan	20
处于	chǔyú	to be situated	7
处处	chùchù	everywhere	2
处所	chùsuǒ	place, location	2
处长	chùzhǎng	head of a department	2
穿	chuān	to wear	15
穿越	chuānyuè	to pass through	15
穿着	chuānzhuó	dress, apparel	15
川剧	Chuānjù	Sichuan opera	16
传	chuán	to pass on, to transmit	1
传达	chuándá	to transmit, to pass on	5
传单	chuándān	leaflet	18
传导	chuándǎo	conduction	24
传道	chuándào	to propagate doctrines	1
传教	chuánjiào	to do missionary work	1
传热	chuánrè	to conduct heat	1
传统	chuántǒng	tradition	7
传闻	chuánwén	it is said that...	10
传真	chuánzhēn	facsimile	1
传奇	chuánqí	legend, romance	1
船	chuán	boat	22
船夫	chuánfū	boat person	22
船员	chuányuán	(ship's) crew	22
船长	chuánzhǎng	captain, skipper	22

船只	chuánzhī	shipping, vessel	22
窗	chuāng	window	15
窗户	chuānghu	window	15
窗口	chuāngkǒu	window (for selling tickets etc.)	15
床	chuáng	bed	9
床单	chuángdān	bed sheet	18
创	chuàng	to create, to achieve	23
创办	chuàngbàn	to establish, to set up	23
创建	chuàngjiàn	to found, to establish	23
创见	chuàngjiàn	an original idea	23
创举	chuàngjǔ	pioneering work	23
创立	chuànglì	to found, to originate	23
创设	chuàngshè	to found, to create; to set up	23
创始人	chuàngshǐrén	founder	23
创新	chuàngxīn	to innovate	23
创业	chuàngyè	to do pioneering work	23
创造	chuàngzào	to create; creation	23
创造性	chuàngzàoxìng	creativity	23
创作	chuàngzuò	to create; creation	23
春季	chūnjì	springtime	24
春节	Chūnjié	Spring Festival	15
春联	chūnlián	spring couplets	15
春暖花开	chūnnuǎnhuākāi	During the warmth of spring all the flowers bloom.	19
词	cí	word	2
词句	cíjù	words, sentences	2
词类	cílèi	parts of speech	4
词头	cítóu	prefix	2
词形	cíxíng	morphology	10
词语	cíyǔ	words and expressions, terms	2
词组	cízǔ	word group, phrase	2
此	cǐ	this	12
此地	cǐdì	this place, here	12
此后	cǐhòu	henceforth	12
此刻	cǐkè	this moment, now	12
此时	cǐshí	this moment, right now	12
此外	cǐwài	besides, in addition, moreover	12
此致	cǐzhì	to give, to extend (greetings, etc.)	17
次货	cìhuò	substandard goods	14
次品	cìpǐn	defective or substandard products	13
从此	cóngcǐ	from now on	12
从而	cóng'ér	thus, thereby	7
从容	cóngróng	calm, unhurried, leisurely	10
从事	cóngshì	to be engaged in, to deal with	23
村	cūn	village	14

293

村落	cūnluò	village	14
村长	cūnzhǎng	village head	14
村庄	cūnzhuāng	village	14
村子	cūnzi	village	14
存	cún	to exist, to store	21
存车处	cúnchēchù	parking lot (for bicycles)	21
存放	cúnfàng	to deposit, to leave with	21
存货	cúnhuò	goods in stock	21
存钱	cúnqián	to deposit money	21
存心	cúnxīn	intentionally	21
存衣处	cúnyīchù	cloakroom	21
存在	cúnzài	to exist; existence	21
存在主义	cúnzàizhǔyì	existentialism	21

D

答	dá	to reply, to answer	7
答道	dádào	to reply	8
答复	dáfù	to reply, to answer	20
答题	dátí	response	7
达	dá	to reach, to extend	5
达成	dáchéng	to reach (an agreement etc.)	5
达到	dádào	to achieve, to reach	5
打断	dǎduàn	to break, to interrupt	7
打官司	dǎguānsi	to go to court	22
打架	dǎjià	to fight	14
打毛衣	dǎmáoyī	to knit (a sweater)	18
打破	dǎpò	to break, to smash	23
打球	dǎqiú	to play ball games	18
打扰	dǎrǎo	to disturb	18
打碎	dǎsuì	to break into pieces, to destroy	18
打通	dǎtōng	to get through (telephone etc.)	5
打印	dǎyìn	to print	13
打杂	dǎzá	to do odd jobs	20
打招呼	dǎzhāohu	to make a sign	3
大部分	dàbùfen	the majority, for the most part	14
大典	dàdiǎn	grand ceremony	25
大队	dàduì	battalion, regiment	13
大概	dàgài	approximately	19
大公无私	dàgōngwúsī	selfless, impartial	24
大号	dàhào	large size	15
大哭	dàkū	to cry, to sob	8
大街	dàjiē	avenue, street	11
大量	dàliàng	in large quantities	13
大脑	dànǎo	brain	2
大桥	dàqiáo	large bridge	25

大杀风景	dàshāfēngjǐng	to spoil the fun	10
大使	dàshǐ	ambassador	2
大使馆	dàshǐguǎn	embassy	2
大象	dàxiàng	elephant	14
大喜过望	dàxǐguòwàng	things turn out better than expected	5
大约	dàyuē	approximately, about	12
大致	dàzhì	roughly, approximately	17
大众	dàzhòng	crowd, masses, public	16
大众化	dàzhònghuà	popular	16
代	dài	era; to replace	1
代办	dàibàn	to act on s. o. 's behalf	1
代表	dàibiǎo	to represent	2
代表大会	dàibiǎodàhuì	congress, assembly	2
代表团	dàibiǎotuán	delegation	15
代词	dàicí	pronoun	2
代价	dàijià	cost	22
代理	dàilǐ	to act on s. o. 's behalf	3
代替	dàitì	to replace, to substitute	10
代言人	dàiyánrén	spokesperson, mouthpiece	1
代用	dàiyòng	to replace	1
待	dài	to treat s. o. , to welcome	7
待人接物	dàirénjiēwù	how one gets along with people	7
待遇	dàiyù	treatment	7
带队	dàiduì	to lead a group	13
带领	dàilǐng	to lead, to guide	24
单	dān	unique, single, odd	18
单程	dānchéng	one way journey	18
单词	dāncí	word	18
单打	dāndǎ	singles match	18
单调	dāndiào	monotone	18
单独	dāndú	alone, single-handed	18
单方	dānfāng	home remedy	18
单个儿	dāngèr	individually, alone	18
单号	dānhào	odd number	18
单间	dānjiān	single room	18
单身汉	dānshēnhàn	bachelor	18
单位	dānwèi	work unit	18
单行线	dānxíngxiàn	one-way street	18
单衣	dānyī	unlined garment	18
单一	dānyī	single, unitary	18
单元	dānyuán	unit	18
单子	dānzi	sheet, list	18
但	dàn	but	8
但是	dànshì	but	8
淡	dàn	pale, light, thin, weak	13
淡红	dànhóng	light red	13

淡水	dànshuǐ	fresh water	13
淡水鱼	dànshuǐyú	fresh water fish	13
蛋	dàn	egg	19
蛋白	dànbái	egg white	19
蛋黄	dànhuáng	egg yolk	19
当初	dāngchū	originally, in the first place	12
当代	dāngdài	contemporary	1
当地	dāngdì	local, at the place	24
当官	dāngguān	to become a bureaucrat	17
当务之急	dāngwùzhījí	an urgent matter	25
当政	dāngzhèng	to be in power	17
当着	dāngzhe	facing, in front of	3
党	dǎng	(political) party	24
党报	dǎngbào	party newspaper	24
党纪	dǎngjì	party discipline	24
党派	dǎngpài	party	24
党员	dǎngyuán	party member	24
党章	dǎngzhāng	party constitution	24
导	dǎo	to lead, to drive, to direct	24
导电	dǎodiàn	electric conduction	24
导火线	dǎohuǒxiàn	fuse	24
导论	dǎolùn	introduction	24
导热	dǎorè	heat conduction	24
导师	dǎoshī	director of studies, tutor	24
导线	dǎoxiàn	lead, conducting wire	24
导言	dǎoyán	introduction	24
导演	dǎoyǎn	to direct (film etc.); director	24
道具	dàojù	stage prop	3
道理	dàolǐ	reason, principle, truth	3
道士	dàoshi	Taoist priest	17
到达	dàodá	to arrive at	5
到底	dàodǐ	finally, after all	4
得势	déshì	to be in power	25
得意忘形	déyìwàngxíng	dizzy with success	10
灯	dēng	lamp, light	24
灯光	dēngguāng	light, lamp light	24
灯火	dēnghuǒ	lights	24
灯具厂	dēngjùchǎng	lamp factory	24
灯头	dēngtóu	lamp holder	24
等待	děngdài	to wait for	7
等级	děngjí	class, rank	25
等于	děngyú	equivalent to, equal to	7
低	dī	low	9
低声	dīshēng	in a low voice, under one's breath	9
低温	dīwēn	low temperature	12
的确	díquè	indeed, really	12

底	dǐ	bottom, base	4
底片	dǐpiàn	negatives (photography)	4
底下	dǐxià	under	4
底子	dǐzi	base	4
弟	dì	younger brother	8
弟弟	dìdi	younger brother	8
弟子	dìzǐ	disciple	8
地步	dìbù	condition, extent	18
地瓜	dìguā	sweet potato	9
地球	dìqiú	the earth, the globe	18
地铁	dìtiě	subway, metro	5, 25
典	diǎn	code, ceremony	25
典范	diǎnfàn	model, example	25
典故	diǎngù	literary quotation	25
典礼	diǎnlǐ	ceremony	25
点放	diǎnfàng	to light (fire crackers etc.)	15
电	diàn	electricity, telegram	24
电传	diànchuán	telex	1
电灯	diàndēng	electric lamp	24
电话局	diànhuàjú	telephone office	25
电疗	diànliáo	electrotherapy	20
电流	diànliú	electric current	9
电视	diànshì	television	13
电视台	diànshìtái	television station	14
电台	diàntái	radio station	14
电线	diànxiàn	electric wire	18
店员	diànyuán	salesperson	13
掉	diào	to fall, to loose	7
掉过儿	diàoguòr	to turn around	7
掉色	diàoshǎi	to discolour	7
掉头	diàotóu	to turn around, make a U-turn	7
掉下	diàoxià	to fall	7
掉转	diàozhuǎn	to turn around	19
调	diào	to transfer, to shift; accent, tune	18
调查	diàochá	inquiry; to inquire, to investigate	18
调动	diàodòng	to transfer, to mobilise	18
调度	diàodù	to dispatch, to manage; dispatcher	18
调号	diàohào	tone mark, key signature	18
调虎离山	diàohǔlíshān	lure the tiger away from the mountain	18
调换	diàohuàn	to change, to exchange	18
调任	diàorèn	to be transferred to another post	22
调子	diàozi	tune, melody	18
丁香	dīngxiāng	lilac, clove	6
定婚	dìnghūn	to get engaged	10
定货	dìnghuò	to order stock	14

F

发表	fābiǎo	to publish	2
发达	fādá	developed	5
发光	fāguāng	to shine, to emit light	6
发怒	fānù	to be angry	21
发生	fāshēng	to happen	8
发笑	fāxiào	to laugh	11
发育	fāyù	growth, development	8
发展	fāzhǎn	development; to develop	19
乏	fá	tired, lack	20
乏味儿	fáwèir	dull, insipid	20
法官	fǎguān	judge	17
法规	fǎguī	rules, regulations	16
法庭	fǎtíng	court, tribunal	23
法则	fǎzé	rule, law	13
法制	fǎzhì	legality	8
反	fǎn	against; to turn over; opposite	7
反常	fǎncháng	unusual, abnormal	7
反动	fǎndòng	reactionary	7
反对	fǎnduì	to oppose, to be against	7
反而	fǎn'ér	on the contrary	7
反封建	fǎnfēngjiàn	anti-feudal	17
反复	fǎnfù	repeatedly, again and again	20
反感	fǎngǎn	aversion; to be disgusted with	7
反话	fǎnhuà	ironic remark	7
反面	fǎnmiàn	reverse side, wrong side, back	7
反问	fǎnwèn	to reply with another question	7
反响	fǎnxiǎng	repercussion	7
反义词	fǎnyìcí	antonym	7
反应	fǎnyìng	to react; reaction	13
反映	fǎnyìng	to reflect; reflection	13
反正	fǎnzheng	anyway...	7
反作用	fǎnzuòyòng	reaction, counteraction	7
范	fàn	pattern, model, example	16
饭量	fànliàng	appetite	13
方式	fāngshì	way, fashion, pattern	16
方形	fāngxíng	square	10
方圆	fāngyuán	circumference	15
方志	fāngzhì	local records	17
防	fáng	to guard against, to prevent, to block	24
防备	fángbèi	to take precautions against	24
防风林	fángfēnglín	windbreak	24
防护	fánghù	to protect	24

防火	fánghuǒ	fire prevention	24
防空	fángkōng	antiaircraft	24
防守	fángshǒu	to defend	24
防水	fángshuǐ	waterproof	24
防卫	fángwèi	to defend	24
防线	fángxiàn	line of defence	24
防止	fángzhǐ	to prevent, to stop	24
访	fǎng	to visit	24
访友	fǎngyǒu	to visit a friend	24
访问	fǎngwèn	to visit, to pay a call on	24
放假	fàngjià	to go on holidays	2
放心	fàngxīn	to put one's mind at rest	4
放映	fàngyìng	to show, to project	7
非洲	Fēizhōu	Africa	9
非...不可	fēi...bùkě	must, to have to	19
飞舞	fēiwǔ	to flutter	16
费	fèi	to spend, to waste; fees	14
费力	fèilì	strenuous, requiring effort	17
费事	fèishì	time consuming	14
费心	fèixīn	to take a lot of trouble	14
费用	fèiyòng	fees, expenses	14
分辨	fēnbiàn	to distinguish, to differentiate	20
分布	fēnbù	to distribute, to disperse	16
分割	fēngē	to break up, to cut up	20
分类	fēnlèi	to classify	4
分清	fēnqīng	to distinguish clearly	1
分析	fēnxī	to analyse; analysis	11
分支	fēnzhī	branch, subsidiary	24
分量	fènliang	weight	13
坟	fén	grave	21
坟地	féndì	cemetery, graveyard	21
封	fēng	[Mw for letters]; to seal	17
封存	fēngcún	to keep sealed	21
封底	fēngdǐ	back cover	17
封地	fēngdì	fief	17
封建	fēngjiàn	feudal	17
封建主义	fēngjiànzhǔyì	feudalism	17
封面	fēngmiàn	cover (of a book)	17
风度	fēngdù	demeanour, bearing	7
风格	fēnggé	style	16
风光	fēngguāng	scenery	6
风景	fēngjǐng	scenery	10
风浪	fēnglàng	storm	14
风流	fēngliú	refined and tastful, romantic	9
风趣	fēngqù	humour, wit	2

风味儿	fēngwèir	local flavour (of cooking)	20
夫妇	fūfù	husband and wife	8
福	fú	happiness	14
福建	Fújiàn	Fujian Province	14
福利	fúlì	well-being	14
福气	fúqì	good fortune	14
福州	Fúzhōu	Fuzhou (city)	14
服务	fúwù	service; to serve	13
服务员	fúwùyuán	attendant, waiter, waitress	13
服装	fúzhuāng	clothing	10
富	fù	rich	5
富贵	fùguì	riches and honour	5
富人	fùrén	a rich person	5
富有	fùyǒu	rich in...	5
富强	fùqiáng	rich and powerful	5
父系	fùxì	patriarchal system	5
副	fù	vice-, assistant	20
副部长	fùbùzhǎng	vice-minister	20
副产品	fùchǎnpǐn	by-product	20
副词	fùcí	adverb	20
副会长	fùhuìzhǎng	vice-president	20
副食	fùshí	foodstuffs	20
副手	fùshǒu	assistant	20
副书记	fùshūjì	assistant secretary	20
副业	fùyè	side occupation, sideline	20
副院长	fùyuànzhǎng	vice-director	20
副总理	fùzǒnglǐ	vice premier	20
副作用	fùzuòyòng	side effect	20
复	fù	to turn around, to recover	20
复本	fùběn	copy, duplicate	20
复发	fùfā	to have a relapse	20
复工	fùgōng	to go back to work	20
复古	fùgǔ	to restore ancient practices	20
复合词	fùhécí	compound word	20
复合元音	fùhéyuányīn	compound vowel	20
复活	fùhuó	to resuscitate, to resurrect	20
复活节	Fùhuójié	Easter	20
复旧	fùjiù	restoration	20
复句	fùjù	a compound sentence	20
复课	fùkè	to resume classes	20
复习	fùxí	to revise	20
复写	fùxiě	to duplicate, make carbon copies	20
复信	fùxìn	to reply to a letter	20
复姓	fùxìng	disyllabic surname	20
复印	fùyìn	to photocopy	20
复原	fùyuán	to cure, to recover	20

复员	fùyuán	to demobilise	20
复杂	fùzá	complicated, complex	20
复制	fùzhì	to reproduce	20
妇	fù	(married) woman	8
妇科	fùkē	gynaecology	8
妇女	fùnǚ	woman	8

G

该	gāi	ought, should, probably	13
该死	gāisǐ	damned!	13
改	gǎi	to change, to alter	23
改变	gǎibiàn	to transform	23
改掉	gǎidiào	to correct	23
改动	gǎidòng	to modify, to alter	23
改革	gǎigé	reform; to reform	23
改革派	gǎigépài	reformist	23
改观	gǎiguān	to change the appearance of	23
改过	gǎiguò	to correct one's faults	23
改行	gǎiháng	to change professions	23
改换	gǎihuàn	to modify	23
改进	gǎijìn	to improve	23
改期	gǎiqī	to change the date, to postpone	23
改善	gǎishàn	improvement; to improve	23
改天	gǎitiān	another day	23
改天换地	gǎitiānhuàndì	to change the world	23
改正	gǎizhèng	to correct	23
改组	gǎizǔ	to reorganise	23
概	gài	general, approximate	19
概况	gàikuàng	general situation	19
概论	gàilùn	outline, introduction	19
概念	gàiniàn	concept	19
概要	gàiyào	essentials, outline	19
干扰	gānrǎo	to disturb	18
干笑	gānxiào	hollow laugh	11
感	gǎn	to feel, to sense	2
感到	gǎndào	to feel, to sense	2
感动	gǎndòng	to move, to touch	2
感官	gǎnguān	sensory organ	17
感化	gǎnhuà	to help s. o. to change by persuasion, etc.	2
感觉	gǎnjué	feeling, sense	2
感情	gǎnqíng	emotion, feeling	3
感情用事	gǎnqíngyòngshì	to act impetuously	3
感人	gǎnrén	moving, touching	2

感受	gǎnshòu	to feel; experience	3
感想	gǎnxiǎng	impression, thoughts	2
感谢	gǎnxiè	to thank	2
感性	gǎnxìng	perceptual	13
感知	gǎnzhī	intuition, perception	2
敢	gǎn	to dare	4
敢于	gǎnyú	to dare	7
敢作敢为	gǎnzuògǎnwéi	to dare to act	4
干部	gànbu	cadre	14
干将	gànjiàng	capable person	5
刚强	gāngqiáng	firm, staunch, unyielding	5
高贵	gāoguì	noble	5
高低	gāodī	height	9
高度	gāodù	height, altitude	7
高干子弟	gāogànzǐdì	son of a high ranking official	8
高级	gāojí	advanced	25
高价	gāojià	high price	22
高温	gāowēn	high temperature	12
搞	gǎo	to do	14
搞对象	gǎoduìxiàng	to find a boy/girlfriend	14
搞鬼	gǎoguǐ	to play tricks on . . .	14
告	gào	to tell, to warn	4
告别	gàobié	to say goodbye to	4
告急	gàojí	to report an emergency	25
告密	gàomì	to inform (against s.o.)	20
告诉	gàosù	to tell, to warn	4
歌词	gēcí	lyrics	2
歌舞	gēwǔ	song and dance	16
歌剧	gējù	opera	16
革	gé	leather; to change	6
革命	gémìng	revolution	6
革命家	gémìngjiā	revolutionary	6
隔	gé	to separate	9
隔断	géduàn	to cut off, to obstruct	9
隔开	gékāi	to separate	9
隔离	gélí	to segregate, to isolate	9
格	gé	standard, norm, style	16
格格不入	gégébúrù	incompatible	16
格式	géshì	form, pattern	16
格外	géwài	especially	16
个人主义	gèrénzhǔyì	individualism	2
个性	gèxìng	individuality, personality	13
各	gè	every	14
各别	gèbié	distinct, different	14
各得其所	gèdéqísuǒ	everything has its rightful place	14

各个	gège	every	14
各式各样	gèshìgèyàng	all types, all sorts	16
各行其是	gèxíngqíshì	everybody goes his own way	14
各有千秋	gèyǒuqiānqiū	everybody has his strong points	14
各种各样	gèzhǒnggèyàng	all types, all sorts	14
根	gēn	root	4
根本	gēnběn	fundamentally, basically	4
根据	gēnjù	according to	4
根据地	gēnjùdì	base area	4
更加	gèngjiā	more	17
公安部	gōng'ānbù	the Ministry of Public Security	14
公安局	gōng'ānjú	public security bureau	25
公布	gōngbù	to announce, to publish	16
公告	gōnggào	announcement	4
公公	gōnggong	father-in-law	8
公斤	gōngjīn	kilogram	25
公历	gōnglì	Gregorian calendar	11
公社	gōngshè	community	23
公式	gōngshì	formula	16
公诉	gōngsù	public prosecution	4
公有制	gōngyǒuzhì	public ownership	8
公章	gōngzhāng	official seal	1
工程	gōngchéng	engineering project	16
工程师	gōngchéngshī	engineer	16
工具	gōngjù	tool	3
工业	gōngyè	industry	13
工业部	gōngyèbù	Ministry of Industry	14
工艺	gōngyì	craft	2
工资	gōngzī	salary	24
工作者	gōngzuòzhě	worker	4
工作证	gōngzuòzhèng	work card	18
弓	gōng	bow (archery)	11
功	gōng	achievement, merit, skill	22
功夫	gōngfu	time, work, *kungfu*, skill	22
功过	gōngguò	merits and faults	22
功课	gōngkè	schoolwork, course	22
功劳	gōngláo	contribution, credit	22
功利	gōnglì	utility	22
功能	gōngnéng	function	22
功效	gōngxiào	efficiency, effect	22
功用	gōngyòng	function	22
共产党	gòngchǎndǎng	Communist Party	24
共产主义	gòngchǎnzhǔyì	Communism	19
狗	gǒu	dog	21
狗头军师	gǒutóujūnshī	a bad or corrupt advisor	22
狗腿子	gǒutuǐzi	a hired thug	21

299

构	gòu	to construct, to compose	2
构成	gòuchéng	to form, to compose	2
构思	gòusī	to conceive a plot (of writers)	2
构图	gòutú	composition (of a picture)	2
构造	gòuzào	structure	22
够	gòu	enough, sufficient	19
够了	gòule	that's enouth!	19
够受的	gòushòude	unbearable	19
姑	gū	paternal aunt	10
姑姑	gūgu	paternal aunt	10
姑父	gūfù	uncle	10
姑妈	gūmā	paternal aunt	10
姑母	gūmǔ	paternal aunt	10
姑娘	gūniang	girl	10
姑且	gūqiě	tentatively	10
姑息	gūxī	to appease, to indulge, to tolerate	10
古代	gǔdài	ancient times	1
古典	gǔdiǎn	classical	25
古怪	gǔguài	eccentric, strange	1
古玩	gǔwán	antiques	14
骨	gǔ	bone	25
骨干	gǔgàn	backbone, mainstay	25
骨架	gǔjià	skeleton, framework	25
骨节	gǔjié	joint	25
骨科	gǔkē	orthopaedics	25
骨气	gǔqì	strength of character	25
骨肉	gǔròu	flesh and blood	25
骨头	gǔtou	bone	25
骨子里	gǔzili	from the bottom of one's heart	25
故居	gùjū	former residence	23
故事	gùshi	story	7
故意	gùyì	on purpose, deliberately	7
顾	gù	to look at, to attend to	12
顾客	gùkè	customer	12
顾虑	gùlǜ	worry, apprehension	20
顾名思义	gùmíngsīyì	as the name suggests	12
顾问	gùwèn	consultant, advisor	12
固	gù	solid, stubborn	16
固定	gùdìng	fixed	16
固然	gùrán	without doubt, true	16
固体	gùtǐ	a solid	16
固有	gùyǒu	intrinsic	16
瓜	guā	melon	9
瓜分	guāfēn	to carve up	9
瓜田李下	guātiánlǐxià	in suspicious circumstances	9
瓜子儿	guāzǐr	melon seeds	9

瓜子脸	guāzǐliǎn	oval shaped face	12
刮	guā	to blow (of the wind)	21
刮风	guāfēng	the wind is blowing	21
刮脸	guāliǎn	to shave	21
挂	guà	to hang, to hang up	4
挂彩	guàcǎi	decorated with garlands	23
挂号	guàhào	registered mail	15
挂面	guàmiàn	dried noodles	4
挂念	guàniàn	to worry about sth.	4
挂图	guàtú	wall chart	4
怪	guài	strange	1
怪不得	guàibude	that's hardly surprising	1
怪物	guàiwu	monster, an eccentric	1
官	guān	bureaucrat	17
官方	guānfāng	official	17
官话	guānhuà	standard language (Mandarin)	17
官气	guānqì	bureaucratic airs	17
官员	guānyuán	bureaucrat	17
关怀	guānhuái	to show solicitude for	4
关节	guānjié	joint, link	15
关联	guānlián	connection	15
关切	guānqiè	to be concerned	24
关系	guānxì	relation, relationship	5
关于	guānyú	with regards to, about...	7
关照	guānzhào	to look after	9
关注	guānzhù	to pay careful attention to	4
观	guān	to look, view	10
观察	guānchá	to observe	10
观光	guānguāng	to visit	10
观看	guānkàn	to see, to watch	10
观念	guānniàn	concept, idea	10
观众	guānzhòng	crowd, audience	16
管	guǎn	tube; to mind, to arrange	8
管理	guǎnlǐ	to manage, to run	8
管事	guǎnshì	to be in charge, to run	8
管用	guǎnyòng	of use, effective	8
管子	guǎnzi	tube, pipe, straw	8
惯	guàn	habitual, customary	3
惯性	guànxìng	inertia	13
惯用语	guànyòngyǔ	habitual expression	3
光	guāng	light, only	6
光彩	guāngcǎi	lustre	23
光景	guāngjǐng	scenery	10
光明	guāngmíng	clarity, radiant	6
光明正大	guāngmíng zhèngdà	to be straight and honest	6

301

合情合理	héqínghélǐ	fair and sensible	12
合身	héshēn	to fit	12
合适	héshì	suitable	15
合算	hésuàn	worthwhile	12
合同	hétong	contract	12
合意	héyì	to be to one's liking	12
合影	héyǐng	group photograph	12
合演	héyǎn	to act together	16
合约	héyuē	agreement	12
合资	hézī	mixed funds	24
合作	hézuò	to cooperate	12
河流	héliú	river, water course	9
和解	héjiě	to reconcile	3
喝彩	hècǎi	to acclaim, to cheer	23
黑暗	hēi'àn	darkness	21
黑板	hēibǎn	blackboard	4
黑货	hēihuò	contraband	14
黑色	hēisè	black	4
恨	hèn	to hate	21
恨不得	hènbude	how one wishes one could	21
红灯	hóngdēng	red light	24
红军	hóngjūn	the Red Army	22
红木	hóngmù	mahogany	4
红色	hóngsè	red	4
红血球	hóngxuèqiú	red blood cell	24
后继无人	hòujìwúrén	without any heirs	5
后者	hòuzhě	following, next	4
呼	hū	bo breathe out, to shout	3
呼叫	hūjiào	to call out	3
呼应	hūyìng	echo	13
忽	hū	sudden; to ignore, to neglect	12
忽…忽…	hū…hū…	sometimes…sometimes…	21
忽地	hūdì	suddenly	12
忽而	hū'ér	now… , now…	12
忽冷忽热	hūlěnghūrè	sometimes hot, sometimes cold	12
忽然	hūrán	suddenly	11
忽然间	hūránjiān	suddenly	12
忽视	hūshì	to ignore	12
乎	hū	[particle]	12
胡	hú	muddled, confused	22
胡话	húhuà	ranting and raving	22
胡来	húlái	to mess things up	22
胡闹	húnào	to be mischievous	22
胡说	húshuō	to talk nonsense	22
胡说八道	húshuōbādào	to talk nonsense	22
胡同	hútòng	alley, lane	22
胡言	húyán	nonsense talk	22
胡子	húzi	beard and moustache	22
户	hù	family, home	15
户口	hùkǒu	residence booklet	15
互	hù	mutual	15
互利	hùlì	mutually beneficial	15
互相	hùxiāng	reciprocal, mutual	15
互助	hùzhù	to help each other	15
护	hù	to protect, to help	21
护城河	hùchénghé	city moat	21
护理	hùlǐ	to nurse, to protect	21
护理人员	hùlǐrényuán	nursing staff	21
护士	hùshi	nurse	21
护送	hùsòng	to escort, to convoy	21
护卫	hùwèi	to protect, to guard; bodyguard	21
护照	hùzhào	passport	21
花朵	huāduǒ	flower	10
花环	huāhuán	flower garland	16
花脸	huāliǎn	painted face (Beijing opera)	12
花生油	huāshēngyóu	peanut oil	19
花言巧语	huāyánqiǎoyǔ	sweet words	23
华	huá	flower, China	24
华北	Huáběi	Northern China	24
华表	huábiǎo	decorative columns	24
华而不实	huá'érbùshí	flashy but without substance	24
华丽	huálì	magnificent	24
华人	Huárén	Chinese person	24
华语	Huáyǔ	Chinese language	24
划	huá	to paddle, to scratch	24
划得来	huádelái	to be worth the effort	24
划算	huásuàn	to calculate; to one's profit	24
划	huà	to delimit, to differentiate	24
划分	huàfēn	to divide	24
划清	huàqīng	to make a clear distinction	24
划时代	huàshídài	epoch-making	24
化工厂	huàgōngchǎng	chemical factory	24
化合物	huàhéwù	chemical compound	12
化验	huàyàn	chemical analysis	24
化装	huàzhuāng	make-up	16
话剧	huàjù	stage play	16
画像	huàxiàng	portrait	21
怀	huái	bosom, to keep in mind	4
怀抱	huáibào	to harbour (a feeling)	5
怀表	huáibiǎo	pocket watch	4
怀恨	huáihèn	to hold a grudge	21
怀念	huáiniàn	to cherish the memory of	4

怀疑	huáiyí	to doubt, to suspect	4
坏	huài	bad; to ruin	14
坏处	huàichu	bad point, disadvantage	14
坏分子	huàifènzǐ	bad element	14
坏人	huàirén	bad person	14
欢呼	huānhū	to hail, to acclaim	3
欢送	huānsòng	to see off	2
环	huán	ring; to surround	16
环抱	huánbào	to surround	16
环境	huánjìng	environment, context	16
换	huàn	to change	5
换班	huànbān	to change shifts	5
换车	huànchē	to change buses／trains etc.	5
换工	huàngōng	to exchange work	5
换钱	huànqián	to change money	5
换句话说	huànjùhuàshuō	in other words	5
黄瓜	huángguā	cucumber	9
黄连	huánglián	rhizome of Chinese goldthread	3
黄色	huángsè	yellow, decadent	4
回避	huíbì	to avoid	21
回答	huídá	to reply, to answer	7
回绝	huíjué	to refuse categorically	21
回响	huíxiǎng	to echo, to reverberate	7
回忆	huíyì	to remember, to think back	11
回转	huízhuǎn	to turn around	19
回族	Huízú	the Hui minority	16
会合	huìhé	to join, to meet	12
会谈	huìtán	talks	11
会议	huìyì	meeting, conference	18
会员	huìyuán	member (of an association)	13
会章	huìzhāng	constitution (of an association)	1
会诊	huìzhěn	consulation of doctors	20
活该	huógāi	it serves s. o. right!	13
活力	huólì	vitality	17
活命	huómìng	life	4
火线	huǒxiàn	front	18
或	huò	or; somebody; perhaps	1
或许	huòxǔ	maybe	20
或者	huòzhě	or	4
货	huò	stock, goods	14
货车	huòchē	goods train	14
货机	huòjī	cargo aeroplane	14
货色	huòsè	goods	12
货物	huòwù	goods, stock	14
获	huò	to obtain, to get	24
获得	huòdé	to obtain, to get	24

获取	huòqǔ	to acquire	24

J

机动	jīdòng	motorised, mechanical	14
机构	jīgòu	mechanism	2
机关	jīguān	mechanism, gear, office	22
机会主义	jīhuìzhǔyì	opportunism	2
机件	jījiàn	parts	23
机密	jīmì	secret	20
机器	jīqì	machine	4
机制	jīzhì	machine made	8
几乎	jīhū	nearly, almost	12
鸡蛋	jīdàn	(hen's) egg	19
积	jī	to amass, to store	19
积存	jīcún	to stock	21
积极	jījí	active, positive	19
积极性	jījíxìng	initiative	19
积木	jīmù	building blocks	19
积少成多	jīshǎochéngduō	little streams make great rivers	19
基	jī	base, foundation	24
基本	jīběn	basic, fundamental	24
基本功	jīběngōng	basic skill	24
基本上	jīběnshang	basically, fundamentally	24
基层	jīcéng	basic level, primary level	24
基地	jīdì	base	24
基点	jīdiǎn	starting point, base	24
基调	jīdiào	main key	24
基建	jījiàn	capital construction	24
基金	jījīn	funds	24
基因	jīyīn	gene	24
极	jí	extremity, very	3
极点	jídiǎn	the limit, the utmost	3
…极了	jíle	extremely	3
极力	jílì	with all one's energy	17
极其	jíqí	very	3
极为	jíwéi	extremely	3
极右派	jíyòupài	extreme right	17
极左派	jízuǒpài	extreme left	17
集	jí	to gather; market	18
集成	jíchéng	integrated	18
集合	jíhé	to gather together	18
集会	jíhuì	assembly, rally	18
集体	jítǐ	collective	18
集团	jítuán	group	18

集中	jízhōng	to concentrate	18	技术	jìshù	technology, technique	19
集资	jízī	to collect funds	24	技术性	jìshùxìng	technical	19
及	jí	to reach; and	18	技术员	jìshùyuán	technician	19
及格	jígé	to pass a test	18	技艺	jìyì	skill, artistry	19
及时	jíshí	timely	18	季	jì	season	24
及时雨	jíshíyǔ	timely rain	18	季度	jìdù	quarter of a year	24
及早	jízǎo	as early as possible	18	季风	jìfēng	monsoon	24
急	jí	anxious, in a hurry	25	季节	jìjié	season	24
急电	jídiàn	urgent telegram	25	计	jì	to count, to compute; plan	22
急件	jíjiàn	urgent message	25	计划	jìhuà	to plan; plan, project	23
急救	jíjiù	first-aid	25	计件	jìjiàn	to calculate by the piece	23
急剧	jíjù	rapid, sharp	25	计较	jìjiào	to haggle over, to fuss about	22
急忙	jímáng	in a hurry	25	计量	jìliàng	to measure, to calculate	22
急切	jíqiè	eager, impatient	25	计数器	jìshùqì	counter	22
急行军	jíxíngjūn	quick march	25	计算	jìsuàn	to count, to compute, to calculate	22
急性病	jíxìngbìng	acute illness	25	计算机	jìsuànjī	calculator, computer	22
急性子	jíxìngzi	impatient	25	记	jì	to remember, to note	12
急需	jíxū	to be in urgent need of	25	记录	jìlù	to record	8
急用	jíyòng	urgent need	25	记得	jìde	to remember	12
急于	jíyú	eager, anxious	25	记功	jìgōng	to record work points	22
急诊室	jízhěnshì	emergency ward	25	记号	jìhào	mark, sign	15
级	jí	grade, level, rank	25	记忆	jìyì	memory; to remember	12
级别	jíbié	rank, grade	25	记忆力	jìyìlì	memory	17
济济	jǐjǐ	(of people) many	14	记者	jìzhě	journalist	12
济济一堂	jǐjǐyìtáng	to gather together	14	记住	jìzhu	to remember, to keep in mind	12
继	jì	to continue, to succeed	5	济	jì	to help, to aid	14
继承	jìchéng	to inherit	5	纪	jì	discipline; to put down in writing	16
继承人	jìchéngrén	heir	5	纪念	jìniàn	to commemorate	16
继而	jì'ér	then, afterwards	5	纪念品	jìniànpǐn	souvenir	16
继父	jìfù	stepfather	5	纪要	jìyào	summary of minutes	16
继母	jìmǔ	stepmother	5	纪元	jìyuán	era	16
继往开来	jìwǎngkāilái	to forge ahead and prepare the future	5	加	jiā	to add	17
继续	jìxù	to continue	20	加班	jiābān	to work overtime	17
寄	jì	to mail, to send	5	加车	jiāchē	extra bus/train etc.	17
寄存	jìcún	to deposit	21	加法	jiāfǎ	addition	17
寄放	jìfàng	to leave with...	5	加工	jiāgōng	process, working	17
寄钱	jìqián	to send money	5	加号	jiāhào	plus sign (+)	17
寄生	jìshēng	parasitic	5	加紧	jiājǐn	to intensify	23
寄生虫	jìshēngchóng	parasite	24	加快	jiākuài	to accelerate	17
寄信	jìxìn	to mail a letter	5	加强	jiāqiáng	to reinforce	17
寄托	jìtuō	to entrust to..., to leave with...	5	加热	jiārè	to heat	17
技	jì	skill, ability	19	加入	jiārù	to add, to put in	17
技工	jìgōng	skilled worker	19	加上	jiāshang	to add	17
技能	jìnéng	technical ability	19	加深	jiāshēn	to deepen	17
技巧	jìqiǎo	skill, technique	23	加以	jiāyǐ	to proceed; moreover	17
				加油	jiāyóu	Come on!	19

加油站	jiāyóuzhàn	petrol station	19
家家户户	jiājiāhùhù	every family and household	15
家具	jiājù	furniture	3
家庭	jiātíng	household, family	23
家务	jiāwù	household chores	13
家乡	jiāxiāng	hometown	23
家用电器	jiāyòngdiànqì	(household) electrical appliance	4
家族	jiāzú	clan	16
假	jiǎ	false	2
假发	jiǎfà	wig	2
假话	jiǎhuà	lie	2
假名	jiǎmíng	kana	2
假如	jiǎrú	if	2
假山	jiǎshān	rockery, rock garden	2
假使	jiǎshǐ	if, in case	2
假托	jiǎtuō	on the pretext of	5
假	jià	holidays	2
假期	jiàqī	holidays	2
架	jià	frame, [Mw for radio sets, etc.]	14
架空	jiàkōng	built on stilts, impracticable	16
架子	jiàzi	frame, haughty manner	14
价	jià	price	22
价格	jiàgé	price	22
价目	jiàmù	marked price	22
价钱	jiàqián	price	22
价值	jiàzhí	value	24
简	jiǎn	letter, simple	25
简报	jiǎnbào	bulletin	25
简便	jiǎnbiàn	convenient	25
简称	jiǎnchēng	abbreviation	25
简单	jiǎndān	simple	25
简单化	jiǎndānhuà	simplification	25
简短	jiǎnduǎn	concise	25
简化	jiǎnhuà	to simplify	25
简历	jiǎnlì	curriculum vitae	25
简练	jiǎnliàn	succinct, pithy	25
简明	jiǎnmíng	concise	25
简体字	jiǎntǐzì	simplified characters	25
简写	jiǎnxiě	simplified writing	25
简要	jiǎnyào	brief, concise	25
简易	jiǎnyì	simple and easy	25
简直	jiǎnzhí	simply, at all	25
间断	jiànduàn	to be interrupted	7
间接	jiànjiē	indirect	3
健	jiàn	strong, robust	17
健康	jiànkāng	healthy	17

健美	jiànměi	beautiful and healthy	17
健全	jiànquán	sound, perfect	17
件	jiàn	[Mw for events]	23
建	jiàn	to build, to found	6
建成	jiànchéng	to finish building	24
建国	jiànguó	to found a state	6
建交	jiànjiāo	to establish diplomatic relations	22
建立	jiànlì	to found, to establish	6
建设	jiànshè	to build, to construct	16
建议	jiànyì	to suggest, to propose	18
见怪	jiànguài	to take offence	1
见解	jiànjiě	opinion	3
见面	jiànmiàn	to meet	3
见死不救	jiànsǐbújiù	not to rescue s. o. in danger	23
见效	jiànxiào	to be effective	20
将	jiāng	to be about to	5
将错就错	jiāngcuòjiù cuò	to leave a mistake and make the most of it	5
将近	jiāngjìn	nearly, close to	12
将就	jiāngjiu	to make do with	5
将来	jiānglái	in the future	5
将要	jiāngyào	to be about to	5
将军	jiāngjūn	a general	22
将	jiàng	a general	5
讲解	jiǎngjiě	to explain	3
讲究	jiǎngjiu	to be particular about	20
讲理	jiǎnglǐ	to reason, to argue	3
讲求	jiǎngqiú	to be particular about	1
讲台	jiǎngtái	platform, rostrum	14
讲义	jiǎngyì	teaching materials	2
讲座	jiǎngzuò	a course of lectures, etc.	8
交	jiāo	to hand over; relationship; mutual	22
交班	jiāobān	to change shifts	22
交错	jiāocuò	to interlock, criss-crossing	22
交道	jiāodao	contact, relation	22
交给	jiāogěi	to give to	22
交换	jiāohuàn	to exchange	22
交际	jiāojì	communication, relations	22
交流	jiāoliú	to exchange; exchange	22
交谈	jiāotán	talks	22
交替	jiāotì	to replace, to supersede	10
交通	jiāotōng	transport	22
交响乐	jiāoxiǎngyuè	symphony	22
交易	jiāoyì	transaction	22
交易所	jiāoyìsuǒ	stock exchange	22
脚	jiǎo	foot	10

紧接	jǐnjiē	closely followed by	23
紧密	jǐnmì	close together	23
紧要	jǐnyào	urgent	23
紧张	jǐnzhāng	nervous, tense	23
仅	jǐn	only	5
仅仅	jǐnjǐn	only	5
尽	jǐn	to the greatest extent	8
尽管	jǐnguǎn	even though...	8
尽快	jǐnkuài	as quickly as possible	8
尽量	jǐnliàng	as much as possible	13
尽先	jǐnxiān	to give first priority to	8
尽早	jǐnzǎo	as soon as possible	8
尽着	jǐnzhe	to give priority to	8
尽	jìn	exhausted, finished	8
尽力	jìnlì	to do one's best	17
尽其所长	jìnqísuǒcháng	to use all one's talents	8
尽其所有	jìngqísuǒyǒu	to give all one has	8
尽头	jìntóu	end, limit	8
尽心	jìnxīn	with all one's heart	8
尽兴	jìnxìng	to enjoy oneself to the full	8
尽意	jìnyì	to one's heart's content	8
进化论	jìnhuàlùn	the theory of evolution	23
进军	jìnjūn	to march	22
进入	jìnrù	to enter	9
进修	jìnxiū	advanced studies	14
进修班	jìnxiūbān	advanced class	14
进展	jìnzhǎn	to make progress	19
近代	jìndài	modern times	1
近况	jìnkuàng	recent developments	5
近视眼	jìnshìyǎn	myopia	13
近似	jìnsì	approximate, similar	11
经	jīng	to go through; scripture	1
经常	jīngcháng	often	1
经常化	jīngchánghuà	to become a regular practice	1
经典	jīngdiǎn	classics, scriptures	25
经费	jīngfèi	funds	14
经过	jīngguò	to pass through	8
经济	jīngjì	economy	14
经理	jīnglǐ	manager	3
经历	jīnglì	to experience	11
经书	jīngshū	Confucian classics	1
经心	jīngxīn	careful, conscientious	1
经意	jīngyì	careful	1
睛	jīng	eye	1
精	jīng	refined, essence, perfect	11
精彩	jīngcǎi	brilliant	23
精读	jīngdú	intensive reading	13
精美	jīngměi	exquisite, elegant	11
精密	jīngmì	precise, accurate	20
精神	jīngshén	spirit, mind	11
精神病	jīngshénbìng	mental illness	11
精神分析学	jīngshénfēnxīxué	psychoanalysis	11
精心	jīngxīn	meticulously	11
京剧	jīngjù	Beijing opera	16
惊吓	jīngxià	to frighten, to scare	4
景	jǐng	view, scenery	10
景色	jǐngsè	scenery, view	10
景山	Jǐngshān	Jingshan (Coal Hill)	10
景象	jǐngxiàng	scene, sight	10
静	jìng	silent, calm, peaceful	6
静候	jìnghòu	to wait patiently	13
静坐	jìngzuò	to sit still	6
境	jìng	border, boundary	16
境界	jìngjiè	boundary	17
境况	jìngkuàng	condition, circumstances	16
敬	jìng	to respect	17
敬爱	jìng'ài	respect and love	17
敬而远之	jìng'éryuǎnzhī	to keep a respectful distance from	17
敬老院	jìnglǎoyuàn	old folks' home	17
敬礼	jìnglǐ	salute; to extend greetings	17
敬意	jìngyì	respect, to pay one's respects	17
敬祝	jìngzhù	to greet with respect	17
究	jiū	to examine in depth	6
久留	jiǔliú	a long stay	1
酒鬼	jiǔguǐ	drunkard	4
酒精	jiǔjīng	ethyl alcohol	11
酒量	jiǔliàng	capacity for drink	13
旧居	jiùjū	former residence	23
旧历	jiùlì	lunar calendar	11
旧式	jiùshì	old type	16
救	jiù	to rescue	23
救护	jiùhù	to give first aid	23
救火	jiùhuǒ	fire fighting	23
救济	jiùjì	to relieve; succour	23
救命	jiùmìng	save s. o. 's life	23
救星	jiùxīng	liberator	23
就业	jiùyè	to find a job	13
就职	jiùzhí	to assume office	16
居	jū	to reside	23
居功	jūgōng	to claim credit for oneself	23
居留证	jūliúzhèng	residence permit	23

居民	jūmín	inhabitant	23
居然	jūrán	unexpectedly	23
居住	jūzhù	to reside	23
局	jú	office, situation, game	25
局部	júbù	part	25
局面	júmiàn	situation, aspect, phase	25
局势	júshì	situation	25
局着	júzhe	to be disturbed by s. o. 's presence	25
举	jǔ	to lift	9
举办	jǔbàn	to organize	9
举杯	jǔbēi	to raise a toast	9
举例	jǔlì	to give an example	19
举行	jǔxíng	to hold (a meeting, etc.)	24
句	jù	sentence	1
句法	jùfǎ	syntax	1
句号	jùhào	full stop	15
句子	jùzi	sentence	1
具	jù	instrument; to possess	3
具备	jùbèi	to possess	11
具体	jùtǐ	concrete, precise	3
具有	jùyǒu	to possess	5
据	jù	according to	14
据点	jùdiǎn	strong point	3
据说	jùshuō	it is said that	3
剧	jù	theatre, opera	16
剧本	jùběn	scenario, script	16
剧场	jùchǎng	theatre	16
剧情	jùqíng	plot	16
剧团	jùtuán	theatrical company	16
剧院	jùyuàn	theatre	16
拒	jù	to refuse, to resist	21
拒绝	jùjué	to refuse	21
角	jué	role, character	16
角色	juésè	role	16
绝	jué	to break; extreme	21
绝笔	juébǐ	last testament	21
绝大多数	juédàduōshù	the majority	21
绝代	juédài	without equal	21
绝对	juéduì	absolute, absolutely	21
绝对多数	juéduìduōshù	the absolute majority	21
绝境	juéjìng	impasse	21
绝密	juémì	top-secret	21
绝命书	juémìngshū	suicide note, last written testament	21
绝食	juéshí	hunger strike	21

绝育	juéyù	sterilisation	21
决	jué	to decide; absolutely	25
决定	juédìng	to decide; decision	25
决断	juéduàn	to decide; decision	25
决口	juékǒu	to break, to breach (dyke, dam, . . .)	25
决议	juéyì	resolution	25
军	jūn	army	22
军队	jūnduì	army	22
军服	jūnfú	military uniform	22
军官	jūnguān	officer	22
军国主义	jūnguózhǔyì	militarism	22
军号	jūnhào	bugle	22
军情	jūnqíng	military situation	22
军区	jūnqū	military region	22
军人	jūnrén	soldier	22
军事	jūnshì	military	22
军校	jūnxiào	military school	22
军医	jūnyī	military doctor	22
军用	jūnyòng	for army use	22

K

开采	kāicǎi	to mine, to extract	22
开除	kāichú	to expel	15
开设	kāishè	to open (a shop etc.), to offer (a course)	16
开头	kāitóu	beginning	17
开玩笑	kāiwánxiào	to joke, to play a trick on	14
开眼	kāiyǎn	to open one's eyes	1
开演	kāiyǎn	to begin a performance	16
开展	kāizhǎn	to develop, to launch	19
开张	kāizhāng	to open (a store)	14
开支	kāizhī	to pay; expenses	24
砍	kǎn	to cut down, to chop	7
砍大山	kǎndàshān	to chat idly, to gossip	7
砍掉	kǎndiào	to cut down	7
看管	kānguǎn	to watch, to supervise	8
看护	kānhù	to look after	21
看守	kānshǒu	to watch, to supervise	15
看情况	kànqíngkuàng	that depends!	5
看破	kànpò	to see through	23
看望	kànwàng	to visit	5
看相	kànxiàng	to practice physiognomy	1
康乐	kānglè	health and happiness	17

考	kǎo	to examine	18
考察	kǎochá	to examine, to inspect	24
考古	kǎogǔ	archaeology	18
考究	kǎojiu	to investigate; particular about, exquisite	18
考虑	kǎolǜ	to ponder, to think over	20
考取	kǎoqǔ	to pass an entrance examination	18
考上	kǎoshang	to pass an exam	18
考生	kǎoshēng	examination candidate	18
考试	kǎoshì	examination	19
考题	kǎotí	examination question	18
考验	kǎoyàn	to test; trial	24
考证	kǎozhèng	textual research	18
靠	kào	to lean against, to depend on	12
靠岸	kào'àn	to pull in to the shore	12
靠边	kàobiān	to pull over, keep to the side	12
靠不住	kàobuzhù	unreliable	12
靠得住	kàodezhù	trustworthy	12
靠近	kàojìn	to approach, to draw near	12
靠山	kàoshān	backing	12
科	kē	branch, section	2
科技	kējì	science and technology	19
科教片	kējiàopiàn	scientific or education film	2
科学	kēxué	science; scientific	2
科学家	kēxuéjiā	scientist	2
科学院	kēxuéyuàn	academy of sciences	2
科研	kēyán	scientific research	6
可不是吗	kěbúshìma	of course! exactly	6
可恨	kěhèn	detestable	21
可靠	kěkào	trustworthy	12
可能补语	kěnéngbǔyǔ	potential complement (grammar)	19
可取	kěqǔ	desirable	25
可笑	kěxiào	funny, laughable	11
客	kè	guest	12
客车	kèchē	passenger train / bus	12
客店	kèdiàn	inn, hostel	12
客饭	kèfàn	set menu, table d'hôte	12
客观	kèguān	objective	12
客户	kèhù	customer, client	15
客家话	kèjiāhuà	Hakka dialect	12
客气	kèqi	polite, courtesy	13
客人	kèrén	guest	12
客体	kètǐ	object (philosophy)	12
课表	kèbiǎo	class timetable	2
课程	kèchéng	curriculum	16
空话	kōnghuà	idle chatter, empty talk	16

空间	kōngjiān	space	16
空军	kōngjūn	airforce	16
空气	kōngqì	air, atmosphere	16
空前	kōngqián	unprecedented	16
空调	kōngtiáo	air-conditioning	18
空想	kōngxiǎng	illusion	16
空运	kōngyùn	air transport	18
空中客车	kōngzhōngkèchē	air-bus	16
空	kòng	to leave empty; free time	16
空白	kòngbái	blank space	16
空子	kòngzi	gap, opening	16
口传	kǒuchuán	to pass down orally	1
口号	kǒuhào	slogan	15
口技	kǒujì	vocal mimicry	19
口角	kǒujué	to quarrel	16
口试	kǒushì	oral examination	19
口味	kǒuwèi	taste	20
哭	kū	to cry	8
哭声	kūshēng	tears, sobs	8
苦	kǔ	bitter, harsh	25
苦处	kǔchù	suffering	25
苦干	kǔgàn	to work hard	25
苦瓜	kǔguā	bitter gourd	25
苦力	kǔlì	coolie	25
苦难	kǔnàn	suffering, misery	25
苦死	kǔsǐ	for the worst	25
苦头	kǔtóu	suffering	25
苦味	kǔwèi	bitter taste	25
苦笑	kǔxiào	forced laugh	25
苦心	kǔxīn	to take great pains, painstaking	25
块	kuài	piece [Mw]	4
快板儿	kuàibǎnr	a story told in rhythmic style	4
快感	kuàigǎn	delight	2
快活	kuàihuo	happy, cheerful	12
会计	kuàijì	accountant	22
况	kuàng	circumstances, moreover	5
困	kùn	poor, difficult, sleepy	10
困难	kùnnan	difficulty	10

L

拉	lā	to pull	25
拉丁文	Lādīngwén	Latin	25
拉丁字母	Lādīngzìmǔ	Latin alphabet	25
拉关系	lāguānxi	to establish a relationship with	25

流汗	liúhàn	to sweat	11
流浪	liúlàng	to roam about; vagabond	14
流利	liúlì	fluent, smooth	9
流通	liútōng	to circulate	9
流行	liúxíng	popular	9
流行病	liúxíngbìng	epidemic	9
流血	liúxuè	to bleed	24
鲁	Lǔ	(family name)	23
鲁班	Lǔ Bān	Lu Ban (great master of carpentry)	23
鲁迅	Lǔ Xùn	Lu Xun	23
路标	lùbiāo	road sign	7
路程	lùchéng	journey, distance travelled	16
路费	lùfèi	travelling expenses	14
路线	lùxiàn	route, itinerary	18
旅	lǚ	to travel	15
旅程	lǚchéng	route, itinerary	16
旅店	lǚdiàn	hotel, hostel	15
旅费	lǚfèi	travelling expenses	15
旅馆	lǚguǎn	hotel	15
旅客	lǚkè	passenger	15
旅社	lǚshè	hotel	23
旅行	lǚxíng	to travel; travel	15
旅行社	lǚxíngshè	travel agency	23
虑	lǜ	to think over, to be worried about	20
《论语》	〈Lúnyǔ〉	*Analects of Confucius*	8
论	lùn	to discuss; opinion	3
论点	lùndiǎn	thesis	3
论断	lùnduàn	inference, thesis	7
论据	lùnjù	argument	3
论理	lùnlǐ	logic; normally; to reason	3
论说	lùnshuō	argumentation	3
论文	lùnwén	thesis, dissertation	6
论证	lùnzhèng	to prove; proof, grounds of argument	18
落	luò	to fall	2
落成	luòchéng	completion, inauguration	2
落后	luòhòu	backward	2
落花流水	luòhuāliúshuǐ	routed, in a sorry plight	9
落花生	luòhuāshēng	peanut	2
落空	luòkōng	to fall through	16
落日	luòrì	setting sun	2
落实	luòshí	workable, to put into effect	11
落叶	luòyè	fallen leaves	10

M

妈	mā	mother	17
妈妈	māma	mamma, mum	17
马达	mǎdá	motor	5
马到成功	mǎdàochénggōng	to win instant success	22
马力	mǎlì	horsepower	17
卖弄	màinong	to show off	19
满意	mǎnyì	satisfied, content	10
满	mǎn	full	10
满不在乎	mǎnbúzàihū	not to worry at all	12
满城风雨	mǎnchéngfēngyǔ	to be the talk of the town	10
满怀	mǎnhuái	to have one's heart filled with	10
满满当当	mǎnmǎndāngdāng	filled to the brim	10
满面春风	mǎnmiànchūnfēng	beaming with happiness	10
满期	mǎnqī	full term, completed term	10
满人	Mǎnrén	a Manchurian	10
满月	mǎnyuè	full moon	10
满洲	Mǎnzhōu	Manchuria	10
满族	Mǎnzú	Manchurian race	16
满足	mǎnzú	satisfied	22
满座	mǎnzuò	full house	10
慢性病	mànxìngbìng	chronic illness	13
毛病	máobìng	problem, breakdown	10
毛料	máoliào	woollen material	25
毛线	máoxiàn	wool thread	18
毛织品	máozhīpǐn	woollen articles	24
毛织物	máozhīwù	woollen articles	24
美称	měichēng	good name, praise	13
美丽	měilì	beautiful	6
美联社	Měiliánshè	Associated Press	24
美满	měimǎn	happy, satisfied	10
美术	měishù	fine arts	2
美味	měiwèi	delicious; delicacy	20
美洲	Měizhōu	America	9
门户	ménhù	door, sect, faction	15
门类	ménlèi	category	4
门诊	ménzhěn	outpatient service	20
猛	měng	fierce, sudden, vigorous	21
猛然	měngrán	suddenly	21

迷	mí	confused, lost, fascinated	4	某某	mǒumǒu	so-and-so, such-and-such	11
迷路	mílù	to lose one's way	4	母系	mǔxì	matriarchal	5
迷人	mírén	charming, bewitching	4	木	mù	tree, wood	4
迷信	míxìn	superstition	4	木板	mùbǎn	wooden plank	4
迷住	mízhù	to be fascinated by	4	木材	mùcái	timber, lumber	7
密	mì	thick, secret	20	木耳	mù'ěr	edible tree fungi	12
密电	mìdiàn	coded telegram	20	木工	mùgōng	woodwork, woodworker	4
密度	mìdù	density	20	木瓜	mùguā	papaya	9
密封	mìfēng	to seal up, to seal hermetically	20	木料	mùliào	timber, lumber	25
密集	mìjí	concentrated, compact	20	木桥	mùqiáo	wooden bridge	25
密件	mìjiàn	secret document	20	木头	mùtou	wood	4
密切	mìqiè	close, intimate	20	目	mù	eye	9
密谈	mìtán	secret talks	20	目标	mùbiāo	objective, target	9
面积	miànji	area, surface area	19	目不识丁	mùbùshídīng	to be totally illiterate	9
面具	miànjù	mask	3	目的	mùdì	aim, goal, purpose	9
面目	miàmù	features, face	9	目的地	mùdìdì	destination	9
面食	miànshí	flour based foods	19	目前	mùqián	now, currently	24
面条	miàntiáo	noodles	1				
面向	miànxiàng	to face	3				
民众	mínzhòng	people	23				
民主	mínzhǔ	democracy; democratic	23				

N

民主党	mínzhǔdǎng	Democratic Party	24
民族	mínzú	race, nation	17
明白	míngbai	to understand	10
明代	Míngdài	Ming Dynasty	1

明来暗往	mínglái'àn wǎng	to have overt and covert contacts with s. o.	21	南瓜	nánguā	pumpkin	9
				南极	Nánjí	the South Pole	3
明亮	míngliàng	clear, bright	4	南极洲	Nánjízhōu	Antarctica	9
明确	míngquè	clear, definite	12	南温带	nánwēndài	south temperate zone	12
名称	míngchēng	name, title	13	难产	nánchǎn	difficult birth	19
名单	míngdān	roll, name list	18	难处	nánchu	difficulty	2
名句	míngjù	famous saying, well-known phrase	1	难度	nándù	degree of difficulty	7
				难怪	nánguài	no wonder	1
名角儿	míngjuér	famous actor / actress	16	难过	nánguò	sad	21
名利	mínglì	fame and wealth	8	难受	nánshòu	to suffer, to feel pain	3
名望	míngwàng	fame and prestige	5	难为情	nánwéiqíng	embarrassed	3
名义	míngyì	name, in the name of ...	2	男性	nánxìng	man, male	13
名著	míngzhù	famous work, masterpiece	8	闹	nào	noisy; to create trouble	4
命	mìng	life, fate; to order	4	闹病	nàobìng	to fall ill	4
命根子	mìnggēnzi	lifeblood	4	闹事	nàoshì	to make trouble	4
命名	mìngmíng	to baptise	4	闹市	nàoshì	bustling part of town	4
命题	mìngtí	to assign a topic; proposition	4	闹意见	nàoyìjian	to be on bad terms with	4
命运	mìngyùn	destiny	18	闹钟	nàozhōng	alarm clock	4
没落	mòluò	in decline	2	内	nèi	inner, inside, internal	15
某	mǒu	some, certain	11	内部	nèibù	internal, inner	15
某地	mǒudì	somewhere	11	内行	nèiháng	expert; adept at	15
				内经	nèijīng	the Internal Canon of Medicine	15
				内科	nèikē	internal medicine	15
				内容	nèiróng	contents	15

内心	nèixīn	heart, in the depths of one's heart	15
内衣	nèiyī	underwear	15
内在	nèizài	inherent, intrinsic	15
内政	nèizhèng	internal affairs	17
能够	nénggòu	to be able to	19
能见度	néngjiàndù	visibility	7
能量	néngliàng	energy, capacity	13
能力	nénglì	energy, capabilities	17
年初	niánchū	beginning of the year	12
年代	niándài	age, era, times	1
年底	niándǐ	end of the year	4
年画	niánhuà	New Year pictures	15
年级	niánjí	grade, year	25
年纪	niánjì	age	16
年历	niánlì	calendar	11
年终	niánzhōng	end of the year	12
念经	niànjīng	to recite the Buddhist scriptures	1
娘	niáng	girl, mother	10
鸟	niǎo	bird	7
牛角	niújiǎo	ox horn	16
牛排	niúpái	steak	13
农	nóng	agriculture, countryside	14
农场	nóngchǎng	farm	14
农村	nóngcūn	countryside	14
农夫	nóngfū	farmer	14
农活	nónghuó	farm work	14
农具	nóngjù	farm tool	14
农历	nónglì	lunar calendar	14
农民	nóngmín	peasant	14
农人	nóngrén	peasant	14
农田	nóngtián	farmland	14
农药	nóngyào	pesticide	14
农业	nóngyè	agriculture	14
农业部	nóngyèbù	Ministry of Agriculture	14
农庄	nóngzhuāng	farm	14
农作物	nóngzuòwù	crops	14
弄	nòng	to play with, to manage, to handle	19
弄假成真	nòngjiǎchéng zhēn	Make-believe has become reality.	19
怒	nù	anger	21
怒冲冲	nùchōngchōng	in a rage	21
怒火	nùhuǒ	fury	21
怒气	nùqì	anger	21
怒视	nùshì	to glare at	21

女士	nǚshì	madam, lady	17
女性	nǚxìng	woman, female	13
暖	nuǎn	mild, warm	19
暖和	nuǎnhuo	mild, warm	19
暖气	nuǎnqì	central heating	19

P

怕	pà	to be afraid	4
怕人	pàrén	scary, dread to meet people	4
怕生	pàshēng	shy with strangers	4
怕事	pàshì	afraid of trouble	4
怕羞	pàxiū	shy	21
排	pái	to arrange, to put in order; row	13
排比	páibǐ	parallelism	13
排场	páichang	extravagance	13
排除	páichú	to remove, to get rid of	15
排队	páiduì	to queue	13
排骨	páigǔ	spareribs	25
排解	páijiě	to mediate	13
排球	páiqiú	volleyball	18
排他性	páitāxìng	exclusiveness	13
排外	páiwài	xenophobia	13
排印	páiyìn	typesetting and printing	13
排长	páizhǎng	platoon leader	13
排字	páizì	composing, typesetting	13
派	pài	group, faction; to send	11
派别	pàibié	school, faction	11
派出所	pàichūsuǒ	local police station	11
派生	pàishēng	derive	11
派头	pàitóu	manner, style	11
判	pàn	to distinguish, to judge, to decide	18
判别	pànbié	to differentiate, to distinguish	18
判处	pànchǔ	to condemn	18
判定	pàndìng	to judge	18
判断	pànduàn	to judge, to determine	18
判决	pànjué	to deliver a verdict; verdict	18
判决书	pànjuéshū	verdict, written judgement	18
判明是非	pànmíngshìfēi	to distinguish between right and wrong	18
旁观者清	pángguānzhě qīng	Onlookers see more clearly than players.	10
跑	pǎo	to run	3
跑表	pǎobiǎo	stopwatch	3
跑步	pǎobù	to run, to jog	18

千虑一得	qiānlǜyìdé	even an idiot can have a good idea	20
千奇百怪	qiānqíbǎiguài	all kinds of weird things	1
千秋万代	qiānqiūwàndài	throughout the ages	1
千真万确	qiānzhēnwànquè	absolutely true	12
前景	qiánjǐng	foreground	10
前例	qiánlì	precedent	19
前线	qiánxiàn	the front, front-line	18
前者	qiánzhě	the former	13
墙	qiáng	wall	1
墙报	qiángbào	wall newspaper	1
强	qiáng	strong	5
强大	qiángdà	strong, powerful	5
强调	qiángdiào	to stress, to emphasise	18
强国	qiángguó	powerful country	5
强化	qiánghuà	to strengthen	5
强加	qiángjiā	to impose, to force	17
强烈	qiángliè	violent; strong, intense	14
强人	qiángrén	strong person	5
强行	qiángxíng	to force	5
强硬	qiángyìng	strong, unyielding	5
强壮	qiángzhuàng	sturdy	19
强	qiǎng	to strive for	5
强求	qiǎngqiú	to insist on, to impose	5
强使	qiǎngshǐ	to force, to compel	5
桥	qiáo	bridge	25
桥头	qiáotóu	end of a bridge	25
切	qiē	to cut, to slice	17
切除	qiēchú	excision, resection; to excise	17
切断	qiēduàn	to cut off	17
切开	qiēkāi	incision	17
切碎	qiēsuì	to cut into tiny pieces	18
切	qiè	to correspond to	17
切合	qièhé	to suit, to fit	17
切记	qièjì	to fix in one's mind	17
切身	qièshēn	personal, of immediate concern to s. o.	17
且说	qiěshuō	let me begin by saying...	8
亲耳	qīn´ěr	with one's own ears	12
亲密	qīnmì	intimate, close	20
亲切	qīnqiè	cordial, affectionate	17
亲眼	qīnyǎn	with one's own eyes	1
青	qīng	green-blue	10
青菜	qīngcài	green vegetables	10
青春	qīngchūn	youth, spring of one's life	10

青海	Qīnghǎi	Qinghai Province	10
青年	qīngnián	youth, young	10
青衣	qīngyī	a female role in Beijing opera	10
清	qīng	clear; to settle	1
清白	qīngbái	pale, spotless, clear	12
清楚	qīngchu	clear; to be clear about	1
清代	Qīngdài	Qing Dynasty	1
清官	qīngguān	honest official	17
清明	qīngmíng	Qingming (Pure Brightness)	1
清明节	Qīngmíngjié	Qingming festival	15
清算	qīngsuàn	to clear, to settle accounts	1
清真	qīngzhēn	Muslim	1
轻工业	qīnggōngyè	light industry	13
轻视	qīngshì	to underestimate	13
情	qíng	feeling, circumstance	1
情报	qíngbào	intelligence, information	3
情感	qínggǎn	feeling	3
情歌	qínggē	love song	3
情节	qíngjié	plot (of a play)	15
情景	qíngjǐng	scene, circumstance	10
情况	qíngkuàng	situation	5
情理	qínglǐ	reason, sense	3
情人	qíngrén	lover	10
情事	qíngshì	state of affairs	3
情书	qíngshū	love letter	3
情形	qíngxíng	circumstance	10
情愿	qíngyuàn	to be willing to	11
请假	qǐngjià	to ask for leave	2
请教	qǐngjiào	to consult, to ask for advice	5
请客	qǐngkè	to invite (and pay for) a guest	12
请求	qǐngqiú	to request	1
请示	qǐngshì	to ask for instructions	3
请托	qǐngtuō	to ask for a service	5
庆	qìng	to celebrate	15
庆祝	qìngzhù	to celebrate	15
穷	qióng	poor; limit	9
穷尽	qióngjìn	limit, end	9
穷困	qióngkùn	destitute, poverty-stricken	10
穷人	qióngrén	a poor person	9
球	qiú	sphere, globe, ball	18
球场	qiúchǎng	ground, court	18
球票	qiúpiào	match ticket	18
求	qiú	to beg, to request	1
求和	qiúhé	to sue for peace	1
求婚	qiúhūn	to propose marriage, to seek marriage	22

求亲	qiúqīn	to propose marriage, look for a spouse	1
求情	qióqíng	to ask a favour of	1
求学	qiúxué	to attend school	1
求人不如求己	qiúrénbùrú qiǔjǐ	better to rely on oneself than others	1
取材	qǔcái	to draw material	25
取长补短	qǔchángbǔduǎn	to offset one's weaknesses by the strengths of others	25
取代	qǔdài	to replace, to substitute	25
取得	qǔdé	to obtain	25
取灯儿	qǔdēngr	matches	25
取而代之	qǔ'érdàizhī	to supersede someone	25
取经	qǔjīng	to learn from others	25
取决	qǔjué	to depend upon, to hinge upon	25
取暖	qǔnuǎn	to warm oneself	25
取巧	qǔqiǎo	to resort to cunning	25
取消	qǔxiāo	to cancel, to call off	25
取笑	qǔxiào	to make fun of	11
去掉	qùdiào	to get rid of	7
去世	qùshì	to die, to pass away	23
趣	qù	interest	2
趣味	qùwèi	interset, delight	20
全	quán	complete, totally	20
全部	quánbù	complete, entire	20
全程	quánchéng	complete journey	20
全国	quánguó	the entire country	20
全集	quánjí	the complete works	20
全面	quánmiàn	overall, comprehensive	20
全能	quánnéng	all-round	20
全球	quánqiú	the whole world	20
全天候	quántiānhòu	all-weather	20
全体	quántǐ	entire, whole	20
全文	quánwén	full text	20
全心全意	quánxīnquányì	wholeheartedly	20
缺	quē	to lack; incomplete	20
缺点	quēdiǎn	defect, shortcoming	20
缺口	quēkǒu	breach, gap	20
缺货	quēhuò	to be out of stock	20
缺少	quēshǎo	to lack, to be short of	20
缺乏	quēfá	to lack	20
却	què	but; to withdraw	5
却步	quèbù	to step back	18
确	què	authentic, true	12
确定	quèdìng	fixed; to determine	12
确立	quèlì	to establish	12

确切	quèqiè	exact, precise	17
确认	quèrèn	to confirm, to acknowledge	12
确认书	quèrènshū	written confirmation	12
确实	quèshí	true, reliable	12
确信	quèxìn	to believe, to be convinced	12
确诊	quèzhěn	to diagnose	20

R

然而	rán'ér	yet, however	7
让步	ràngbù	to give way, to make a concession	18
让座	ràngzuò	to give up one's seat	8
扰	rǎo	to disturb	18
热烈	rèliè	warm, enthusiastic	14
热闹	rènao	bustling, noisy, lively	4
热情	rèqíng	warm, enthusiastic	3
热水器	rèshuǐqì	kettle, water-heater	4
人才济济	réncáijǐjǐ	a galexy of talent	14
人道主义	réndàozhǔyì	humanism	2
人格	réngé	personality	16
人类	rénlèi	humanity	4
人力	rénlì	labour	17
人参	rénshēn	ginseng	10
人生观	rénshēngguān	outlook on life	10
人士	rénshì	personage, figure	17
人像	rénxiàng	portrait	21
人选	rénxuǎn	candidate	5
人员	rényuán	staff	13
人造	rénzào	artificial, human made	22
人之常情	rénzhīchángqíng	the way of the world	6
认清	rènqīng	to see clearly	1
认识论	rènshilùn	theory of knowledge	20
任	rèn	to appoint, to take up a post	22
任何	rènhé	any, whatever	22
任教	rènjiào	to be a teacher	22
任命	rènmìng	to name	22
任期	rènqī	term of office	22
任务	rènwu	task, job, duty	22
任意	rènyì	wilfully	22
日程	rìchéng	daily programme, schedule	16
日光	rìguāng	sunbeam	6
日记	rìjì	diary	12
日历	rìlì	calendar	11
日食	rìshí	solar eclipse	19

神话	shénhuà	legend	4	实际	shíjì	in reality, in practise	11
神经	shénjīng	nerves	4	实况	shíkuàng	real situation	11
神色	shénsè	expression, mood	4	实物	shíwù	material object	11
甚	shèn	very	13	实习	shíxí	fieldwork, practice	11
甚而	shèn'ér	even. . . , as far as. . .	13	实现	shíxiàn	to realise, to achieve	11
甚至	shènzhì	even. . .	13	实行	shíxíng	to put into practise	11
生产	shēngchǎn	to produce, to manufacture	19	实用	shíyòng	practical	11
生产力	shēngchǎnlì	productive forces	19	实在	shízài	really, truly	11
生词	shēngcí	new word, new vocabulary	2	食	shí	food; to eat	19
生计	shēngjì	livelihood	22	食品	shípǐn	foodstuffs	19
生理	shēnglǐ	physiology	3	食品店	shípǐndiàn	grocery store	19
生命	shēngmìng	life	4	食用	shíyòng	edible	19
生怕	shēngpà	for fear that. . .	4	食欲	shíyù	appetite	19
生死	shēngsǐ	life and death; vital	8	食物	shíwù	food, foodstuffs	19
生育	shēngyù	to give birth to	8	识破	shípò	to see through, to penetrate	23
声调	shēngdiào	tones	18	始终	shǐzhōng	from beginning to end	12
声势	shēngshì	impetus, momentum	25	使	shǐ	to send, to use, to make	2
升级	shēngjí	to go up a grade	25	使不得	shǐbude	useless, undesirable	2
省	shěng	to economise, to omit; province	22	使得	shǐde	usable, workable	2
省得	shěngde	so as to avoid	22	使馆	shǐguǎn	embassy	2
省掉	shěngdiào	to omit	22	使命	shǐmìng	mission	4
省份	shěngfèn	province	22	使用	shǐyòng	to use, to employ	2
省会	shěnghuì	provincial capital	22	使者	shǐzhě	emissary, messenger	4
省钱	shěngqián	to save money	22	史诗	shǐshī	epic poem	19
省心	shěngxīn	to save worry	22	史实	shǐshí	historical fact	19
师范学校	shīfànxuéxiào	teachers' school	16	史书	shǐshū	historical record	19
师范学院	shīfànxuéyuàn	teacher's college	16	史无前例	shǐwúqiánlì	unprecedented	19
师资	shīzī	qualified teacher	24	史学	shǐxué	historiography	19
诗	shī	poem	9	示	shì	to show	3
诗词	shīcí	poetry	9	示范	shìfàn	to set an example	16
词歌	shīgē	poetry	9	示意图	shìyìtú	sketch map	3
诗集	shījí	poetry anthology	18	市民	shìmín	city or town resident	6
诗人	shīrén	poet	9	市委	shìwěi	municipal party committee	25
十足	shízú	pure, completely	22	世	shì	lifetime, generation, world	7
石	shí	rock, stone	9	世代	shìdài	from generation to generation	7
石板	shíbǎn	flagstone, slad	9	世道	shìdào	the way of the world	7
石刻	shíkè	inscription in stone	9	世纪	shìjì	century	16
石头	shítou	stone	9	世界	shìjiè	world	17
石像	shíxiàng	statue	21	世界语	shìjièyǔ	Esperanto	17
石油	shíyóu	petroleum	19	世面	shìmiàn	aspects of society	7
时代	shídài	era, epoch	1	世上	shìshang	in the world	7
时节	shíjié	time, season	15	式样	shìyàng	style, model	16
时量补语	shíliàngbǔyǔ	complement of duration	19	试	shì	to try	19
实	shí	solid, real, honest; fruit	11	试点	shìdiǎn	to make tests at selected points	19
实词	shící	notional word	11	试题	shìtí	exam question	19
实话	shíhuà	truth	11	试验	shìyàn	experiment	24

试用	shìyòng	to try out; on probation	19
试图	shìtú	to attempt	19
试验室	shìyànshì	laboratory	24
视	shì	vision, sight	13
视而不见	shì'érbújiàn	to look without seeing	13
视觉	shìjué	sight, the sense of sight	13
视力	shìlì	vision, sight	17
视听	shìtīng	audio-visual	13
适	shì	to suit; fitting, opportune	15
适当	shìdàng	suitable	15
适合	shìhé	to suit	15
适口	shìkǒu	palatable	15
适应	shìyìng	to adapt to	15
适用	shìyòng	to be applicable, to suit	15/22
适中	shìzhōng	moderate, well-situated	15
士	shì	scholar, soldier	17
士大夫	shìdàfu	literati	23
事变	shìbiàn	incident	23
事故	shìgù	accident	7
事件	shìjiàn	event	23
事例	shìlì	example, case	19
事情	shìqing	thing, affair, matter	3
事实	shìshí	fact, reality	11
事物	shìwù	object	13
事项	shìxiàng	item, matter	22
事业	shìyè	cause, undertaking	13
势	shì	power, influence	25
势必	shìbì	inevitably, certainly	25
势力	shìlì	force, power, influence	25
势能	shìnéng	potential energy	25
收成	shōuchéng	harvest	24
收获	shōuhuò	to gather, to harvest	24
收集	shōují	to collect	18
收据	shōujù	receipt	3
收取	shōuqǔ	to receive	25
收入	shōurù	income	9
首	shǒu	head; first; [Mw for poems, etc.]	6
首创	shǒuchuàng	to initiate	23
首次	shǒucì	first time	6
首都	shǒudū	capital	6
首脑	shǒunǎo	head of government	6
首先	shǒuxiān	first	6
首相	shǒuxiàng	prime minister	6
守	shǒu	to guard, to watch	15
守旧	shǒujiù	to stick to old ways	15
守门	shǒumén	goalkeeper	15

守势	shǒushì	defensive	25
守岁	shǒusuì	to bring in the new year	15
手表	shǒubiǎo	wrist watch	2
手段	shǒuduàn	means	25
手法	shǒufǎ	skill, technique	23
手工业	shǒugōngyè	handicraft industry	13
手球	shǒuqiú	hand ball	18
手势	shǒushì	gesture, sign	25
手术	shǒushù	surgical operation	2
手下留情	shǒuxiàliúqíng	to be lenient	3
手艺	shǒuyì	workmanship	2
手指	shǒuzhǐ	finger	1
受	shòu	to receive, to accept	3
受不了	shòubuliǎo	intolerable	3
受害	shòuhài	to fall victim to, to suffer from	8
受话机	shòuhuàjī	receiver	3
受苦	shòukǔ	to suffer	25
受气	shòuqì	to be bullied, to suffer	3
受伤	shòushāng	to be wounded	8
受托	shòutuō	to be entrusted with	5
书记	shūji	secretary	12
书架	shūjià	bookshelf	14
书经	shūjīng	*The Book of History*	1
书评	shūpíng	book review	18
舒	shū	to stretch; easy	11
舒服	shūfu	comfortable	11
舒适	shūshì	comfortable, cosy	15
舒心	shūxīn	serene	11
熟	shú	ripe, mature, familiar	12
熟菜	shúcài	cooked food, prepared food	12
熟练	shúliàn	skilled, experienced	25
熟人	shúrén	acquaintance	12
熟习	shúxí	to be skilled at	12
数	shǔ	to count	9
数数	shǔshù	to count, to reckon	9
数	shù	number, figure	9
数量	shùliàng	quantity	9
数目	shùmù	number, amount	9
数学	shùxué	mathematics	9
数字	shùzì	numeral, figure	9
术	shù	art, skill, technique	2
术语	shùyǔ	terminology	2
树	shù	tree	7
树立	shùlì	to establish	7
树林	shùlín	forest	7
树木	shùmù	trees	7

树叶	shùyè	tree leaves	10
霜	shuāng	frost	9
双	shuāng	pair, two	10
双边	shuāngbiān	bilateral	10
双重	shuāngchóng	double, dual	10
双打	shuāngdǎ	doubles match	10
双方	shuāngfāng	both sides	10
双关语	shuāngguānyǔ	pun, double meaning	10
双名	shuāngmíng	disyllabic given name	10
双亲	shuāngqīn	mother and father	10
双喜	shuāngxǐ	double happiness	10
水管	shuǐguǎn	water pipe	8
水流	shuǐliú	watercourse, river	9
水准	shuǐzhǔn	level, standard	7
顺	shùn	along, in the same direction as, suitable	17
顺便	shùnbiàn	in passing	17
顺从	shùncóng	to submit to	17
顺当	shùndang	smoothly	17
顺耳	shùn'ěr	pleasing to the ear	17
顺利	shùnlì	smoothly	17
顺手	shùnshǒu	smoothly, in passing	17
顺水	shùnshuǐ	with the current	17
顺心	shùnxīn	satisfactory	17
顺眼	shùnyǎn	pleasing to the eye	17
顺着	shùnzhe	following	17
说服	shuōfú	to persuade, to convince	11
说理	shuōlǐ	to reason, to argue	3
《说文解字》	〈shuōwénjiězì〉	An Analysis and Explanation of Characters	3
思考	sīkǎo	to ponder, to reflect	18
思虑	sīlǜ	to examine	20
思索	sīsuǒ	to ponder, to reflect	21
私	sī	private	24
私产	sīchǎn	private property	24
私房	sīfáng	confidential	24
私货	sīhuò	contraband	24
私交	sījiāo	personal friend	24
私利	sīlì	private interests	24
私立	sīlì	privately run	24
私情	sīqíng	personal relationship	24
私人	sīrén	private	24
私生活	sīshēnghuó	private life	24
私生子	sīshēngzǐ	illegitimate child	24
私事	sīshì	private matter	24
私心	sīxīn	selfish motives	24
私有	sīyǒu	private	24
私有制	sīyǒuzhì	private ownership	24
私自	sīzì	secretly, without permission	24
司	sī	to manage; department	22
司法	sīfǎ	judicial, judicature	22
司机	sījī	driver	22
死	sǐ	to die	8
死板	sǐbǎn	rigid, stiff	8
死党	sǐdǎng	die-hard followers	24
死得其所	sǐdéqísuǒ	to die a worthy death	8
死活	sǐhuó	life or death, fate	8
死记	sǐjì	to memorise mechanically	12
死路	sǐlù	blind alley, the road to ruin	8
死去	sǐqu	to die	8
死人	sǐrén	dead person	8
死心	sǐxīn	to give up an idea completely	8
四季	sìjì	four seasons	24
四人帮	sìrénbāng	the Gang of Four	11
四书	sìshū	the Four Books	23
四通八达	sìtōngbādá	to extend in all directions	5
似	sì	to be like	11
似乎	sìhū	it seems as if	12
似是而非	sìshì'érfēi	apparently correct but in fact wrong	11
送	sòng	to deliver, to carry	2
送别	sòngbié	to see someone off	2
送给	sònggěi	to give, to offer	2
送行	sòngxíng	to see someone off	2
诉	sù	to tell, to accuse	4
诉说	sùshuō	to tell, to relate	4
算	suàn	to count	4
算法	suànfǎ	algorithm	4
算了	suànle	forget it!	4
算命	suànmìng	to tell fortunes	4
算术	suànshù	arithmetic	2
随	suí	to follow	5
随便	suíbiàn	casual as one wishes, careless	5
随从	suícóng	to accompany	5
随地	suídì	anywhere	5
随和	suíhe	amiable	5
随口	suíkǒu	to speak thoughtlessly	5
随身	suíshēn	to carry on one's person	5
随时	suíshí	at all times	5
随手	suíshǒu	in passing, at your convenience	5
随意	suíyì	as one pleases	5
碎	suì	to break, to smash	18

索	suǒ	rope; to search, to ask for	21	体谅	tǐliàng	to show sympathy for	21
索道	suǒdào	cable way	21	体温	tǐwēn	body temperature	12
索取	suǒqǔ	to demand, to extort, to ask for	21	体温计	tǐwēnjì	thermometer	12
索性	suǒxìng	may as well	21	体系	tǐxì	system	5
				体育	tǐyù	physical education	8

T

				体育界	tǐyùjiè	sports world	17
				体制	tǐzhì	system, structure	8
台	tái	platform; [Mw]	14	替	tì	in place of, for	10
台北	Táiběi	Taibei	14	替代	tìdài	to replace	10
台灯	táidēng	desk lamp	24	替换	tìhuàn	to substitute	10
台风	táifēng	typhoon	14	天命	tiānmìng	heavenly mandate	4
台阶	táijiē	a flight of steps	25	天桥	tiānqiáo	overline bridge	25
台湾	Táiwān	Taiwan	14	天使	tiānshǐ	angel	2
态	tài	form, appearance, state	7	条	tiáo	[Mw]; clause	1
态度	tàidu	attitude	7	条件	tiáojiàn	condition	23
太极	tàijí	the supreme ultimate	3	条理	tiáolǐ	proper order	3
谈	tán	to talk, to chat	11	条例	tiáolì	regulations	19
谈虎色变	tánhǔsèbiàn	turn pale at the mention of...	23	条目	tiáomù	clause, subclause	9
谈话	tánhuà	to discuss; talks	11	条文	tiáowén	article, clause	1
谈判	tánpàn	negotiations	18	条子	tiáozi	strip, note	1
谈天	tántiān	to chat	11	调	tiáo	to mix, to adjust	18
谈心	tánxīn	heart to heart talk	11	调和	tiáohé	harmonious; to reconcile	18
特	tè	special, particular	1	调节	tiáojié	to regulate, to adjust	18
特别	tèbié	especially, particularly	1	调解	tiáojiě	to mediate	18
特产	tèchǎn	local product	19	调皮	tiáopí	naughty	18
特长	tècháng	strong point	1	调情	tiáoqíng	to flirt	18
特殊	tèshū	outstanding, prominent	1	调味	tiáowèi	flavour, seasoning	20
特此	tècǐ	especially	12	调整	tiáozhěng	to adjust, to regulate	18
特等	tèděng	special grade	1	贴	tiē	to stick	15
特地	tèdì	for a special purpose	1	贴切	tiēqiè	apt, suitable	17
特点	tèdiǎn	characteristic	1	铁板	tiěbǎn	iron plate	25
特级	tèjí	special grade	25	铁板一块	tiěbǎnyíkuài	a monolithic block; rigid	25
特技	tèjì	stunt, trick	19	铁道	tiědào	railway	25
特色	tèsè	characteristic	1	铁道部	tiědàobù	Railway Ministry	25
特务	tèwu	special agent, special task	13	铁饭碗	tiěfànwǎn	iron rice bowl (secure job)	25
特性	tèxìng	characteristic	18	铁路	tiělù	railroad	25
特意	tèyì	specially	1	铁器	tiěqì	ironware	25
特约	tèyuē	by special arrangement	12	铁桥	tiěqiáo	metal bridge	25
特制	tèzhì	specially made	8	铁水	tiěshuǐ	molten iron	25
题材	tícái	subject, theme	7	铁证	tiězhèng	irrefutable evidence	25
题词	tící	to prompt; inscription	2	听觉	tīngjué	hearing	18
提取	tíqǔ	to draw, to pick up	25	听力	tīnglì	listening comprehension	17
体格	tǐgé	physique, build	16	听取	tīngqǔ	to listen to	25
体积	tǐjī	volume, bulk	19	听任	tīngrèn	to allow	22
体力	tǐlì	physical strength	17	听诊器	tīngzhěnqì	stethoscope	20
				听众	tīngzhòng	audience, listener	16

庭	tíng	hall, courtyard	23	图章	túzhāng	seal, stamp	1
庭院	tíngyuàn	courtyard	23	土	tǔ	earth	19
停	tíng	to stop	25	土布	tǔbù	hand-woven cloth	19
停车	tíngchē	to park, to stop a vehicle	25	土产	tǔchǎn	local product	19
停车场	tíngchēchǎng	parking lot	25	土地	tǔdì	earth	19
停当	tíngdang	ready	25	土耳其	Tǔěrqí	Turkey	19
停放	tíngfàng	to park, to place	25	土法	tǔfǎ	local method	19
停工	tínggōng	to stop work	25	土工	tǔgōng	earthworker	19
停火	tínghuǒ	to cease fire	25	土话	tǔhuà	local dialect	19
停留	tíngliú	to stay	25	土货	tǔhuò	local product	19
停业	tíngyè	to close down, to stop a business	25	土块	tǔkuài	clod of earth	19
停职	tíngzhí	to suspend someone from work	25	土里土气	tǔlitǔqì	country person	19
停止	tíngzhǐ	to stop	25	土木工程	tǔmùgōngchéng	civil engineering	19
通	tōng	open, through; to go through	5	土生土长	tǔshēngtǔzhǎng	locally born and bred	19
通报	tōngbào	to notify; bulletin	5	土星	Tǔxīng	Saturn	19
通病	tōngbìng	common fault	5	土性	tǔxìng	soil quality	19
通常	tōngcháng	general, normal	5	土音	tǔyīn	local accent	19
通车	tōngchē	to be open to traffic	5	土语	tǔyǔ	local dialect	19
通道	tōngdào	thoroughfare	5	团	tuán	group	15
通电	tōngdiàn	to electrify; open telegram	5	团体	tuántǐ	organisation	15
通风	tōngfēng	to ventilate	5	团圆	tuányuán	reunion	15
通告	tōnggào	to announce	5	团长	tuánzhǎng	group leader	15
通过	tōngguò	to pass through, to traverse	16	推	tuī	to push, to choose	22
通顺	tōngshùn	smooth, clear, coherent	17	推出	tuīchū	to promote	22
通信	tōngxìn	to write letters to	5	推动	tuīdòng	to promote, to push	22
通行	tōngxíng	to pass through	5	推断	tuīduàn	to infer, to deduce	22
通用	tōngyòng	in common use	5	推广	tuīguǎng	to popularise, to spread	22
通知	tōngzhī	to inform, to notify	5	推进	tuījìn	to advance	22
同居	tóngjū	to live together	23	推举	tuījǔ	to elect, to choose	22
同类	tónglèi	similar	4	推理	tuīlǐ	inference, reasoning	22
同期	tóngqī	contemporary (in the same		推论	tuīlùn	deduction	22
		period）	24	推却	tuīquè	to decline, to refuse	22
同情	tóngqíng	sympathy	3	推让	tuīràng	to decline	22
同乡	tóngxiāng	person from the same village or		推算	tuīsuàn	to calculate, to reckon	22
		town	6	推土机	tuītǔjī	bulldozer	22
同义词	tóngyìcí	synonym	2	推托	tuītuō	to give an excuse	22
同志	tóngzhì	comrade	17	推想	tuīxiǎng	to imagine	22
统	tǒng	to gather, to unite; all together	7	推行	tuīxíng	to carry out, to pursue	22
统称	tǒngchēng	joint name, general name	14	推选	tuīxuǎn	to elect, to choose	22
统一	tǒngyī	to unify	7	托	tuō	to hold, to support, to ask	5
统治	tǒngzhì	to rule, to dominate	8	托词	tuōcí	to find a pretext	5
痛苦	tòngkǔ	pain, suffering	25	托儿所	tuōérsuǒ	child-care centre, nursery	5
突	tū	sudden; to dash forward	1	托人情	tuōrénqíng	to seek the good offices of s. o.	5
突出	tūchū	protruding, projecting	1	托生	tuōshēng	reincarnation	5
突破	tūpò	to break through	23	托运	tuōyùn	to consign (shipping)	18
突然	tūrán	sudden; suddenly	1	托子	tuōzi	base, support	5

W

外号	wàihào	nickname	15
外交	wàijiāo	diplomatic relations	22
外界	wàijiè	the outside world	17
外科	wàikē	surgical department	2
外省	wàishěng	other provinces	22
玩	wán	to have fun, to play	14
玩具	wánjù	toy	14
玩弄	wánnòng	to play with	19
玩儿	wánr	to have fun, to play	14
玩儿命	wánrmìng	to gamble with one's life	14
玩意儿	wányìr	toy, thing	14
完备	wánbèi	complete, perfect	11
完蛋	wándàn	to be done for	19
完满	wánmǎn	satisfactory	10
完全	wánquán	complete, totally	20
完整	wánzhěng	complete, intact	12
碗	wǎn	bowl; [Mw]	12
晚婚	wǎnhūn	late marriage	10
万古长存	wàngǔchángcún	to exist forever	21
万古长青	wàngǔchángqīng	to remain fresh forever	10
王八蛋	wángbādàn	bastard!	19
忘掉	wàngdiào	to forget	7
忘记	wàngjì	to forget	12
忘却	wàngquè	to forget	4
望	wàng	to look, to call on; reputation, hope	5
围	wéi	to surround	18
围墙	wéiqiáng	enclosing wall	18
为止	wéizhǐ	until	20
委	wěi	to entrust; indirect; committee	25
委冬儿	wěidōngr	to stay idly at home in winter	25
委派	wěipài	to delegate, to designate	25
委任	wěirèn	to appoint	25
委托	wěituō	to entrust	25
委员	wěiyuán	committee member	25
委员会	wěiyuánhuì	committee, commission	25
为此	wèicǐ	for this purpose, for this reason	12
为了	wèile	for, so as to ...	3
卫	wèi	to defend, to guard	6
卫生	wèishēng	hygiene	6

卫生部	wèishēngbù	Ministry of Health and Hygiene	14
卫生间	wèishēngjiān	bathroom	6
卫生局	wèishēngjú	public health bureau	25
卫生所	wèishēngsuǒ	public dispensary, clinic	6
卫星	wèixīng	satellite	6
味	wèi	taste, flavour	20
味道	wèidao	taste, flavour	20
味精	wèijīng	monosodium glutamate	20
味觉	wèijué	sense of taste	20
温	wēn	warm; to warm up	12
温带	wēndài	temperate zone	12
温度	wēndù	temperature	12
温度计	wēndùjì	thermometer	12
温故知新	wēngùzhīxīn	to gain new insights by studying the past	12
温和	wēnhé	mild, moderate	12
温和	wēnhuo	warm	12
温课	wēnkè	to go over one's lessons	12
温暖	wēnnuǎn	warm	19
温情	wēnqíng	tender feelings	12
温室	wēnshì	hothouse, greenhouse	12
温习	wēnxí	to review, to revise	12
文官	wénguān	civil official	17
文件	wénjiàn	document	23
文具	wénjù	writing materials	3
文剧	wénjù	opera score	16
文科	wénkē	liberal arts	2
文如其人	wénrúqírén	style makes the man	2
文艺	wényì	literature and art	2
文艺复兴	wényìfùxīng	the Renaissance	20
文艺界	wényìjiè	literary and art circles	17
文章	wénzhāng	article, text	1
闻	wén	to hear, to smell	10
闻风而动	wénfēng'érdòng	to respond immediately to a call	10
闻名	wénmíng	famous, renowned	10
问答	wèndá	question and answer	7
问候	wènhòu	to give one's regards to	15
问候语	wènhòuyǔ	expression of one's respects, greetings	17
问世	wènshì	to be published, to be released	7
屋	wū	house, room	21
屋子	wūzi	room	21
无	wú	without	7
无比	wúbǐ	unparalleled	4
无不	wúbù	without exception	4

无产者	wúchǎnzhě	proletarian	19
无从	wúcóng	to have no way of doing sth.	4
无法	wúfǎ	to be unable to . . .	4
无法无天	wúfǎwútiān	to defy the laws of God and man	4
无非	wúfēi	nothing but	4
无故	wúgù	without reason	7
无关	wúguān	to have nothing to do with	4
无害	wúhài	inoffensive	8
无济于事	wújìyúshì	to no avail	14
无际	wújì	unlimited	11
无理	wúlǐ	unreasonable, unjustifiable	3
无论	wúlùn	no matter. . .	3
无论如何	wúlùnrúhé	in any case	6
无论怎样	wúlùnzěnyàng	in any case, no matter what	4
无名指	wúmíngzhǐ	the ring finger	1
无能	wúnéng	unable	4
无穷	wúqióng	infinite, boundless	9
无神论者	wúshénlùnzhě	atheist	4
无条件	wútiáojiàn	unconditional	22
无望	wúwàng	hopeless	4
无为	wúwéi	nonaction (Taoism)	4
无味	wúwèi	tasteless	20
无限	wúxiàn	infinitely	21
无线电	wúxiàndiàn	wireless, radio	18
无效	wúxiào	to no avail, with no effect	20
无形	wúxíng	invisible	10
无疑	wúyí	undoubtedly	4
无中生有	wúzhōngshēngyǒu	completely fabricated, fictitious	4
无足轻重	wúzúqīngzhòng	of little or no importance	22
五官	wǔguān	the five senses	17
五经	wǔjīng	the Five Classics	23
五色	wǔsè	the five colours	4
五颜六色	wǔyánliùsè	multicoloured	18
舞	wǔ	to dance; dance	16
武官	wǔguān	military officer	17
舞会	wǔhuì	dance, ball	16
舞剧	wǔjù	ballet, dance	16
舞台	wǔtái	stage	16
武	wǔ	soldier, military	16
武打	wǔdǎ	acrobatic fighting, combat	16
武汉	Wǔhàn	Wuhan (city)	16
武剧	wǔjù	military opera	16
武器	wǔqì	arms	16
武生	wǔshēng	role of a warrior	16

武术	wǔshù	martial arts	16
武装	wǔzhuāng	armour, arms, battle gear	16
午睡	wǔshuì	siesta	15
物极必反	wùjíbìfǎn	when pushed to the extreme, things go the other way	21
物价	wùjià	price	22
物件	wùjiàn	object, article	23
物理	wùlǐ	physics	3
物品	wùpǐn	object, article	13
务	wù	business; to be engaged in, must	13
务必	wùbì	must	21
务农	wùnóng	to work in the fields	13
务实	wùshí	to deal with things realistically	13

X

西部	xībù	west	14
西瓜	xīguā	watermelon	9
西式	xīshì	western style	16
西装	xīzhuāng	western style clothing, suit	10
希	xī	to hope; rare	5
希奇	xīqí	curious, rare	5
希少	xīshǎo	rare	5
希有	xīyǒu	rare	5
析	xī	to analyse, to separate	11
习	xí	to practise; exercise	3
习非成是	xífēichéngshì	what is wrong eventually becomes right	3
习惯	xíguàn	habit; to get used to	3
习见	xíjiàn	commonly seen	3
习气	xíqì	bad habits	3
习题	xítí	exercise, problem	3
习以为常	xíyǐwéicháng	to be used to	3
习字	xízì	to practise writing	3
喜剧	xǐjù	comedy	16
喜庆	xǐqìng	joyous, jubilant	15
喜笑颜开	xǐxiàoyánkāi	to glow with delight	18
洗	xǐ	to wash	14
洗礼	xǐlǐ	baptism	14
洗脸	xǐliǎn	to wash one's face	14
洗衣机	xǐyījī	washing machine	14
细	xì	thin, fine, careful	6
细长	xìcháng	long and thin	6
细细	xìxì	in detail, very carefully	13
细小	xìxiǎo	tiny	6

向着	xiàngzhe	towards, facing	19
象形字	xiàngxíngzì	pictogram (pictographic character)	10
象牙	xiàngyá	elephant's tusk, ivory	20
像	xiàng	likeness, portrait, picture	21
像话	xiànghuà	reasonable, proper	21
像...似的	xiàng...shìde	just like...	21
项	xiàng	nape, sum, term	22
项目	xiàngmù	item	22
消	xiāo	to vanish, to eliminate	25
消除	xiāochú	to eliminate, to remove	25
消防队	xiāofángduì	fire brigade	25
消费	xiāofèi	to consume	25
消费品	xiāofèipǐn	consumer goods	25
消费者	xiāofèizhě	consumer	25
消化	xiāohuà	digestion	25
消极	xiāojí	negative, passive	25
消息	xiāoxī	news, a piece of news	25
小吃部	xiǎochībù	snack counter	14
小费	xiǎofèi	tip (gratuity)	14
小分队	xiǎofēnduì	small group	24
小鬼	xiǎoguǐ	little devil	4
小姐	xiǎojiě	miss, young lady	17
小卖部	xiǎomàibù	small shop	14
小品	xiǎopǐn	a short work, sketch	13
小指	xiǎozhǐ	the little finger	1
小组	xiǎozǔ	small group	2
笑	xiào	to laugh, to smile	11
笑话	xiàohua	joke, funny story	11
效	xiào	effect; to imitate	20
效法	xiàofǎ	to follow the example of	20
效果	xiàoguǒ	effect, result	20
效力	xiàolì	to serve; effect	20
效能	xiàonéng	efficacy, usefulness	20
效用	xiàoyòng	effectiveness, usefulness	20
鞋	xié	shoes	22
鞋带儿	xiédàir	shoe lace	22
鞋跟	xiégēn	heel	22
写实	xiěshí	to describe realistically	11
写作	xiězuò	writings	23
谢绝	xièyué	to decline politely	21
新华社	Xīnhuáshè	Xinhua News Agency	24
新娘	xīnniáng	bride	10
新式	xīnshì	new style	16
新闻	xīnwén	news, information	10
新鲜	xīnxiān	fresh, new	23
新约	xīnyuē	the New Testament	12
心计	xīnjì	calculation, scheming	22
心里美	xīnlǐměi	a type of turnip with green peel and purple red flesh	25
心里有鬼	xīnlǐyǒuguǐ	to have sth. on one's conscience	4
心理	xīnlǐ	psychology, mentality	3
心理学	xīnlǐxué	psychology	3
心明眼亮	xīnmíngyǎnliàng	to see and think clearly	4
心目	xīnmù	mood, mind	9
心情	xīnqíng	mood, frame of mind	3
心愿	xīnyuàn	wish	11
信封	xìnfēng	envelope	17
信号	xìnhào	signal	15
信件	xìnjiàn	mail, letters	23
信任	xìnrèn	to trust	22
信托	xìntuō	trust; to trust, to entrust	5
信纸	xìnzhǐ	letter paper	17
行草	xíngcǎo	half cursive half free style of calligraphy	20
行为	xíngwéi	behaviour, conduct, action	8
行政	xíngzhèng	administration	17
形成	xíngchéng	to form, to take shape	10
形而上学	xíng'érshàngxué	metaphysics	10
形容	xíngróng	to describe, to qualify (grammar)	10
形容词	xíngróngcí	adjective	10
形声字	xíngshēngzì	ideophonogram	10
形式	xíngshì	form, shape	16
形势	xíngshì	situation, circumstances	25
形态	xíngtài	form, shape	10
形体	xíngtǐ	shape	10
形象	xíngxiàng	image, form	10
形形色色	xíngxíngsèsè	of every description	10
形影不离	xíngyǐngbùlí	as inseparable as one's shadow	10
兴趣	xìngqu	interest, motivation	2
幸	xìng	good luck, fortune	8
幸得	xìngdé	fortunately	8
幸而	xìng'ér	fortunately	8
幸福	xìngfú	happiness	14
幸好	xìnghǎo	fortunate, fortunately	8
幸运	xìngyùn	good luck	18
性	xìng	nature, quality, sex	13
性别	xìngbié	sex, gender	13
性病	xìngbìng	venereal disease	13
性格	xìnggé	temperament, character	16

性交	xìngjiāo	sexual intercourse	22
性能	xìngnéng	function, performance	13
休假	xiūjià	to have a holiday	2
修	xiū	to decorate, to repair	14
修道院	xiūdàoyuàn	monastery, convent	14
修复	xiūfù	to repair, to restore	20
修改	xiūgǎi	to correct	23
修建	xiūjiàn	to build, to construct	24
修理部	xiūlǐbù	repair shop	14
修路	xiūlù	road repairing, to repair a road	14
修养	xiūyǎng	accomplishment, training	14
修业	xiūyè	to study (at school etc.)	14
修正	xiūzhèng	to revise, to emend	14
羞	xiū	shy, shame	21
羞答答	xiūdādā	shy	21
需	xū	to need, to want	19
需求	xūqiú	requirement, demand	19
需要	xūyào	to need, to want; need, want	19
许	xǔ	to praise, to allow; maybe	20
许多	xǔduō	many	20
许久	xǔjiǔ	for a very long time	20
许可	xǔkě	to permit, to allow; permission	20
续	xù	to continue; successive	20
续假	xùjià	to extend one's leave	20
选	xuǎn	to choose, to select	5
选段	xuǎnduàn	extract, selected extract	25
选民	xuǎnmín	voter	5
选票	xuǎnpiào	vote, ballot	5
选手	xuǎnshǒu	representative(athlete), contestant	5
选种	xuǎnzhǒng	seed selection	5
学费	xuéfèi	school fees	14
学派	xuépài	school of thought	11
学生证	xuéshēngzhèng	student card	18
学士	xuéshì	bachelor, scholar	17
学术	xuéshù	learning	2
学术界	xuéshùjiè	academic circles	17
学无止境	xuéwúzhǐjìng	learning is infinite	20
学习	xuéxí	to study	3
学员	xuéyuán	student	13
学者	xuézhě	scholar	4
雪	xuě	snow	6
雪花	xuěhuā	snowflake	6
雪人	xuěrén	snowman	6
血	xuè	blood	24
血管	xuèguǎn	blood vessel	24
血统	xuètǒng	origin, bloodline, descent	24

血小板	xuèxiǎobǎn	(blood) platelet	24
寻	xún	to look for, to search	22
寻常	xúncháng	ordinary, usual	22
寻根究底	xúngēnjiūdǐ	to get to the bottom of the matter	22
寻求	xúnqiú	to explore, to seek	22
寻找	xúnzhǎo	to look for	22
迅	xùn	fast	23
迅猛	xùnměng	swift, violent	23

Y

牙	yá	tooth	20
牙科	yákē	dentistry	20
牙医	yáyī	dentist	20
研	yán	to grind, to study	6
研究	yánjiū	to research	6
研究生	yánjiūshēng	postgraduate student	6
研究员	yánjiūyuán	research worker	6
颜	yán	face, prestige, colour	18
颜色	yánsè	colour	18
言必有据	yánbìyǒujù	words need to have a point	21
言论	yánlùn	opinion	3
眼	yǎn	eye	1
眼界	yǎnjiè	field of vision	17
眼睛	yǎnjīng	eye	1
眼看	yǎnkàn	soon, in a moment	1
眼科	yǎnkē	ophthalmology	2
眼明手快	yǎnmíngshǒukuài	quick of eye and deft of hand	1
眼皮	yǎnpí	eyelid	1
眼前	yǎnqián	before one's eyes, now	1
眼神	yǎnshén	look, look in one's eyes	4
眼熟	yǎnshú	to look familiar	12
眼下	yǎnxià	at present	1
眼中钉	yǎnzhōngdīng	thorn in one's side	1
演	yǎn	to develop, to evolve, to perform	16
演变	yǎnbiàn	evolution	23
演唱	yǎnchàng	to perform a song, to sing	16
演出	yǎnchū	to perform, to put on a show	16
演讲	yǎnjiǎng	to give a lecture, to make a speech	16
演说	yǎnshuō	to make an address	16
演员	yǎnyuán	actor, actress	16
验	yàn	to check, to prove, to test	24

验光	yànguāng	optometry	24	疑虑	yílǜ	doubt, worry	20
验货	yànhuò	goods control	24	疑问	yíwèn	query, question	4
验收	yànshōu	to check and accept	24	已	yǐ	already	3
验算	yànsuàn	to check a calculation	24	已经	yǐjīng	already	3
验血	yànxuè	blood test	24	已知	yǐzhī	already known	3
验证	yànzhèng	to test, to verify	24	乙	yǐ	second	12
阳光	yángguāng	sunlight	6	以内	yǐnèi	within, less than	15
阳历	yánglì	solar calendar	10	以身作则	yǐshēnzuòzé	to set an example	13
阳台	yángtái	balcony	14	以…为	yǐ…wéi	to regard as, to consider as	18
阳性	yángxìng	male, masculine	13	以下	yǐxià	below, underneath	18
养	yǎng	to support, to foster	7	以致	yǐzhì	so that...	17
养成	yǎngchéng	to foster, to maintain	7	意境	yìjìng	artistic conception	16
养活	yǎnghuo	to support, to feed	7	意味	yìwèi	meaning	20
养老院	yǎnglǎoyuàn	old people's home	7	意义	yìyì	meaning	2
养路	yǎnglù	to maintain a route	7	意志	yìzhì	will	17
样品	yàngpǐn	sample	13	义	yì	justice, righteous	2
样子	yàngzi	appearance, shape	10	义和团	Yìhétuán	the Boxers	15
要求	yāoqiú	to ask, to require; demand, request	1	义气	yìqi	personal loyalty	2
				义务	yìwù	duty, obligation	13
要不然	yàoburán	otherwise	21	艺	yì	skill, art	2
要紧	yàojǐn	important, essential	23	艺名	yìmíng	stage name	2
要命	yàomìng	to drive s. o. to his death	4	艺人	yìrén	actor, actress	2
要义	yàoyì	important idea	2	艺术	yìshu	art	2
要员	yàoyuán	important official	13	艺术家	yìshujiā	artist	2
药材	yàocái	drug, medicinal drug	7	忆	yì	to recall	11
药品	yàopǐn	medicines	13	易	yì	easy; to change	18
爷	yé	grandfather, father	25	《易经》	〈Yìjīng〉	*The Book of Changes*	18
爷爷	yéye	grandfather	25	议	yì	opinion, view	18
也许	yěxǔ	maybe	20	议会	yìhuì	parliament	18
叶	yè	leaf	10	议会制	yìhuìzhì	parliamentary system	18
叶公好龙	Yègōnghàolóng	to say one loves what one fears most	10	议论	yìlùn	to comment, to discuss	18
				议题	yìtí	topic for discussion	18
叶子	yèzi	leaf	10	议员	yìyuán	member of parliament	18
业	yè	industry, trade, profession	13	一般	yìbān	just like, general, ordinary	5
业务	yèwù	professional/vocational work	13	一般地	yìbānde	generally	5
夜景	yèjǐng	night scene	10	一般化	yìbānhuà	vague generalisation	5
依	yī	to depend on, according to	9	一般来说	yìbānláishuō	usually, generally speaking	5
依据	yījù	according to	9	一般人	yìbānrén	ordinary person	5
依照	yīzhào	according to	9	一得之功	yìdézhīgōng	minor success	22
衣架	yījià	coat hanger	14	一概	yígài	totally, without exception	19
衣食住行	yīshízhùxíng	food, clothing, shelter and transportation	19	一举两得	yìjǔliǎngdé	to kill two birds with one stone	9
				一路顺风	yílùshùnfēng	Have a smooth trip!	17
医	yī	doctor; to cure, to treat	20	一切	yíqiè	all	17
医疗	yīliáo	treatment, medical care	20	一清早	yìqīngzǎo	early in the morning	1
医务所	yīwùsuǒ	clinic	13	一望无际	yíwàngwújì	as far as the eye can see	11
疑	yí	to doubt, to suspect	4	一向	yíxiàng	all along, always	3

一言一行	yìyányìxíng	every word and action	13	优点	yōudiǎn	merit, strong point	2
一元论	yìyuánlùn	monism	3	优美	yōuměi	fine, exquisite	2
一直	yìzhí	straight, continuously	15	优生学	yōushēngxué	science of healthy birth	2
一致	yízhì	identical, unanimous	17	优势	yōushì	superiority	25
因此	yīncǐ	therefore	12	优先	yōuxiān	to take precedence	2
因而	yīn'ér	thus, as a result	7	由	yóu	cause, reason, by, through	2
阴	yīn	Yin; sinister, cloudy	19	由不得	yóubude	to be out of one's control	2
阴暗	yīn'àn	dark, gloomy	21	由此可见	yóucǐkějiàn	thus showing that...	12
阴电	yīndiàn	negative electric current	19	由来	yóulái	origin	2
阴极	yīnjí	negative pole	19	由于	yóuyú	owing to, due to	7
阴间	jīnjiān	the nether world	19	油	yóu	oil	19
阴历	yīnlì	lunar calendar	19	油菜	yóucài	rape (plant)	19
阴性	yīnxìng	female, feminine	19	油灯	yóudēng	oil lamp	24
印	yìn	seal, stamp; to print	13	油画	yóuhuà	oil painting	19
印度	Yìndù	India	13	油田	yóutián	oil field	19
印象	yìnxiàng	impression	13	油条	yóutiáo	deep fried dough sticks	19
应	yīng	to answer, to agree, must	13	有底	yǒudǐ	to be prepared for	4
应当	yīngdāng	should, ought to	13	有关	yǒuguān	to have sth. to do with	5
应得	yīngdé	deserved, due	13	有害	yǒuhài	harmful	8
应该	yīnggāi	must, should	13	有机	yǒujī	organic	20
应有	yīngyǒu	due, owing	13	有教无类	yǒujiàowúlèi	to teach everybody without bias	4
应	yìng	to respond, to grant, to deal with	13	有空儿	yǒukòngr	to have free time	16
应承	yìngchéng	to agree to	13	有理	yǒulǐ	to be right, reasonable	3
应声	yìngshēng	to reply	13	有利	yǒulì	beneficial, favourable	8
应用	yìngyòng	to apply, to use	13	有求必应	yǒuqiúbìyìng	to answer every request	21
应用文	yìngyòngwén	practical writing	13	有趣	yǒuqù	interesting, amusing	2
英	yīng	flower, hero	17	有无	yǒuwú	to have or not to have	4
英国	Yīngguó	Great Britain, England	17	有限	yǒuxiàn	limited	21
英国人	Yīngguórén	the British, an English person	17	右	yòu	right, ritht-hand side	17
英明	yīngmíng	wise	17	右边	yòubiān	the right side	17
英文	Yīngwén	English	17	右上角	yòushàngjiǎo	top right corner	17
英语	Yīngyǔ	English	17	于	yú	by, as, for	7
影迷	yǐngmí	movie buff, film fanatic	4	于是	yúshì	hence, as a result	8
影评	yǐngpíng	film review	18	与	yǔ	and, with	20
影响	yǐngxiǎng	influence; to influence	7	与此同时	yǔcǐtóngshí	at the same time as	23
影子	yǐngzi	shadow, shade	4	与众不同	yǔzhòngbùtóng	out of the ordinary	20
映	yìng	to reflect	7	语感	yǔgǎn	feel for a language	2
用处	yòngchu	use, good	2	语系	yǔxì	language family	5
用功	yònggōng	diligent, hard working	22	雨季	yǔjì	wet season, rainy season	24
用户	yònghù	consumer	15	雨量	yǔliàng	rainfall	13
用尽	yòngjìn	to use thoroughly	8	雨鞋	yǔxié	rubber boots	22
用具	yòngjù	tool, utensil	3	遇	yù	to meet, (by chance); chance	3
用品	yòngpǐn	object, article (to be used)	13	遇到	yùdào	to meet	3
用语	yòngyǔ	expression	3	遇见	yùjiàn	to meet	3
优	yōu	excellent	2	遇难	yùnàn	to be killed in an accident	3
优等	yōuděng	high-class	2	育	yù	to give birth to, to rear, to bring up	8

欲	yù	to wish, to want	9
欲望	yùwàng	to desire, to wish	9
原	yuán	original, raw, pardon, plain	2
原本	yuánběn	original; originally	2
原价	yuánjià	original price	22
原件	yuánjiàn	the original	23
原来	yuánlái	originally, formerly	3
原理	yuánlǐ	principle	3
原谅	yuánliàng	to forgive, to pardon	21
原料	yuánliào	raw material	25
原始	yuánshǐ	original, primitive	2
原文	yuánwén	original text	2
原先	yuánxiān	original, formerly, at first	2
原因	yuányīn	cause, reason	2
原则	yuánzé	principle	13
原著	yuánzhù	original work	8
原子	yuánzǐ	atom	2
原子能	yuánzǐnéng	atomic energy	2
员	yuán	member	13
圆	yuán	round, spherical, circle	15
圆规	yuánguī	compasses	16
圆满	yuánmǎn	satisfactory	15
圆形	yuánxíng	circular, round	15
元代	Yuándài	Yuan Dynasty	1
元首	yuánshǒu	head of state	6
园艺	yuányì	horticulture	2
愿	yuàn	to want, to hope, to be willing	11
愿望	yuànwàng	to desir; to wish	11
愿意	yuànyì	to be willing to	11
约	yuē	to arrange; agreement, appointment	12
约定	yuēdìng	to agree on, to appoint	12
约会	yuēhuì	date, meeting, appointment	12
约请	yuēqǐng	to invite, to talk	12
越	yuè	to jump over, to exceed	2
越过	yuèguò	to cross	2
越剧	Yuèjù	Shaoxing opera	16
越来越	yuèláiyuè	more and more	2
越南	Yuènán	Vietnam	2
越…越…	yuè…yuè…	the more… the more…	2
乐队	yuèduì	orchestra	13
乐器	yuèqì	musical instrument	4
乐团	yuètuán	orchestra	15
月初	yuèchū	the beginning of the month	12
月底	yuèdǐ	the end of the month	4
月份	yuèfèn	month	15
月光	yuèguāng	moonlight	6

月经	yuèjīng	menstruation	1
月亮	yuèliang	moon	4
月食	yuèshí	lunar eclipse	19
月牙儿	yuèyár	crescent moon	21
月终	yuèzhōng	end of the month	12
云	yún	cloud	22
云层	yúncéng	layer of clouds	22
运	yùn	motion, transport, fate	18
运动	yùndòng	sport, movement	18
运动会	yùndònghuì	sports meet	18
运动员	yùndòngyuán	sports person	18
运河	yùnhé	canal	18
运气	yùnqi	chance, luck	18
运送	yùnsòng	to transport	18
运行	yùnxíng	to move	18
运用	yùnyòng	to utilise, to wield	18

Z

杂	zá	miscellaneous, mixed	20
杂感	zágǎn	stray thoughts	20
杂货	záhuò	various goods	20
杂技	zájì	acrobatics	20
杂文	záwén	essay	20
杂志	zázhì	magazine	20
再婚	zàihūn	to get remarried	10
再者	zàizhě	moreover, furthermore	4
在座	zàizuò	to be present at	8
咱	zán	we, us (inclusive)	20
咱们	zánmen	we, us (inclusive)	20
早产	zǎochǎn	premature delivery	19
早婚	zǎohūn	early marriage	10
造	zào	to make, to create, to build	22
造成	zàochéng	to crate	22
造船厂	zàochuánchǎng	shipyard	22
造反	zàofǎn	to rebel, to revolt	22
造价	zàojià	cost price	22
造就	zàojiù	to bring up, to train	22
造句	zàojù	to make sentences	22
造林	zàolín	afforestation	22
造作	zàozuo	artificial, affected	22
则	zé	rule, standard; therefore	13
增	zēng	to increase, to add	22
增产	zēngchǎn	to increase production	22
增光	zēngguāng	to do credit to	22

增加	zēngjiā	to increase, to augment	22
增进	zēngjìn	to promote, to further	22
增强	zēngqiáng	to strengthen, to reinforce	22
增长	zēngzhǎng	to increase, to rise	22
怎么一回事	zěnmeyìhuíshì	what's happening?	4
展	zhǎn	to open up; exhibition	19
展出	zhǎnchū	to expose, to put on display	19
展开	zhǎnkāi	to spread, to unfold	19
展品	zhǎnpǐn	item on display	19
展示	zhǎnshì	to reveal, to show	19
展现	zhǎnxiàn	to emerge	19
站台	zhàntái	(train) platform	14
张嘴	zhāngzuǐ	to open one's mouth	21
章	zhāng	chapter, section, seal, stamp	1
章法	zhāngfǎ	composition of a written work	1
章回小说	zhānghuíxiǎoshuō	novel in chapters	1
长相	zhǎngxiàng	looks, features	22
丈	zhàng	man, a unit of length	8
丈夫	zhàngfu	husband	8
着急	zháojí	to worry, to feel nervous	25
招	zhāo	to call, to attract, to recruit	3
招待	zhāodài	to receive guests	7
招待会	zhāodàihuì	reception	7
招待所	zhāodàisuǒ	guest house	7
招呼	zhāohu	to call, to greet	13
招生	zhāoshēng	to recruit students	3
招收	zhāoshōu	to recruit	3
招手	zhāoshǒu	to wave, to beckon	3
照	zhào	to shine, to photograph; according to	9
照办	zhàobàn	to act in accordance with	9
照常	zhàocháng	as usual	9
照顾	zhàogu	to take care of	12
照旧	zhàojiù	as before	9
照片	zhàopiàn	photograph	9
照相	zhàoxiàng	to photograph	9
照相机	zhàoxiàngjī	camera	9
者	zhě	[suffix, the one who...]	4
真实	zhēnshí	real, authentic	11
真理	zhēnlǐ	truth	3
诊	zhěn	to examine a patient	20
诊断	zhěnduàn	to diagnose	20
诊断书	zhěnduànshū	medical certificate	20
诊所	zhěnsuǒ	clinic	20

诊治	zhěnzhì	to diagnose and treat	20
整	zhěng	complete, entire	12
整风	zhěngfēng	to correct work styles	12
整个	zhěnggè	whole, entire	12
整理	zhěnglǐ	to arrange, to order	12
整年	zhěngnián	all year	12
整体	zhěngtǐ	whole, entire	12
整天	zhěngtiān	all day	12
整整	zhěngzhěng	whole, entire	12
正规	zhèngguī	regular, standard	15
正派	zhèngpài	honest, upright	11
正巧	zhèngqiǎo	just in time, perfect timing	23
正确	zhèngquè	correct	12
正式	zhèngshì	official	16
正统	zhèngtǒng	orthodox	7
正义	zhèngyì	justice	2
正月	zhēngyuè	first lunar month	15
正直	zhèngzhí	honest, upright	15
政	zhèng	government, politics	17
政变	zhèngbiàn	coup d'état	23
政党	zhèngdǎng	political party	24
政府	zhèngfǔ	government	24
政见	zhèngjiàn	political opinion	17
政教分离	zhèngjiàofēnlí	to separate religion and politics	17
政客	zhèngkè	politician	17
政论	zhènglùn	political commentary	17
政体	zhèngtǐ	political regime	17
政治	zhèngzhì	politics	17
政治家	zhèngzhìjiā	statesperson	17
证	zhèng	to prove; evidence, certificate, card	18
证件	zhèngjiàn	papers, credentials	23
证据	zhèngjù	proof	18
证明	zhèngmíng	to proof; certificate	18
证人	zhèngrén	witness	18
证实	zhèngshí	to proof; to demonstrate	18
证书	zhèngshū	certificate	18
之	zhī	[indicating possession], this	3
之后	zhīhòu	after...	3
之乎者也	zhīhūzhěyě	pedantic terms	12
之间	zhījiān	between	3
之类	zhīlèi	of that sort	4
之前	zhīqián	before...	3
支	zhī	branch; [Mw]; to support	24
支部	zhībù	branch of a party	24
支出	zhīchū	to pay; expenses	24

支架	zhījià	support, stand, trestle	24
支解	zhījiě	dismemberment	24
支流	zhīliú	tributary, branch of a river	24
支票	zhīpiào	cheque	24
支取	zhīqǔ	to draw, to withdraw money	24
支使	zhīshǐ	to order s. o.	24
支书	zhīshū	party secretary	24
织	zhī	to weave, to knit	24
织布	zhībù	weaving	24
织女星	zhīnǚxīng	Vega	24
直	zhí	straight	15
直观	zhíguān	ocular, audio-visual	15
直接	zhíjiē	direct	15
值	zhí	value, worth; on duty	24
值班	zhíbān	to be on duty	24
值当	zhídàng	to be worthwhile	24
值得	zhídé	to be worth, to deserve	24
值钱	zhíqián	costly, valuable	24
值日	zhírì	day duty, to be on day duty	24
职	zhí	duty, post; to manage	16
职称	zhíchēng	work title	16
职工	zhígōng	staff and workers	16
职位	zhíwèi	post, position	16
职务	zhíwù	duty, job, post	16
职业	zhíyè	profession	16
职员	zhíyuán	employee	16
指	zhǐ	finger; to point	1
指出	zhǐchū	to point out	1
指导	zhǐdǎo	to direct, to guide	24
指点	zhǐdiǎn	to give directions	1
指定	zhǐdìng	to appoint, to assign	1
指东画西	zhǐdōnghuàxī	to talk with a hidden meaning	1
指教	zhǐjiào	to give advice	1
指明	zhǐmíng	to show clearly	1
指名	zhǐmíng	to mention by name	1
指南	zhǐnán	compass	1
指事	zhǐshì	pictogram, symbol	1
指头	zhǐtou	finger, toe	1
指正	zhǐzhèng	to point out errors, constructive criticism	1
纸	zhǐ	paper	15
纸钱	zhǐqián	paper money burnt as offering to the dead	17
纸张	zhǐzhāng	paper	17
纸包不住火	zhǐbāobúzhùhuǒ	truth will out	15

止	zhǐ	to stop	20
止步	zhǐbù	to stop, to halt	20
止境	zhǐjìng	limit, end	20
止痛	zhǐtòng	to relieve pain	20
止住	zhǐzhù	to stop	21
至	zhì	until, extremely; to reach	7
至此	zhìcǐ	up to this point	12
至多	zhìduō	at most	7
至今	zhìjīn	up to today	7
至少	zhìshǎo	at least	7
至于	zhìyú	as for . . .	7
治	zhì	to rule, to govern, to control, to cure	8
治安	zhì'ān	public order	8
治病	zhìbìng	to treat, to cure	8
治疗	zhìliáo	to treat, to cure; treatment	20
致	zhì	to send, to deliver	17
致电	zhìdiàn	to send a telegram	17
致敬	zhìjìng	to pay one's respects	17
致使	zhìshǐ	to cause, to result in	17
致意	zhìyì	to give one's regards to	17
志	zhì	will, ideal, records	17
志气	zhìqi	ambition, aspiration	17
志趣	zhìqù	interest, aspiration	17
志士	zhìshì	person of ideals and integrity	17
志向	zhìxiàng	ideal, aspiration, ambition	17
志愿	zhìyuàn	wish, ideal, aspiration	17
制	zhì	to make, to manufacture	8
制定	zhìdìng	to formulate, to draw up	8
制动器	zhìdòngqì	brake	8
制度	zhìdù	system	8
制革	zhìgé	tanning (of leather)	8
制片厂	zhìpiànchǎng	film studio	22
制片人	zhìpiànrén	film producer	8
制造	zhìzào	to manufacture	22
制止	zhìzhǐ	to check, to curb	20
制作	zhìzuò	to make, to manufacture	8
中断	zhōngduàn	to interrupt, to discontinue	7
中国通	Zhōngguótōng	specialist on Chinese affairs	5
中华人民共和国	Zhōnghuá Rénmín Gònghéguó	the People's Republic of China	24
中级	zhōngjí	intermediate, middle	25
中肯	zhòngkěn	to the point, pertinent	25
中篇小说	zhōngpiānxiǎoshuō	(medium sized) novel	6
中秋	zhōngqiū	mid-autumn	12

专政	zhuānzhèng	dictatorship	17	资格	zīgé	qualifications	24
专制	zhuānzhì	autocratic, despotic, autocracy	8	资金	zījīn	funds	24
转	zhuǎn	to turn, to change	19	资历	zīlì	qualifications and work record	24
转变	zhuǎnbiàn	to change, to transform	19	资料	zīliào	data, material	25
转车	zhuǎnchē	to change buses／trains etc.	19	资助	zīzhù	to aid financially, to subsidise	24
转达	zhuǎndá	to pass on, to convey	19	子实	zǐshí	seed, grain	11
转告	zhuǎngào	to pass on, to communicate	19	仔	zǐ	young (animal)	6
转给	zhuǎngěi	to give to, to pass on to	19	仔细	zǐxì	careful	6
转化	zhuǎnhuà	to change, to transform	19	字典	zìdiǎn	dictionary	25
转换	zhuǎnhuàn	to change, to transform	19	字据	zìjù	written pledge	3
转换期	zhuǎnhuànqī	transitional period	19	字母表	zìmǔbiǎo	alphabet	2
转机	zhuǎnjī	a turn for the better	19	字眼	zìyǎn	wording, diction	6
转交	zhuǎnjiāo	to transmit, to pass on	19	自此	zìcǐ	from now on	12
转让	zhuǎnràng	to transfer the ownership of	19	自给自足	zìjǐzìzú	self-sufficiency	22
转身	zhuǎnshēn	to turn around	19	自理	zìlǐ	to provide for oneself	3
转眼	zhuǎnyǎn	in the twinkling of an eye	19	自满	zìmǎn	self satisfied	10
转	zhuàn	to turn, to revolve	19	自…起	zì…qǐ	from. . .	23
转动	zhuàndòng	to turn, to revolve	19	自然界	zìránjiè	nature, the natural world	19
转向	zhuànxiàng	to lose one's hearings	19	自杀	zìshā	suicide	7
转转	zhuànzhuan	to go for a stroll	19	自私	zìsī	selfish	24
传记	zhuànjì	biography	12	自习	zìxí	to study by oneself, self-study	3
庄子	Zhuāngzǐ	Zhuangzi	7	自信	zìxìn	confident	1
装	zhuāng	to pretend to act; clothing, makeup	10	自由	zìyóu	free; liberty	2
				自治区	zìzhìqū	autonomous region	8
装出	zhuāngchū	to put on airs	10	自知之明	zìzhīzhīmíng	to know oneself well	3
装作	zhuāngzuò	to pretend	10	自传	zìzhuàn	autobiography	1
壮	zhuàng	strong, robust	19	总	zǒng	to sum up; general, always	4
壮大	zhuàngdà	to strengthen, to expand	19	总而言之	zǒng'éryánzhī	in a word	7
壮观	zhuàngguān	grand, grandiose	19	总共	zǒnggòng	in all, altogether	4
壮举	zhuàngjǔ	a magnificent feat, heroic undertaking	19	总会	zǒnghuì	central association	4
				总机	zǒngjī	swichboard	4
壮丽	zhuànglì	majestic, magnificent	19	总结	zǒngjié	to sum up, to summarise; summary	10
壮年	zhuàngnián	prime of life	19	总理	zǒnglǐm,	prime minister	4
壮阳	zhuàngyáng	to strengthen the Yang	19	总是	zǒngshì	always	12
准	zhǔn	to allow, to follow; standard	7	总书记	zǒngshūjì	secretary general	12
准备	zhǔnbèi	to prepare	11	总算	zǒngsuàn	finally, at long last	4
准确	zhǔnquè	exact, precise	12	总统	zǒngtǒng	president	7
准时	zhǔnshí	punctual, on schedule	7	总统府	zǒngtǒngfǔ	presidential palace	24
准许	zhǔnxǔ	to allow, to permit	20	总之	zǒngzhī	in short, brief	4
准则	zhǔnzé	standard, criterion	13	走访	zǒufǎng	to interview, to go and see	24
资	zī	money, qualifications; to provide	24	走狗	zǒugǒu	running dog, stooge	21
资本	zīběn	capital (money)	24	走马观花	zǒumǎguānhuā	to skim the surface	10
资本家	zīběnjiā	capitalist	24				
资本主义	zīběnzhǔyì	capitalism	24	走私	zǒuxī	to smuggle	24
资产	zīchǎn	property, capital	24	租界	zūjiè	concession	17
资方	zīfāng	people with capital	24	族	zú	race, ethnic group, clan	16

足	zú	foot; sufficient	22	作保	zuòbǎo	to sponsor, to be guarantor	14
足够	zúgòu	to suffice	22	作怪	zuòguài	to make trouble	1
足球	zúqiú	football	22	作官	zuòguān	to be a bureaucrat	17
足以	zúyǐ	enough, sufficient	22	作客	zuòkè	to be a guest	12
组	zǔ	to organise; group	2	作料	zuóliao	seasoning, condiments	25
组成	zǔchéng	to make up, to compose	2	作品	zuòpǐn	(art or literature) work	13
组合	zǔhé	to constitute, to make up	19	作业	zuòyè	homework	13
组长	zǔzhǎng	group leader	2	作者	zuòzhě	author	4
组织	zǔzhī	to organise; organization	24	作证	zuòzhèng	to witness	18
嘴	zuǐ	mouth	21	坐视不救	zuòshìbújiù	to watch without going to s.o.'s	
嘴脸	zuǐliǎn	looks, features	21			rescue	23
最初	zuìchū	initial, beginning	12	座	zuò	seat; [Mw]	8
左	zuǒ	left	17	座次	zuòcì	seating arrangements	8
左边	zuǒbiān	on the left	17	座位	zuòwèi	place, seat	8
左上角	zuǒshàngjiǎo	upper left corner	17	座钟	zuòzhōng	desk clock	8
左右	zuǒyòu	more or less	17	座子	zuòzi	stand, pedestal, saddle	8

FREQUENCY TABLE

Frequency of usage of characters in modern readings.

(Source: *Chinese Character Frequency Dictionary*, Beijing 1986)

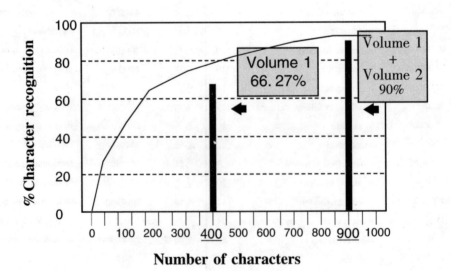

TAPES

TAPE 1	Side A	Lesson 1 to 7
	Side B	Lesson 8 to 14
TAPE 2	Side A	Lesson 15 to 20
	Side B	Lesson 21 to 25

责任编辑　周奎杰　郁 苓

封面设计　唐少文

插　　图　Christian Buthigieg　李士伋

版面设计　René Daire　　贾寅淮

汉语语言文字启蒙(Ⅱ)

Joël Bellassen (白乐桑)　张朋朋

※

ⓒ华语教学出版社

华语教学出版社出版

(中国北京百万庄路 24 号)

邮政编码 100037

北京外文印刷厂印刷

中国国际图书贸易总公司发行

(中国北京车公庄西路 35 号)

北京邮政信箱第 399 号　邮政编码 100044

1997 年(16 开)第一版

(汉英)

ISBN 7-80052-508-2／H·683 (外)

05800

9—CE—3204 PB